A PLAGUE OF ANGELS

A PLAGUE OF ANGELS

Patricia Finney writing as

P.F. Chisholm

Hodder & Stoughton

First published in Great Britain in 1998
by Hodder and Stoughton
A division of Hodder Headline PLC

10 9 8 7 6 5 4 3 2 1

Chisholm, P. F.
A plague of angels
1. Carey, Sir Robert (Fictitious character) – Fiction
2. Borders of England (England) – Fiction 3. Detective
and mystery stories
I. Title II. Finney, Patricia
823.9'14 [F]

ISBN 0 340 67162 9

Typeset by Hewer Text Ltd, Edinburgh
Printed and bound in Great Britain by
Mackays of Chatham PLC, Chatham, Kent

Hodder and Stoughton
A division of Hodder Headline PLC
338 Euston Road
London NW1 3BH

To Kay,
with thanks

Some of the diabolical liberties I have taken with two famous playwrights were inspired by Samuel Schoenbaum's *William Shakespeare*, A. L. Rowse's *Shakespeare's Dark Lady* and Charles Nicholl's *The Reckoning*. The Topographical Society's *A to Z of Elizabethan London* was indispensable as was my father's enthusiastic willingness to delve through his library in search of obscure nuggets of information.

Wednesday, 30th August 1592,
late afternoon

1

You could always tell when you were near a town from the bodies hanging on the gibbets by the main road, thought Sergeant Dodd. London was no different from anywhere else they had passed on the interminable way south. As their horses toiled up the long hill from Golders Farm, Dodd could just glimpse a robber's corpse dangling from a big elm tree, up on the brow. Of course Sir Robert Carey had told him how close they were to London when they turned off the Great North Road and passed through the village of Hendon, but they had been delayed by Carey's horse throwing a shoe. The afternoon crowds of people were gone now so that the dusty rutted road was quite empty. It could have been anywhere.

A bit of knowledge gleaned from Carey's manservant floated to the front of his mind.

'Ay,' he said with interest, and turned in the saddle to speak to Barnabus himself who trailed lumpenly along behind them on a sulky looking horse. 'Would that be Tyburn Tree up ahead there?'

Barnabus was frowning with concentration as he tried to get his mount to move faster up the hill.

'Nah, mate,' he puffed, kicking viciously at the horse's flanks. 'Tyburn's off to the west, where the Edgeware Road meets the Oxford Road, and it's a lot fancier than that. That's only the Hampstead Hanging Elm.'

The road was curving round into a deep cutting with scrubby heathland trees growing on the banks. Ahead, the Courtier's ugly and obstinate replacement horse was balking at something again, probably the smell of rot from the corpse. Carey had glanced

3

without interest at the Elm with its judicial fruit. The horse neighed, tossed his head and skittered sideways.

'God damn it,' Carey snarled to the horse. 'You flyblown lump of dogsmeat, get over!' He brought his whip down on the animal's flank and the horse crow-hopped and tried to turn to run back down the hill to its home in Golders Green.

Dodd wasn't liking the look of the place either. You couldn't see past the curve of the road and those high banks on both sides were perfect siting for an ambush.

He tried to urge his own horse up to a canter to bring him level with Carey, but the mare had her head up too, and her nostrils flared. Forelegs straight and the hairs of her mane up, she refused to pick up the pace. Dodd frowned.

'Whit's ahead of us, sir?' he called to Carey whose nag was slowly turning round in circles and shaking his head.

'The Cut, then Hampstead horse pond,' said the Courtier and whacked the animal again. 'Will you get on, blast you . . .!' he roared at it.

Drawing his sword, Dodd slid from the saddle, took the mare's bridle and led her forward at a run, then dodged behind and hit her on the rump with the flat of the sword. The mare reared and bolted past the Courtier and young Simon Barnet on his pony.

As she galloped up the road through the Cut, whinnying and shaking her head, Dodd heard the unmistakeable *whip-chunk!* of a crossbow being fired.

'Och,' he said to himself as he instantly changed direction and sprinted softly up the narrow path he had spotted on the right hand side of the Cut. 'Ah might have guessed.'

The bank reared higher on the right of the road, soft sandy earth held together by tree roots and bushes. Just below him, overlooking the narrowest part, he saw a man hunched in hiding, a bolt ready in his crossbow as he squinted down the sight ready for them to pass by.

Dodd had been storing up an awful lot of rage on the journey south from Carlisle. He gave an inarticulate roar at the sight, hopped like a goat down the high crumbling earthbank and cut down on the man with his sword.

4

The footpad had heard something coming, turned just in time to see his death, dropped the crossbow and reflexively put up his hands to defend himself. He took Dodd's swordblade straight down through his armbone and the middle of his face. Dodd slashed sideways to finish the job, then turned at another man who was lungeing out of a bramble bush waving the biggest sword Dodd had ever seen in his life, a great long monster of a thing that the robber was wielding two-handed, his face purple with effort.

Somewhere behind him, Dodd heard one of Carey's dags fire and an incoherent screaming follow it. As he dodged the whirling blade in front of him, a particle of thought noted that for the first time in his memory, Carey had finally managed to shoot somebody with his fancy weapon.

Balancing in a crouch, Dodd watched how the robber handled his stupid great sword, ducked again and waited for the instant when the momentum of it was whirling it round the back of the robber's head. That was when Dodd jumped inside the man's guard, slashed once with his sword and kicked as hard as he could at the man's balls.

The soft earth crumbled under him, he missed his target as he toppled and slipped on his bum down the bank. The robber danced after him, hefted up the long blade to bring it down on Dodd's head; the blade arced through the sky and Dodd rolled and slithered frantically, caught a rowan trunk to stop himself pitching eight feet down, and then saw the man grunt, stand still for a moment with his mouth wide open. The double-handed sword thudded to the ground and its wielder pitched headfirst down the bank and into the road.

Barnabus stood behind him, puffing for breath and dusting off his hands. Dodd nodded his thanks, clambered back up to the tiny narrow path and ran on to find the rest of the bastards, his blood properly up, just itching to find someone else to kill.

He saw the flash of legs and then glimpsed three more men off across the bare hill, running as fast as they could past the Hanging Elm. He sprinted after them, roaring 'A Tynedale, A Tynedale, Out! Out!' and the cowardly southron pigs only ran faster, splitting up as they dodged down the other side of the hill through the brambles and bushes.

Years spent on the Border not getting himself killed won through Dodd's rage and he stopped. They might have kin within hailing range, there might be men and horses lying in wait behind one of the hedges, hiding in a double ambush to catch them when they thought they'd won the fight. No. He was a Dodd from Upper Tynedale and he'd pulled that trick too often himself in the past to be fooled by it.

He caught his breath and wiped his swordblade with some of the tussocky grass next to the Elm, where the sandy soil was more fertile, glanced up at the corpse in its soiled suit of brown wool with black velvet trimmings. A bit prosperous-looking for a thief; must have been a murderer. The smell wasn't bad at all, though the face was a terrible mess.

Horsehooves beat the earth behind him, and Dodd whisked round into a crouch again, sword at the ready. It was only the Courtier though, laughing fit to burst his ribs, dag in his left hand and his sword in his right.

'By God, Sergeant,' he said. 'That was a bloody good piece of work.'

Dodd tried hard not to look pleased. 'Ay,' he said. 'They've run though.'

'Of course they have. No soft southern footpad is a match for a Tynedaler and never will be.'

As this was undoubtedly true, Dodd nodded his head. 'How long afore they fetch their kin?' he asked, squinting around himself. Apart from the Elm, there were no proper trees, though a multiplicity of hedges split the fields below. Not much cover up here, he thought, plenty down there, I don't like it.

Carey was laughing again, putting his still-wound second dag back into its case on the horse's withers, and twirling his sword around his gloved fingers in an absurd swordmaster's flourish.

'They won't,' he said with the unwarranted certainty that always enraged Dodd. 'This is Hampstead Heath, not the Bewcastle Waste. Every man jack of them will have to change his breeches now they've lost three of their friends, including the big ugly bastard that almost fell on Simon, who I think was their leader.'

'Ye killed one, then, sir?' Dodd said as he followed Carey down the slightly better path that led back to the road on the southern side of the Cut.

'Shot one, slashed another.'

'Nae trouble wi' yer hands now?'

Carey grinned with satisfaction and flexed the fingers of his left hand in the embroidered kid gloves he was wearing. 'No, my grip's as good as it ever was,' he said. 'The kick didn't even hurt.'

Dodd nodded once, unwilling to be as delighted with Carey as Carey was with himself.

'I swapped a couple of blows with somebody who had a polearm, might have got him with a slash, and then you killed the big one and the lot of them ran like rabbits.'

'Nay sir, that werenae me, it were Barnabus,' Dodd said dolefully, annoyed with himself for not doing better. 'Got him in the back with a throwing knife. I killed anither man with a crossbow.'

Carey laughed again and sheathed his sword. 'I've never regretted the day I hired Barnabus,' he said untruthfully. 'Even though I was drunk at the time. Come on, let's make sure he doesn't strip all the corpses.'

Dodd glowered at the thought of being bilked out of his rightful spoils and ran back through the Cut to find Barnabus bending over the man Carey had evidently shot, since his chest was a mashed mess of bone and blood. He was still flopping feebly and Barnabus appeared to be trying to act as a surgeon on him.

'Barnabus, really,' admonished Carey from his horse, which was spinning and sidling again. 'Wait until the poor bugger's dead.'

Barnabus looked furtive. 'Well, sir, I was . . . ah . . . going to put him out of his misery, so to speak.'

'Ay,' said Dodd, coming close and looking down. 'Were ye now? What are they, then?' He pointed at the round bright gold coins scattered about the dying man, some of them embedded in the ruined flesh of his chest. 'Buttercups?'

Barnabus had the grace to look embarrassed. 'Just wondering,' he muttered.

Even the sniff of gold had the Courtier off his horse, tying it to a bush and coming over to look.

'Hm,' he said. 'That's peculiar.'

Dodd was gathering up the coins on the ground, though he couldn't quite bring himself to start plucking coins out of the man's body. Barnabus wasn't so fussy.

'What's a scrawny Hampstead footpad doing with a purseful of gold?' Carey asked. 'And why did they try it on with us if they already had money?'

Dodd shrugged and went to look at the big bruiser that Barnabus had killed. Somebody else had got there first though, and he scowled at Barnabus who coughed and brought out the purse he had taken.

Simon came trotting down from the bank looking disappointed. 'Nothing up there, Uncle Barney,' he said. 'Sorry.'

Pointedly, Carey held out his hand for the spoils which Barnabus handed over. Dodd was very reluctant to give up a purse full of money, even if it had blood and chips of bone mixed in, but wasn't quite annoyed enough with the Courtier to hold onto it.

Carey hefted the purses and frowned. 'What wealthy little footpads,' he said, and bent over the man he had shot, who was finally still. Staring eyes told him he'd get no information.

'Hm,' said Carey again, putting the purses into one of his saddle bags. 'Come on, let's get the horses watered and try and make it into London before nightfall.'

As expected, Dodd's nag was at the horsepond slurping up greenish water and swishing at flies with her tail. She made a great drama about shying when she saw him and trotting further round the pool. Dodd pretended he wasn't interested in her, wandered up to the trampled banks of the pond, looked everywhere but at the horse and then when she put her wary head down again, nipped her bridle.

'Got ye,' he whispered to her and she snorted resignedly.

Carey's mount was still pulling on the reins and sidling stupidly until he caught the smell of water and then he lunged for it. Carey tied him to one of the posts and disappeared into a bramble bush a

little way off. Simon came up from the Cut with Barnabus, leading
the other two horses. They had no packponies and were riding
strange southern horses because Carey had been in a hurry and
they had been riding post. They were due to change mounts again
at the Holly Tree in Hampstead, and Dodd, for one, couldn't wait
to be rid of the latest batch of useless knacker's rejects. Also, he was
thirsty, but he would have to be a great deal worse off to consider
the stuff in the horsepond. What he wanted was a quart of ale,
Bessie's for preference, bread, cheese, a meat pie, pickled onions
... Dodd sighed. Maybe the Holly Tree would have some food.
Maybe Carey would let them stop for half an hour to drink.

Maybe he wouldn't. Dodd wasn't very hopeful. Out of sheer
habit, he stared out across the horsepond at the countryside
around them and at the thatched roofs of the village which began
a little way down the other side of the hill. His horse had finished
and was looking at him expectantly, but he didn't have a feedbag
hidden anywhere on him, so he tied her to the hitching post near
the pond. Then he wandered to the other side of the hilltop, to
see if he could spy London town yet, even though the milestone
had said they were five miles away still.

His mouth fell open. It was a fine lookout spot, that hill, good
siting for a pele tower, not that the soft southrons had thought
of building one. They had a pathetic beacon on a raised bracket,
that must have been put up in the Armada year from the rust on
it, but there was no wood around to light it with. You could see
for miles when it was clear, which it was, a pale golden evening
with not a hint of autumn.

And if you looked southwards, there it lay, a baleful brackish
sea of houses, the foremost city in England. The craggy flotsam of
church steeples poked up among the cluttered roofs, with smoke
dirtying the sky above even on a warm day. Dodd had never seen
such a thing. The day before he had been impressed with York,
but this ... A city that had burst its walls in all directions with
so many people that came and stayed, as if the city ate them and
got fatter each time. Dodd narrowed his eyes and pursed his lips.
London might impress him, but eat him it would not.

'Makes yer heart sing, don't it?' said a guttural voice beside him. Barnabus Cooke was standing there, squinting in the south-westering light of the sun. Either the light was stronger than Dodd thought, or the ferret-faced little man had tears in his eyes. 'Seems a hundred years gone since I left,' he sighed.

'Hmphm,' said Dodd noncommitally.

Barnabus heard his lack of enthusiasm and waved an expressive arm. 'That, Sergeant Dodd, is the greatest city in Christendom. Everything any sane man could ever want you can get right there, no trouble, money to be made, never any reason to be bored.'

'Ay, and the streets are all paved wi' gold,' said Dodd straight-faced, 'so I've heard tell.'

'No, they ain't,' piped up Simon. 'Don't you listen to 'em, Sergeant. Me and my friend Tom, we dug down for two days solid, looking for gold paving stones and we never found nuffing except more paving stones.'

Dodd nodded at Simon. At some time on the long weary journey, a mystery had happened to the lad's speech again. From sounding quite Christian really, at least as comprehensible as the Carlisle stable lads, Simon had turned back into the guttural creature with hiccups for 't's that he had been when he first came north. God save me, Dodd thought, feeling for the little lump of his wife's amulet under his shirt, alien men with alien notions and words like cobblestones.

'Nay lad,' he said gravely to Simon. 'I never thought it were, or why are the Grahams no' laying siege to it.'

'Figures of speech, Sergeant,' said Barnabus patronisingly. 'Only true in a manner of speaking. Like what you get at the playhouse? You ever seen a play?'

'I've seen the players that come to Carlisle some years,' said Dodd, who hadn't thought much of them. 'Garish folk, and ay arguing.'

Barnabus tutted. 'Nah. Plays. At a playhouse. With guns for thunder and the boys tricked out in velvets and satin and trumpets and a jig at the end. Best bit, the jig, I've always thought. Worf waiting for.'

'Why?'

Barnabus grinned knowingly and tapped his bulbous nose. 'You'll see.'

Dodd grunted and looked around for the cause of this whole stupid expedition into foreign parts. Carey came striding impatiently out of his sorry-looking stand of thorns, his good humour after a fight obviously destroyed by what had sent him hurrying into it. Dodd was quite recovered from the vicious Scottish flux they had both picked up in Dumfries, but Carey's bowels were clearly made of weaker stuff. He saw them gazing into the distance and turned to look as well, scowling at the view of London before turning back to scowl at all of them. To his clear dissatisfaction, the horses were all drinking nicely, none of them was lame for a change, and there was nothing to complain about. God, but he was in a nasty temper and had been all the way south, starting with an eyeblinking explosion of profanity when he first got the letter from his father. Dodd had heard it in the new barracks building while Carey was in the Carlisle castle yard.

It had been very wearying, riding with a man as chancy as a bad gun, all the way to Newcastle and every step of the Roman road south. They had changed horses luxuriously twice a day and pressed on at a pace that Dodd thought indecent, even with the Courtier having to stop and find cover every couple of hours. It wasn't the length of time it took – Dodd was no stranger to long rides and three days was not the longest he'd been on by several days – it was the sheer dullness of the business. Hour after hour of cavalry pace, walk a mile, trot a mile, canter for two, then lead the horses again, and never a familiar face to greet nor a known tower to sight by. Dodd felt marooned. Even with the straight dusty Roman road, he doubted he could find his way back home again from so far away, though Carey knew the way well enough. After all, he was used to flinging himself across the entire country on the Queen's account.

The countryside had changed around them as they went, so you might think they were still and the country moving, changing itself magically from rocky to flat and back to hills, fat and golden with straw after the harvest, the gleaners still combing painstakingly through the fields. They passed orchards – Dodd had not been certain what the little woods full of fruit trees might be, but had found out from Simon; they passed fields full of sheep and kine and only children guarding them, so it made you sad to think how many you could reive if only the distances weren't so great. Even the size of the fields changed, from small and stone-walled to vast striped prairies and then back to small squares quilted with hedges. The road was generally full of strangers as well, crowded with packponies, carriers' wagons, even newfangled coaches jolting along with silkclad green-faced women suffering inside them. Once a courier carrying the Queen's dispatches had galloped down the grassy verge, shouting for them to make room, and leaving the rest of the travellers bathed in dust. Carey had coughed and brightened up a little, and they had talked for an hour about the technicalities of riding post. They had agreed that the key to speed was in making the change of horses every ten miles as fast as possible and paradoxically in taking the first half mile slowly so the animal had a chance to warm up.

Once a trotting train carrying fish from Norwich went past them, little light carts pulled by perkily trotting ponies, trailing a smell of the ocean behind the smart clatter. Once they had passed a band of beggars and Dodd had loosened his sword, but the upright man at the head of them had not liked the look of three men and a boy, well-armed and with the gentleman at the head of them ostentatiously opening his dag case before him. Dodd had thought it was a pity, really, he'd heard tell of southern beggars and a fight would at least have broken the monotony. Dodd was also short of sleep, thanks to Carey's efforts at economising. At each inn they stayed at, Carey had put them all in the one room so Dodd could get the full benefit of Carey and Barnabus's outrageous snoring. In desperation he had offered to sleep with the horses in the stables, but Carey had turned the idea down.

The south was a dreamworld where all the familiar normal animals had suddenly turned fat and handsome and he could only understand one word in three that was spoken to him. Dodd felt naked without his jack and morion, and thought wistfully that it would have been nice if his brother could have come too so he could have had someone to talk to. But Carey had refused to pay for any more followers than he had to on the grounds that it was Dodd himself

12

that the Lord Chamberlain his father wanted to speak to, not Red Sandy.

'What do you make of it, Sergeant?' Carey asked him, nodding at the ambush of houses ahead of them.

'Ah dinna ken, sir,' said Dodd at his most stolid. 'I've no' been there yet.' Was Carey actually planning to keep all the spoils for himself? Damn him for a selfish grasping miser; he'd only killed one of the footpads and if it hadn't been for Dodd, they would have been helpless in the Cut when the robbers attacked . . .

As if reading Dodd's mind, Carey had squatted down and was emptying out the gold and silver coins onto a flat stone, sorting them briskly into shillings and crowns and angels, and then into three piles which he then doled out. The few pennies left over he gave to Simon.

'Will we get to see the Queen, sir?' asked Simon as he stowed his money away.

Carey shrugged. 'We might, if she's in London. She's more likely to be on progress.'

'Will yer father no' be with her then, sir?' Dodd said, having picked up the vague notion that Lord Chamberlains were supposed to look after courtiers and the court and such. 'How will we tell him our tale if he isnae there?'

'How the hell should I know?' snapped Carey. 'Father's brains have addled, I expect. Bloody London. What the devil's the point of making me come back to London now?'

'Ay, the Grahams will be riding, and the Armstrongs forbye,' said Dodd dolefully. 'Once the Assize judge has gone home after Lammas torches, and the horses are strong and the kine are fat, that's when we run our rodes.'

Carey snorted. Dodd, who was tired of treating Carey with tact, decided to live dangerously. 'Ah, that'll be it, sir,' he said comfortably. 'Your father will have got wind the Grahams have a price on yer head and he'll want ye safe in the south again.'

Lord, Carey could glare fit to split a stone when he wanted. 'I very much doubt it,' he said frostily, 'seeing he knows perfectly well I'd rather be in Carlisle and take my chances with the Grahams.'

'Hm,' said Barnabus. 'Not an easy choice, is it, sir? With all the people wanting to see you in London.'

Carey didn't answer, but went to his horse and started turning up hooves looking for stones. The animal nickered and licked at his neck, searching for salt and knocking his hat off in the process. Uncharacteristically, Carey elbowed the enquiring muzzle away with a growled 'Get over, you stupid animal.'

'Mr Skeres will want to talk to you, won't he, sir?' Barnabus went on, sucking his teeth and scratching his bum. 'And Mr Barnet and Mr Palavicino's agent and Mr Bullard and then there's Mr Pickering's men . . .'

Involuntarily, Carey winced.

'Got some feuds waiting for ye, have ye, sir?' asked Dodd with interest. It didn't surprise him at all, knowing Carey by now, but he wouldn't have thought southerners would have the spirit.

'No,' Carey admitted as he checked the girth and mounted. 'Not feuds. Much worse.'

'Och ay?'

'Much much worse,' Barnabus explained gloomily, using the mounting stone to clamber into the saddle.

'What then?'

'Creditors,' Carey said hollowly. 'London's bloody crawling with my creditors.'

The nags supplied by the Holly Tree were, if anything, worse than the ones they had been riding before and true to Dodd's gloomy expectation, Carey refused even to pause long enough for a quart of beer. Nor would he roust out the village Watch to go and find the footpads, though that was sensible enough since they were more than likely the same people or at least their relatives.

As they clopped briskly down Haverstock Hill, Carey's face got longer and longer. He looked just like a man whose blackrent to the Grahams was late, waiting for the torch in his thatch.

'Could ye not pay 'em off with the spoils fra the footpads?' Dodd asked solicitously.

Carey blinked at him, as if checking to see whether he was making fun, and then laughed hollowly.

'Christ, Dodd, you've no idea,' he said. 'I wish I could. The only thing I've got going for me is the fact they don't know I'm coming.'

'Wouldn't be too sure of that, sir,' said Barnabus from behind them.

Carey had been in a tearing hurry all the way south, but now he slowed to a walk.

'I don't know,' he said. 'What do you think, Barnabus? I was hoping to come down Gray's Inn Road and into Holborn just about the time when the law students come out of dinner and use them as cover, but we're too late for that.'

'Mm,' said Barnabus thoughtfully. 'I shouldn't think there'll be too many duns out on Holborn – why bother? If I was trying to catch you, I'd hang around Somerset House, wiv a boat on the river. After all, they don't know which way you're coming.'

'If they know I'm coming at all.'

'You're planning to rely on that, are you, sir?'

Carey shook his head. 'It's the Strand that's the problem then.' He nibbled the stitching on the thumb of his glove. 'I simply can't afford to wind up in the Fleet.'

'What's that, sir?'

'A debtor's prison,' said Carey in a voice of doom.

'Och,' said Dodd and considered. 'Have ye kin in London? Yer father's there, is he no'?'

'I hope so, since he's forced me to ride a couple of hundred miles just to talk to him face to face and do business that could be perfectly well done by letter.'

'Ay. It's no' difficult, then. They willnae ken ma face as one o' yourn, so ye tell me the lie of the land and where your father's castle is, I ride hell fer leather intae it, he calls out yer kin and comes out to meet ye and none o' yer enemies can do a thing about it.'

A short silence greeted this excellent plan which Dodd realised was not the silence of admiration. Carey cleared his throat in a way which Dodd knew meant he was trying hard not to laugh and Simon sniggered behind his hand.

'Well?' demanded Dodd truculently. 'What's wrong with that idea?' He could feel his neck reddening.

15

'Among other things, the fact that Somerset House is only one of the palaces on the Strand and I doubt you could find it,' said Carey. 'Not to mention the fact that the Queen is highly averse to pitched battles being fought on the streets of London.'

'You could let 'em take you, we talk to your dad and he bails you tomorrow,' suggested Barnabus. 'You'd only need to spend one night inside . . .'

'Absolutely not,' snapped Carey, and his face was pale.

Dodd thought he was being overdramatic and called his bluff. 'Ye can allus change clothes wi' me, sir, if ye're so feart o' being seen; none will know you in my clothes,' he offered. Perhaps it was cruel to tease the Courtier; Dodd knew perfectly well that Carey would probably rather die than enter even London's suburbs wearing Dodd's sturdy best suit of homespun russet. Certainly he would hang before going into his father's house like that.

Carey's blue glare narrowed again but it seemed he was learning to know when Dodd was pulling his leg. He coughed.

'Thank you for your offer, Dodd,' he said, 'but I doubt your duds would fit me.'

'Ay, they would,' said Dodd, who was only a couple of inches shorter than Carey and not far off the same build. Though he thought no one would actually confuse them in a thousand years since Carey had dark chestnut hair, hooded blue eyes, a striking family resemblance to the Queen along his cheekbones and slightly hooked nose, and a breezy swagger that breathed of the court. Dodd knew he was no beauty though he felt it was unfair the way his wife sometimes compared his usual expression to a wet winter's day. The best you could say about his brown hair was that it was quite clean and he still had all of it.

'We dinna have to go straight in,' Dodd pointed out. 'There's surely no shortage of fine inns. Ye could stay at one o' them, Barnabus could scout out yer dad's castle for ye, see was the approaches laid wi' ambush, and then we could bring out a covered litter for ye and take ye in that way.'

'That might work,' said Barnabus. 'At least we could bring out some of your father's liverymen for cover.' Dodd forebore to point out that this was exactly the plan he had first suggested and they had laughed at.

For once Carey looked as if he was being tempted to act sensibly but as Dodd expected, it didn't last.

'No,' Carey said. 'News travels fast in London. If anyone spots you, Barnabus, they'll know I'm back and come looking for me when you return. Dodd wouldn't know the way and Simon's too young. Also nobody knows them at Somerset House so they might have trouble getting in. Besides I'm not skulking into my father's house in a blasted litter like some bloody trollop from the stews. No, if we move fast enough and quietly enough, by the time they realise it's me, we'll be in.'

'And yer father's henchmen can see 'em off.'

'No,' said Carey. 'My father's lawyers.'

'Whit use are lawyers?' laughed Dodd, who had never heard good of one. 'It's fighting men we lack, as usual.'

'You'd be surprised, Sergeant. Right, so it's down Gray's Inn Road to Holborn, turn right on Holborn and past Chancery Lane, cut across Lincoln's Inn Fields, then down Little Drury Lane at a trot, turn right into the Strand where we'll walk so as not to be too dramatic and besides the ground's awful there, then in at my father's gatehouse. Stick close, Dodd, I don't want you getting lost.'

What did a London bailiff look like? wondered Dodd as they cut across the fields to the gate at the top of Gray's Inn Lane, cattle almost blocking it as they stood waiting to be taken in for milking. They were lovely beasts, fat as butter, huge udders groaning. As they manoevred round the herd, Dodd rode up behind Carey and let out a soft cough.

'Look at them,' he said longingly. 'Could we no' . . . er . . . borrow a few, sir? I could drive at least five o' them maself, and more if ye gave me a hand. We could use 'em to pay off yer creditors.'

Carey stared for a moment and then shouted with humourless laughter. 'For God's sake, Dodd, keep your sticky hands off those beasts, they're the Earl of Essex's. See the bear and ragged staff brand? Don't touch 'em.'

'Och,' said Dodd sadly, not very surprised. 'He's a big lord, is he, sir?'

'Er . . . yes,' said Carey. 'Also, I'm still his man and you'd get me in a lot of trouble.'

Gray's Inn Road must have been a horror in winter, what with the depth of dust. It was lined with houses, like streets in Edinburgh, and then they came out on a wide road. Carey was looking about him and had his hat pulled down. They crossed some fields criss-crossed with paths that looked badly overgrazed and came through a gate beside a high garden wall. Across another dusty road was a lane that led due south between tall narrow houses. Simon shut the gate and they unconsciously bunched together as they went into the lane. The sun was a low copper bowl now and the people milling around not paying them any attention. Dodd thought that Londoners were very rude folk, not to wave, even. Carey was biting the corner of his lip and looking nervous, while Barnabus had the narrow-eyed thoughtful expression he wore when he was waiting for trouble. Dodd loosened his sword and wished for a bow.

'Don't kill anybody, Sergeant,' Carey said. 'Even if there's a fight.'

'Why not?'

'You've no idea what a bloody nuisance it is to fix juries in London,' Carey snapped. 'So don't get yourself hanged.'

Their horses' hooves slipped and scuffed on the dusty clay as they negotiated a whole fine litter of red piglets plugged into their dam across the middle of the lane. There was a stone water conduit at the end of the lane, where city women stood waiting to draw water – fine ladies too, by the looks of their velvet trimmed kirtles and outrageously feathered hats. The Strand was wide and choking with dust, the biggest houses Dodd had ever seen in his life rearing up like cliffs on either side of it.

'Hell's teeth,' said Carey, catching sight of the decorative gathering at the conduit. 'The wives are out to watch.'

Dodd gestured at an impressive house opposite the conduit. 'Is that yer father's house . . .?' he asked. Carey shook his head and pointed at the gatehouse of a towering elaboration of a palace that Dodd had taken for the Queen's court itself.

'And here they come,' said Barnabus, as a crowd of large men in buff coats, waving pieces of paper and clubs and coshes, moved suddenly in their direction.

Just for a second, Dodd saw Carey on the verge of running like a rabbit. If he hadn't known why Carey was so afraid of arrest, he would have thought it funny, but since he did, he decided that he wasn't going to allow it and the hell with London juries, they had to catch him first.

Dodd drew his sword and drove his horse into the thick of the shouting crowd of men. As he'd thought, they wanted their bounties for arresting Carey, but not at the expense of their heads, and they fell back in front of him. At least Carey, Barnabus and Simon had the sense to stick close behind him. The boom of Carey's second dag rang out by Dodd's ear as he discharged it into the air. A couple of bailiffs clutched desperately for Carey's reins and stirrup leathers. One fell back with a broken nose from a vicious kick from Carey's boot, and Barnabus's horse co-operatively trod on another one's foot, making him howl.

And then they were through, the whole bunch scattering at the edges, the other people in the street staring, a couple of children laughing and pointing and the women round the conduit clapping.

They clattered inside the shelter of the gatehouse, Dodd turning at the opening with his sword ready and his teeth bared. The bailiffs had followed them, though at a safe distance. A hubbub rose from them in which the words 'writs', 'warrants' and 'Westminster Hall' could be heard and more papers were waved.

'Och,' said Dodd, spitting deliberately at the feet of the biggest one. 'If ye think ye can take a Dodd fra Tynedale, come on and try it.'

Carey was shouting at the gatekeeper in his lodge. Surely to God they weren't at the wrong place? Was Carey's father not there? What was going on? Dodd had his horse placed sideways on to block any rushes, but he didn't think the bailiffs had the stomach for a real fight.

'Ay tell you what,' he said conversationally, and trying hard to talk as much like Barnabus as he could so they would understand him. 'Since ye're all a bunch o' catamites wi' nae bollocks at all, I'll take three o' ye at once so I dinnae outnumber ye.'

The biggest bailiff stopped and frowned in puzzlement. How much longer would it take Carey to get into his father's house? If this had been anywhere in Cumberland, they would all have been dead by now. A coach bowled past like the Devil himself.

Surely somebody would have a go soon? Even Londoners couldn't be that soft. Dodd gripped his sword more tightly and wished again for his nice comfortable jack and helmet, and a lance as well while he was at it. He looked about in case the bailiffs had sent for reinforcements. How far did a messenger have to go to find men? How long would Carey be chatting in the gatehouse . . .?

The postern gate opened finally and Carey beckoned. Instinctively Dodd sent the boy in first leading the horses, then Barnabus, before backing his own horse through the gate. That was the bailiffs' last chance to hit him but by that time his already low opinion of southerners was at rock bottom.

'Off ye go, lads,' he sneered at the bewildered bunch. 'Ye've lost us. Best get back to yer mams and yer fancy-boys.' He gave a hard final stare at the biggest bailiff as the postern gate shut and Carey barred it.

He turned to see a small yard beetled over by high stone and brick walls. A groom came to take the horses. Someone else in yellow and black livery, wearing a badge that looked like a duck in the throes of delirium, came hurrying out, bowing to Carey who greeted the plump little man with a familiar clap on the shoulder. The servant led them through a stunning marble entrance hall and into a small parlour lined with painted cloths and dotted with benches and stools padded in primrose yellow. In a corner was a virginals, painted with enamel people, mostly naked and winged, with the cover on. Another man in glaring livery brought wine which Dodd tasted with habitual suspicion before finding it quite smooth and hardly sour at all. Carey knocked his back in one and held out the silver goblet for a refill. Then he threw himself onto a bench, stretched his long legs in front of him, crossed them at the ankles and grinned.

'Can't think what I was so worried about,' he said to Dodd.

Dodd himself was still worried. Magnificent and palatial though Carey's family house was, it didn't look very defensible, with no proper pele tower, no battlements, no moat, no mound, no visible ordnance. There didn't seem many men around either.

'Ay,' he said. 'But how long before we have your . . . creditors around our ears like flies?'

Carey laughed. 'Well, they won't have pikes and muskets like the Grahams' debt-collectors.'

'Oh? What then?' asked Dodd, interested to know what weapons Londoners preferred.

'Writs,' said Carey. 'Blizzards of paper.'

Dodd began wondering irritably what all the fuss had been about. Barnabus took Simon off with him to see to the small amount of luggage they had brought with them in their saddlebags and Carey wandered familiarly round the room with another goblet of wine in his hand.

'Place seems deserted,' he commented. 'Where the devil's Father gone?'

On that instant there was the sound of a female voice raised in argument outside the door which opened to let the owner of the voice come in. It was a young woman trailed by a maidservant and a young man in Hunsdon's livery who was still arguing with her back.

'Mistress, this is unwise, this is very very foolish, my lord Hunsdon will . . .' droned the servingman in a voice that sounded as if it had been flattened with a hot iron. The maidservant elbowed him and he finally fell silent, looking crestfallen.

Dodd gawked. For all the cunning cut of her green velvet English gown, it was quite obvious the lady was pregnant. She was also tall, lushly built with a haughty expression on her face, light hazel eyes, skin creamy and hardly painted at all, and magnificent rich glossy black hair tumbling down her back in a proudly maidenlike display, only slightly controlled by a rope of pearls and emeralds wound about it.

Dodd felt quite pleased to see something so restful to the eye, especially as her neckline was cut temptingly low. He heard Carey's breath check infinitesimally beside him. A second later Carey was on his feet, sweeping a tremendous bow. Dodd's eyes were trapped by the velvet valley above the short bodice as she curtseyed in response. Then the lovely view was cut off because the lady had opened her arms, put her head on one side and Carey had folded her to his chest with a most disrespectfully thorough kiss on her mouth.

'Mistress Bassano,' he said caressingly when he had come up for air. 'What a splendid joy to see you again.'

Mistress Bassano laughed, put up a hand to stroke Carey's cheek. 'Whatever are you doing in London, Robin?' she asked. 'I thought you'd run away from me forever.'

Good God, thought Dodd in despair, not another loose bitch, and then bitterly, and not for the first time, how the devil does he draw the women to him like that?

'I could say that my despair at being parted from you so poisoned my meat and drink that in order to survive I was forced to return,' Carey suggested.

Mistress Bassano tossed her head haughtily. 'And I would say you were lying to me.'

'Well, I am,' Carey admitted, his blue eyes sparkling. 'My blasted father ordered me south.' A worrying thought obviously struck him. 'It isn't . . . er . . . He hasn't . . . er . . .?'

Mistress Bassano shook her head. 'No, no. I'm sure he doesn't know.'

Dodd caught the knowing glance from the maidservant to the servingman and felt his heart sink even further. What the hell was going on here?

'His lordship was in Chelsea this afternoon,' put in the man-servant. 'We expect him at any minute. He . . . er . . . didn't leave any orders about you, sir.'

'Mm,' Carey smiled kindly on the man. 'How is it with you, Will, any luck?'

Will shook his head, looking doleful. 'No, sir. If it weren't for your father giving me his livery, I'd be in the Fleet.'

'Bit of a comedown, isn't it, after this spring?'

Will shrugged. 'Can't be helped, sir.'

Mistress Bassano had swept a glance at Dodd which instantly dismissed him, moved to the virginals in the corner and lifted the cover. She sat down and pressed some of the notes, tilted her head consideringly and then leaned down to find the tuning key. Dodd tried to stop himself from staring at those milky plump breasts that seemed fashionably on the point of bursting out of the bodice. Would they? Could they?

She caught him at it and gave him a coldly knowing glare as she twiddled one of the pegs that was not to her satisfaction. Then she put the key back on its hook and placed her fingers to play.

Carey stood over her, no doubt getting a leisurely eyeful of the view and she smiled over her shoulder at the manservant.

'Will,' she said. 'Would you fetch me the Italian songsheets?'

Will's pointed face went pink. 'Yes, mistress,' he said and hurried over to delve in a chest by the wall, bringing out sheafs of paper dotted over with music. When he brought them to her, Dodd saw his hands shake as he arranged them on the music stand. He too seemed to be fighting the urge to stare and then Dodd was shocked to see one of Mistress Bassano's slim hands lift from the keyboard and briefly brush his leg. Carey was craning over, ostensibly to read the music, and Mistress Bassano's other hand went quietly out of sight somewhere in the vicinity of Carey's trunkhose.

Dodd's mouth had to be shut consciously. It turned down in stern disapproval of the whole proceedings.

'Sir,' said Mistress Bassano, turning from between her two admirers and finally favouring him with a dazzling smile that seemed to promise worlds of pleasure. 'Robin has been very rude to you, not introducing you.'

Dodd coughed, pulled off his hat, did the best bow he could muster which he knew, to his despair, was a lumpen misshapen thing in comparison to Carey's grace.

'Sergeant Henry Dodd,' he growled. 'Land Sergeant of Gilsland.'

The pointed chin on its proudly held neck tilted a little in acknowledgement. 'Can you sing, Sergeant Dodd?'

'Ay I can, a bit,' he allowed.

'And what is your voice?'

Her own voice was deeper than most women's but as velvet as the rest of her. Dodd's mouth had gone dry as the old Adam in him went skipping off into sinful daydreams. He licked his lips.

'Ah. I dinna ken. It's just a voice.'

Carey was smiling knowingly at him, over the top of Mistress Bassano's gleaming head. 'I've never heard you sing, Dodd?'

You bastard, thought Dodd. 'Ay, well, I wouldnae claim to be a gleeman, see,' he said. 'But I can hold ma own wi' a lay.'

Delicate frown lines appeared on Mistress Bassano's smooth forehead. 'What is he saying, Robin?' she asked. 'Is he a northerner?'

Carey bent and whispered in her ear and her magnetic smile dimmed a little to become patronising. 'Well, but I am disappointed. Robin and Will are both tenors, and it would be good if we had a basso. Do you have a deep voice, Sergeant?'

Dodd coughed again, suppressing the wistful wish that she would call him Henry. 'Ay, I reckon. But I cannae read music, mistress. Words, ay, but not notes.'

The full pink lips pouted in disappointment as Carey whispered his translation. 'Oh what a pity. Never mind. You can be our audience and make useful criticisms.'

I could criticise you, mistress, Dodd thought, as he watched a blush going all the way up into what was left of the manservant's hair under his cap, I could criticise you with a will, ay, criticise you till ye squealed for more, but it doesnae suit me to take thirds. Mistress Bassano's hands reappeared to place on the keyboards and she launched into the beginning of one of Carey's favourite Court songs, a ditty that had all the pointless complexity of a lace ruff.

Carey's voice rang out, taking the main part and Mistress Bassano's voice rose with his. Somewhere in the background Will was adding his own voice, in a key that was awkward for him so he growled in the deeps.

It was very good. Even Dodd had to admit that Carey's voice was far better than ordinary and Mistress Bassano's was a marvel of poured cream, while the ruthlessly pre-empted Will still seemed to know what he was about. Personally, Dodd had no taste for foreign songs, preferring familiar tunes like the Ballad of Chevy Chase, but you could tell it was a clever thing they were doing even if you couldn't understand a word of it and the shape of the music was strange.

They wound sinuously to a halt, Mistress Bassano gazing full into Carey's eyes while he smiled down at her, both mouths open, carolling like birds in spring. Will had been completely outbid, and he knew it, for once his part finished he moved away from the virginals to stand by the door with a face as miserable as a leaking roof.

A trumpet sounded from the water just as Carey bent to kiss Mistress Bassano's mouth again. Jesus, did the man have no shame? But then Dodd was honest enough to admit to himself that if he had the chances Carey seemed to attract, he wouldn't waste one of them either. What would it be like to kiss that curving mouth, Dodd wondered, could you get your hand between the bodice and the tit or would you have to mess about with her lacings first? Carey seemed to know the answers to these important questions. Over by the door, Will looked deliberately away from the scandalous sight, his mouth and nose pinched with distress.

The shouting and trumpets from the other side of the house grew louder. Dodd moved swiftly to the windows facing the noise and found himself looking out on a vast garden, as big as the Maxwells' or bigger, where more men in yellow livery were hurrying up the paths from a gate in a wall. Doors crashed open, someone shouted something about my Lord Chamberlain Hunsdon and Mr Vice Chamberlain Thomas Heneage. At the last possible minute, Carey straightened up, moved smoothly away from Mistress Bassano and sat down at his ease on a bench again.

The doors to the parlour burst open.

Standing framed there was a broad elderly man in black velvet and gold brocade, his hair rusty grey, his face red, his eyes a shrewd dark grey. He was wearing a terrifying expression of disgust and rage. The sheer physical presence of the man almost blotted out the second richly-dressed courtier standing next to him, not as tall, not quite as broad in the shoulder, but a great deal more fleshy. That one had a round face and a prim mouth, though his face was presently decorated with a smile.

Carey leapt to his feet.

'Robert!' boomed Lord Hunsdon. 'What the Devil are you doing here, God damn your eyes?!'

Carey swept a bow to his father so poetical in its elaboration of courtesy that it came out the other side into insolence. Hunsdon glowered, swept forward to bring his white Chamberlain's staff slamming down on a nearby table. 'By Christ, Robert,' he roared. 'I've told Heneage here, if you've got yourself into trouble with Her Majesty again, I'll disinherit you.'

Dodd, who had lost his own father to an Elliot polearm at the age of twelve, watched in fascination. Something shifted subtly inside Carey. He bowed again, including the other rich courtier this time.

'My good lord and respected Father, and Mr Vice Chamberlain, may I present my most able second-in-command at Carlisle, Mr Henry Dodd, Land Sergeant of Gilsland.'

Not knowing what else to do with himself, Dodd managed a clutch at his cap and an ungainly bow. The small parlour was suddenly crowded with people. A liveryman bustling about behind him, lighting unnecessary candles, made him twitch. Another man brought up a carved armchair for his lord, yet another poured more wine. Plates of wafers and nuts appeared seemingly invisibly.

Hunsdon threw his bulk into the armchair which creaked under him. Mr Vice Chamberlain Heneage sat more circumspectly a little behind and to the right on a yellow padded stool. Hunsdon rapped his white staff on the floor.

'Right,' he growled. 'Scotland.'

'Most reverend sir,' said Carey. 'I would prefer to have cleaned off the dust of our rather hurried journey before I rendered my report to . . .'

'Ay, no doubt. But we want to hear it now, since you're here, you bloody idiot.'

The tips of Carey's ears had gone red. He put his hat back on his head and sat himself back down on the bench very pointedly, without being asked. Dodd decided to stay standing.

'Where should I start, my lord?' Nobody smiled that sweetly without intending it as an insult. Hunsdon's bushy eyebrows almost met over his nose.

'How is His Majesty of Scotland?' put in Heneage, mellifluously.

'Very well indeed and received me most kindly on account of the love he bears Her Majesty the Queen.'

Hunsdon grunted. 'And the business over the guns? Lowther sent some nonsensical tale that you had substituted them for scrap iron. Is that true?'

Carey waved gloved fingers airily. 'A complete mare's nest, sir. There was indeed an arrangement between His Majesty of Scotland and the Wardenry of Carlisle, as it turned out, only no one saw fit to inform me.'

'I'd heard that some of the guns we sent were faulty,' said Heneage with oily concern. 'I do hope no one was hurt?'

'One man lost his hand and died of it, but no other harm done,' Carey told him callously. 'Really, the guns were a side-issue. We rode to congratulate my Lord Maxwell on being made Warden and of course to learn what support the King might want when he harried Liddesdale . . .'

Dodd's eyes were nearly popping out with shock. The tale Carey told his father . . . Improved was too mild. A tissue of lies spun convincingly from Carey's smiling mouth. There had been no problems whatever at the Scottish Court. Lord Maxwell had been kindness itself and of course Sir John Carmichael sent his regards. The King had been at his most affable, only a little sad at the smallness of his bribe . . . er, pension. Spanish spies? What Spanish spies? Oh, those Spanish spies. Well, Carey had not suspected the Italian wine merchant and his charming wife, but he had heard that Lord Spynie was deep in dangerous business with the Papists, for what that was worth. These rumours will fly around, won't they, Mr Vice Chamberlain, shocking really, what people will say in the hope of payment. Sir Henry Widdrington? Well, yes, admitted Carey, he had met the man. A little too warm to the Scots perhaps, and another one with Papist leanings, he was sure. My Lord Hunsdon might want to warn his Deputy Warden, brother John, up in Berwick, about the Widdringtons, seeing how powerful they were . . .

After a while Dodd stopped trying to follow exactly where Carey was sticking to the truth and where he was lying to his father, and sat back to admire the barefaced way he did it. Heneage and Hunsdon both asked pointed questions that sounded as if Lowther had been busy with his pen. Carey actually laughed when Heneage wanted to know if King James had given him a pension. No, said Carey, he had been lucky with some bets, that was all. And of course he had sold Thunder to the King.

'Hmf,' said Hunsdon. 'Pity. Best piece of horseflesh you ever owned.'

'I know sir,' said Carey with genuine regret. 'But what could I do? The King wanted him. I was quite pleased he paid for the nag, really.'

'Hah!' said his father, standing and striding out into the entrance hall while he shouted for the steward. Carey elaborately gave way to Heneage as they followed and then muttered quietly over his shoulder, 'Back me up, Dodd.'

Before Dodd could answer, Carey had hurried after his father. Dodd was pressed to keep up, reflecting that the Carey family were very tiring people, the way they were always rushing about. Hunsdon had decided to take a turn in the garden while they waited for supper to be readied, which displeased Dodd who would have been perfectly happy with a hunk of bread and some cheese, so long as he could put something in his growling belly immediately. But no, it seemed courtiers did things differently.

Dodd had never seen the point of gardens really, except for herbs and salads and the like. Janet had a garden at their tower in Gilsland and Lord knows, she had given him grief when his favourite horse got out and ate all the pea plants. This was nothing like anything he had seen. In the pale blue dusk, the garden stretched itself down to the wall, everything in it shouting of wealth, from the rose bushes and the maze to the grass which was scythed short and green as velvet, to the trees which were politely trimmed. Dodd wandered across the grass and peeked out of the gate which gave onto the water. He saw a little landing with yellow boats drawn up and a man standing watching them. The man touched his cap to Dodd and Dodd nodded back in lordly fashion, thoroughly enjoying himself. There was an hysterical duck carved in the stone lintel of the watergate and another one on the boatman's sleeve. Dodd wondered why Lord Hunsdon had chosen such a daft badge for himself. He was impressed with the Thames, though. It was wide and fast flowing and looked an unchancy water to cross even at low tide. Good thing there was the Bridge. Even Dodd had heard tell of the glories of London Bridge, though mostly from Barnabus who couldn't really be trusted.

Someone coughed softly at his elbow and Dodd looked sideways to find he was being quietly accosted by the Vice Chamberlain.

'Mr Dodd.'

'Ay, sir,' said Dodd, wondering had the man not heard he was Land Sergeant of Gilsland or did he not know how to address him?

'Perhaps you can help me.'

'If Ah can, sir.'

'What was your impression of the King's court in Scotland?'

Dodd thought for a moment. Heneage's face was full of friendliness and affability, which was all wrong. Dodd knew he was very small fry compared to the Vice Chamberlain of the Queen's court, and no great lord was that affable to his inferiors without he wanted something.

'Ah dinna ken, sir,' he said. 'I've no' seen any ither court, sir, for comparison.'

'Did the King seem well-affected?'

What the Devil did the man mean by that? Well-affected?

'Ah dinna ken, sir.'

'Well, did His Majesty grant Sir Robert an audience?'

'Oh ay, sir, he did that.'

'And what happened?'

'Ah dinna ken, sir, I wasnae there.'

'Sir Robert was alone, unattended?'

'I didnae say that, sir, only I wasnae there.'

'Well, was my Lord Spynie present at the audience?'

'Ah dinna ken, sir.'

Heneage coughed. 'Come, Mr Dodd, you're a man of parts, I can see, Sir Robert wouldn't employ you if you weren't.' Dodd felt pricklish. He wasn't Carey's servant, even if he was under the Courtier's command. He was a free man, with his own tower and kin to back him. What the Devil did Heneage think he was, some kind of hanger-on?

Heneage was smiling. Was Dodd supposed to be pleased he thought well of Dodd? Bugger that, thought Dodd.

'Do you think Sir Robert will be returning to the Scottish court soon?' From the casual way in which it was asked, that sounded an important question.

Dodd took refuge in stolidity. 'Ah dinna ken, sir. And it isnae my place to say, forbye, sir.'

Heneage coughed again, but would he leave off? No, he would not. Where the hell was Carey when he was needed?

'Well, perhaps you can tell me how Signor and Signora Bonnetti fare?'

'Eh, sir?'

Heneage's round little smile was becoming somewhat fixed. 'The Italian wine merchant and his wife. Perhaps you recall them?'

Dodd thought about it for a while. 'Ay, I mind 'em.'

Another silence. Heneage took a deep breath, held it and coughed again. 'Did . . . ah . . . did Signora Bonnetti seem well-affected to Sir Robert?'

Dodd looked even more blank. 'Sir?'

'Surely you met the lady?'

Heneage had come closer, had taken Dodd's elbow in a proprietorial fashion. 'Come, Dodd, we can deal together,' he said softly. 'Do you know who I am?'

'Ay, sir,' said Dodd, wishing to flick Heneage's importunate fingers off his arm but controlling himself. 'Ye're the Queen's Vice Chamberlain.'

'One of my offices is to thoroughly investigate all potential . . . ah . . . foreign problems. You can be sure I ask my questions with good reason.'

'Ay, sir.' Was there some kind of threat in Heneage's silky confiding manner? Did he expect Dodd to be frightened or flattered? The plump fingers were nipping quite hard now, they were stronger than they looked. Dodd's eyes narrowed and he could feel anger starting to wash up the back of his neck. Was the fat courtier trying to bully him? *Him?*

'I have other sources regarding Signora Bonnetti,' breathed Heneage. 'You needn't fear that you will tell me anything I don't already know about your master. I am only looking for confirmation.'

Carey was standing over by a tree next to his father. Their eyes met briefly and Dodd could have sworn the Courtier winked knowingly at him. Dodd had never been so angry in his life without he punched somebody, but Carey steadied him. He took a deep shaky breath.

'I'm sorry, sir, but I cannae help ye, for I never met the lady.'

'Surely you saw her, for she danced with Sir Robert.' Jesus, would Heneage never let up?

'Ay, she did, sir, but I niver spoke to her.'

'Sir Robert was friendly with her? Hm?'

'She's a fair lady,' said Dodd, not bothering to keep his voice as low as Heneage's. 'I never saw Sir Robert but he was friendly to a good-looking woman.'

Heneage chuckled softly. 'Did they deal together?'

Much more of this, thought Dodd, and I surely will punch the bugger. Once again Carey caught his eye, still speaking to his father. Looking very amused, the Courtier shook his head infinitesimally.

Dodd felt as if he was drowning. What did Carey want him to do? Lie? But he didn't know what to say.

'Ah'm sorry, sir,' he said to Heneage at last when he was sure his voice wouldn't shake. 'But I cannae help ye as ye think I can. I'm no' Sir Robert's servant, I'm nobbut a Sergeant o' the Carlisle garrison.'

At last Heneage let go of him, leaving tingling prints on Dodd's elbow. He didn't seem dissuaded, only calculating. 'Perhaps we can talk at some other time. Perhaps I should invite you to my residence at Chelsea.'

Even Dodd could hear that there was a threat in the man's voice, though the words seemed harmless enough.

31

'That's kind of ye, sir,' he said, struggling to be urbane.

Heneage frowned as if Dodd had insulted him. 'Don't under-estimate me, Dodd.'

What the hell had he said that was wrong? 'I dinna follow ye, sir.'

'No? Perhaps you should ask your Captain to elucidate.'

'Ay, sir,' said Dodd, taking refuge in stolidity again.

Heneage sighed and shook his head. 'Was there nothing at all that struck you about the Scottish court?'

Dodd took a deep breath. 'They was an awfy lot of buggers there, sir. Ah didnae take to it mesen.'

Heneage's brow wrinkled as he tried to make out what Dodd was saying.

'I'm afraid Sergeant Dodd thoroughly disapproved of the Scots court and the whole proceedings generally, didn't you, Sergeant?' translated Sir Robert who had finally drifted over to them. His father was still under the apple tree, poking with his staff at the green apples weighing the branches.

'Ay, sir. I'm no' a courtier, sir.'

Both men heard the compressed distaste in his voice. Heneage smiled; Carey's eyebrows went up quizzically.

'Well, each to his own,' he said comfortably. 'Eh, Mr Vice Chamberlain? Good thing not everyone is desperate for the court, or the place would be even more infernally crowded than it is now. How are the accommodations at Oxford? Colleges being co-operative?'

Heneage sniffed. 'Helpful enough, though not perhaps as willing as one would like, Sir Robert.'

'You'll be doubling up the Gentlemen, no doubt. I remember one Progress when I had to share a bed with Sir Walter Raleigh. Though he was still a plain mister then – it was a few years ago now. And the only reason we didn't have a third man in bed with us was because we bribed him to sleep on the floor.'

Dodd found to his astonishment that his hands were shaking. Never had he felt such pure rage and been forced to do nothing about it. His arm felt unclean where Heneage had dared to pinch it. And what the hell was he hinting about his residence in Chelsea? Dodd would personally eat his helmet if the Queen's Vice Chamberlain was planning to invite him to a dinner party, no matter how eager he was to pick Dodd's brains on the subject of Carey's doings in Scotland.

They were moving back towards the house, Carey prattling about Raleigh's sleeping habits. Raleigh, it seemed, had been unreasonably insulting to Carey, claiming he snored like a wild sow in farrow, which was manifestly unfair. Was it true that Raleigh was in the Tower now, over one of the Queen's maids of honour? Heneage allowed that it was and Carey displayed an almost infantile pleasure at the juicy nugget of gossip – Bess Throgmorton, well, he was damned, would never have thought she'd have it in her, though he knew Raleigh did, and now it seemed she had more in her than she rightfully should . . . Carey put his head back and laughed. Serve Raleigh right, the man's arrogance was insufferable.

Mistress Bassano came out, gliding over the grass, very lithe and graceful for a woman in her condition, with two of her women, one on either side of her and her bald manservant trotting at her heels like a bloodhound. A small hairy dog followed close behind him completing the symmetry.

Hunsdon joined them from the apple tree, and Mistress Bassano smiled like a cat as he caught her hand and put a large arm proprietorially around her shoulders. She kissed Hunsdon as lingeringly on the lips as she had earlier kissed Carey. Dodd could almost feel his eyes bulging from their sockets. Was Carey really ploughing his father's field? Was that why he had come to be Deputy Warden in Carlisle? By God, it made sense of why a popinjay Courtier would want to move north in a hurry.

Carey was showing not a single sign of guilt. He was laughing and chatting to Heneage in the most natural and carefree way, taking the trouble to flatter the Vice Chamberlain as he had buttered up Lord Maxwell in Scotland.

A liveryman came out and announced that supper was served, and as he followed Hunsdon and his mistress, Carey, Heneage and flocks of attendants, Dodd's head was reeling.

*　　　*　　　*

Supper involved eight different kinds of meat in sixteen different sauces, salads decorated with orange nasturtium flowers, a piece of a pie which must originally have been the size and weight of a millstone, and yet more of the wine. Dodd had always thought he didn't like wine but now realised that what he didn't like was cheap wine. If this was the way the better stuff tasted, he felt he could well get used to it.

The pity of it was having to sit down with Carey, his dad, his dad's mistress, and Heneage in another room hung with tapestries. Servants filed in with the food under silver covers on silver dishes as ceremoniously as if this were some fine feast, which only meant further delay before Dodd could fill his belly. Lord Hunsdon said grace. After all that, Dodd had almost lost his appetite again. Heneage tucked in enthusiastically, though.

Dodd concentrated on eating as neatly as he could, despite the way the Vice Chamberlain had soured his stomach. He watched out of the corner of his eye to see how Carey handled his eating knife and silver spoon and tried hard to copy him. The funny foreign sauces on the meats didn't help and he dropped a big piece of pheasant into the rushes. Mistress Bassano's lapdog was onto the tidbit at once, slurping and growling at it. Trying to pretend he had meant to drop the food, Dodd patted the hairy head and had his fingers nipped at for his pains, which made Mistress Bassano smile at him again.

'Little Willie is a very naughty dog,' she told him with a teasing note in her voice. 'You really must not indulge him, Sergeant, or he'll get fat.'

Dodd smiled at her apologetically while he mentally took all her clothes off and bulled her up against a wall. As if reading his mind and enjoying it, she bent over and scooped the dog into her arms, while Dodd tried desperately to stop himself wondering if her arse was as smooth and round as her tits. He concentrated on the meat again. Much more of this, he thought, and he wouldn't be able to rise from the table.

The talk went right over his head too, though it seemed to be swirling repeatedly around the twin whirlpools of Carey's relations with the Scottish King and the question of the Italian woman. Mistress Bassano must have been foreign herself with that name but spoke like any other southerner. She was sitting next to Lord Hunsdon and leant against him scandalously. Carey's father seemed not exactly smitten – more pleased and smug like a bull next to his favourite heifer. Carey sat opposite her and next to Heneage. Thank God, the Courtier was studiously avoiding the lady's eye.

Mistress Bassano talked, laughed, preened and, unless Dodd was much mistaken, the whole pleasing display was aimed straight at Carey and not his dad. That was distinctly tactless and Carey seemed a little worried by it. He struck up another gossipy conversation with Heneage in a bid to avoid the noonday glare of Mistress Bassano's dangerous flirtation. It didn't work, for she kept interrupting.

At last the food was finished – or at least they had eaten their fill for there was too much to be got down in one sitting. Dodd wondered what happened to the leftovers – the Hunsdon pigs must live like kings and be fat as butter.

The leavetaking was prolonged and jovial, Carey talking rather at random as Heneage and his followers went down to the river again and took a few of the boats. Dodd was more than ready for his bed. Mistress Bassano went ostentatiously to her chamber, kissing Lord Hunsdon fondly on the lips and giving Carey's fingers a squeeze when he bent to kiss her hand.

Dodd had half-expected to be put in the servants' quarters or on a truckle bed in Carey's room, but it seemed the Hunsdon steward knew more about what a Land Sergeant was than did Heneage. He was stunned at the magnificence of his bedchamber – a fashionably golden oak-panelled cavern and no less than a four-poster bed complete with a tester and pale summer curtains. The servingman who led him there through a bewildering number of corridors and rooms advised him to shut his bed curtains against bad ague airs from the Thames and asked with a careful lack of expression and no hint of a glance at his homespun if the Land Sergeant would require a man to help him undress. Dodd told him no and decided on his usual ale and bread for breakfast at a restful 7 o'clock in the morning, well after sun-up. Now that was something to look forward to – a nice lie-in when he was neither wounded nor sick.

For a while, Dodd wandered around the room admiring the vast quantity of things in it; the painted cloths, the clothes chests, the carved folding chair, the fireplace laid with logs in case he should feel cold and a tinderbox beside it. There were candles everywhere, at least five of them and not a speck of tallow but the finest beeswax. Dodd firmly crushed the urge to slide them into his pocket. The rushes on the floor were new all the way down to the floor and the windows were glass with wooden shutters, so that not only was there no draught but you could even look out of them quite well. In awe Dodd touched the carved babies rioting with grape vines across the mantelpiece: he liked to whittle on wood himself and appreciated fine workmanship.

At last he shucked his clothes down to his shirt, left them folded on the chest, drew the curtains around the bed and climbed gingerly in, sliding between ice-smooth linen sheets that had not only never been slept in by another body but must have been ironed as well. By God, what it was to have hordes of servants, he thought, as he shut his eyes and snuggled into the softness of the pillows.

Half an hour later he turned over for the forty-fourth time and opened his eyes. It was no good. He couldn't sleep. He was used to sleeping alone – the jealously guarded privilege of his own cubbyhole next to the bunkroom of the barracks at Carlisle was normally his sole domain. But the fact remained that this bed was bigger than that entire tiny room. The vast spaces of the chamber outside the curtains, unpeopled by friendly farting snoring humanity, made him as nervous as a horse in an empty stable.

He got up, wandered around the room again, peered out of the window, swatted an enterprising mosquito and then found the jug of spiced wine. That was a blessing. Sipping lukewarm spiced syrup from the silver goblet provided, he looked again out of the window and saw someone moving on the Strand. Those bailiffs weren't giving up; two men in buff coats were watching the gatehouse like cats at a mousehole.

Thursday, 31st August 1592, morning

2

Next morning Dodd had a slight headache from the spiced wine but felt happier than he could remember after sleeping so late and waking in solitary state with no one hammering on the door telling him the Grahams were over the Border or Gilsland was under siege. God knew what was going on at home with the whole Border Country as stirred up as it was, but what could he do about it? A man-servant brought in his breakfast on a tray and seemed surprised to find him already up and dressed.

Sitting by the window again, he ate fine white manchet bread with fresh-made butter and cheese and drank ale as nutty and sweet as Bessie's. It was fine to look down on all the folk milling around, working hard, and the shops opening up with a rattle of shutters. And it was staggering the wealth here; even the prentices had velvet sleeves and the kitchen maids wore silk ribbons and fine hats. How would you pillage London, Dodd wondered, where would you begin? Fetching the spoils away might be a problem – there didn't seem to be many horses around. Most people were on foot.

There was a knock on the door and Carey entered, resplendent in black velvet and brocade, a suit Dodd didn't think he had seen before. He had obviously been up since well before sunrise and was full of plans. He instantly destroyed the restful peace of the morning.

'Morning, Sergeant,' he said cheerfully, strode to the window and peered out. His brows knitted. 'Christ, we're under siege.'

Dodd looked out again at once, but couldn't see any armed

39

concourse of men, so assumed the Courtier was exaggerating about debt-collectors again. 'Oh ay?'

Carey paced up and down tiringly. 'I was going to slip out by river this morning, have a look round, but there was a whole boatload of 'em waiting by the steps. And there are four that I recognise on the Strand now.'

Dodd nodded mournfully, though in fact he had rarely been more tickled by a situation in his life. God, whatever else you could say about the Courtier, he was very entertaining.

'Ay, they were keepin' watch here last night.'

'Were they?' Carey was only confirmed in his disgust. Off he went pacing again.

'Er . . . sir,' said Dodd tactfully. 'Yer father's a man o' substance and wealth.'

'Yes?'

'Could he not . . . er . . . pay 'em off, sir?'

The Courtier smiled sadly, wandered over to check the wine jug, lifted his eyebrows at Dodd and then poured himself a gobletful and knocked it back.

'Well, he could and he won't,' said Carey. 'He's rich, certainly, but most of it's in land and buildings. Very hard to get liquid cash off property like that; if you sell them you lose badly on the deal and mortgaging's even worse. Plus my esteemed eldest brother George would have a fit if Father sold any of his patrimony to pay more of my debts.'

'More?'

'He's already settled about four thousand pounds for me and lent me another thousand.'

Dodd's jaw dropped. He could not get used to the way Carey casually bandied about sums that he had never even thought about before, much less owned or spent.

'And then there's brother Edmund who's not cheap to maintain either, and John's expenses in Berwick are crippling. Father says if he kept paying off his sons' debts he'd be begging at Temple Gate in a year and stark raving mad into the bargain.'

'But sir! What on earth d'ye spend all this money on? Not just clothes, surely?'

'Oh clothes, armour, horses, masquing, occasional little bets, women, plays, cockfighting . . . God, I don't know. It just flows away from me somehow.'

'Ay. So how much d'ye owe?'

Carey shook his head. 'I'm not sure. Somewhere about another two or three thousand, I should think. Thereabouts.'

Very carefully Dodd shut his mouth and swallowed hard.

'Two or three thousand pounds?' he asked, just to get it straight. Carey looked mildly irritated.

'Well, it's not pennies, unfortunately.'

'And the creditors are feeling a mite impatient?'

'They're terrified because I got away from them last time and they think I'll do it again – go north and stay there until the lot of them are dead or in debtors' gaol themselves.' Dodd blinked at this admission. Even Carey had the grace to look a little shamefaced. 'Well, what else could I do?'

'Ay, sir. What?' echoed Dodd, thinking of a whole variety of sensible and economical things.

'Anyway, you have to spend money to get money. Which reminds me – did Heneage give you a bribe?'

'Nay, sir, he didnae,' said Dodd, feeling aggrieved. 'Nae such thing. He said he might invite me tae his residence in Chelsea, but nae more than that . . .'

Carey frowned. 'That was bloody cheeky of him.'

Dodd felt confused. 'It was?'

'Who does he think he is, threatening you in front of me and my father?'

'Ah . . . Was that what he wis doing, sir?'

Carey's frown lightened. 'Well, you'll have confused him at least. What did you say?'

'I said he wis kind, sir. Nae more.'

Carey shouted with laughter. 'I wish I'd been closer to see his reaction. You must be the first person he's said that to who didn't instantly quiver with fright.'

'Ay, he seemed puzzled. He said I should ask you, sir.'

'How would you react if Richie Graham invited you to Brackenhill to discuss your blackrent payments?'

'Och.' Dodd sucked his teeth. 'I see. What is Mr Heneage, exactly, sir?'

'One of the most powerful men in the kingdom and getting stronger every day. I'd say he's even keeping the Cecils up at nights.'

'Why? He disnae seem much of a fighting man.'

'Did you ever hear of Sir Francis Walsingham?'

'Ay, sir, ye've told me about him. The Queen's Secretary.'

'And chief intelligencer, until his death. Well, Heneage has taken over Walsingham's activities in collecting information here and abroad, and in hunting down Papist priests. Unlike Walsingham, he isn't an honest man. Interrogations of suspected traitors used to take place in the Tower of London, under warrant from the Queen. Now they happen at Chelsea.'

'But he couldnae arrest me, could he, Sir Robert? I'm no' a traitor.'

Carey said nothing to that, just looked at him until Dodd felt embarrassed by his naivety.

'It is certainly true,' said Carey eventually, in a distant tone of voice, 'that all suspected traitors who are taken to Heneage's house in Chelsea eventually confess to treason.'

'Ay,' said Dodd, his mouth gone dry. 'I see now what he was trying. What should I do, sir? He seems to think I know what went on in Scotland. And I dinna, sir, I was wi' the Johnstones when ye . . . er . . . when ye were talking to the King.'

'A piece of advice for you, Dodd,' Carey said, fiddling with the embroidered cuffs of his fancy gloves. 'If Heneage offers you a bribe, take it. Answer his questions, tell him whatever you can; by all means play stupid, but convince him that you are frightened enough of him to want to co-operate. He likes that.'

'Ay.'

Carey squinted through the window glass again and then sat down and ran his hand through his hair.

'My blasted father's disappeared off with Heneage to have a look at some property Mr Vice wants to buy. God knows why they're both here when the Queen's on progress in Oxford and they're thick as thieves as well. I thought Father loathed the man.'

'Perhaps Heneage wants blackrent fra yer father?' offered Dodd. Carey gave him one of those very blue considering looks of his.

'You catch on fast, don't you Dodd?' he said. 'Yes, I'm beginning to think something like that is going on, but I'm damned if I can work out what. Father ought to be untouchable by the likes of Heneage.'

Dodd knew this was because Lord Hunsdon was in fact the Queen's bastard half-brother. Carey was staring out of the window and the expression on his face was one that Dodd had never seen there before; a cold, wary, calculating look.

'Anyway, he says he wants me to write a report for him about Scotland. Presumably, one he can show to Heneage.'

'Ay, sir. Which tale will ye tell?'

Carey looked amused at Dodd's tone. 'The one for public consumption, of course. It seems nobody the Cecils or Heneage is paying for news from Scotland actually recognised me at the crucial time, which is a blessed relief. Thanks for backing me with Heneage, by the way, you did it perfectly. I nearly bust a gut trying not to laugh at his expression when you were stonewalling him.'

Dodd tilted his head in acknowledgement. 'Ay, sir. I'll own I was surprised to hear ye . . . er . . . tell such a strange tale to your dad.'

'What? You mean, lie to him?' Carey grinned, who would have instantly called Dodd out if he'd said the word himself. 'I didn't. He's already got the real report from me. He warned me to be tactful with Heneage, so I was.'

'Er . . . how?'

'Called me Robert. Never does that, not ever. Usually it's Robin, boy or bloody idiot, depending. I wanted to talk to him about it last night but his man said he was . . . ah . . . busy and passed the message about the report. Now it seems I'm stuck here indoors scribbling away like some damned clerk – God, how I hate paperwork. But I want you and Barnabus to go and do some scouting for me. See what's going on. Barnabus will want to put a notice up in St Paul's to find a new master and if you see any likely looking northerners who might make a decent *valet de chambre* for me, get their names. I may have to borrow somebody from Father, seeing the Court's not in town and the law term not started yet. And something's wrong here but I'm not sure what.'

'With your father?'

'And with London too. It's too quiet. Strand's half-empty. Where is everybody? Bartolmy's fair just packed up and Southwark due to start, but all the traders seem to have made off as fast as they can with their woolsacks and bolts of cloth. I want to know why. Stick close to Barnabus, and if you get lost, head south for the river and then go westwards until you find Somerset House. Or take a boat.'

'Ay, sir.'

'And leave any of your money behind that you don't want stolen. London pick-pockets are famous the world over.'

As Dodd had brought what had once seemed to him like the large sum of three shillings from his pay and also had an angel and some shillings from the footpads, he nodded at this good advice.

St Paul's was surrounded by a market full of little stalls filled up with booksellers and papersellers, more books than Dodd had ever seen in his entire life before. Even the Reverend Gilpin had never had such a lot of books. How could a man tell which he wanted to read? It was indecent. And the place was full of people standing around reading books or talking and arguing with each other. Two poorly-dressed hungry-looking men were arguing loudly with a fat man in an ink-stained apron who they seemed to think owed them money for their writing of a book, which he was strenuously denying.

Barnabus threaded through purposefully, swatting boys away from his pockets and disentangling Dodd from a pretty young piece in a mockado gown who seemed to think Dodd was her long-lost cousin.

They climbed the steps and went into the cathedral of London town, which was a great echoing monster of a building. The nave was full of little stalls, and scriveners tables, the aisle was full of young men who paraded in clothes that made Dodd gasp for the colours of them, the outrageous size of their cartwheel ruffs, the velvets, damasks and satins, the vast padded breeches and the long peascod bellies, the slashings and panes and embroideries. The human butterflies were in constant motion, bowing to each other, talking, laughing.

'Mm,' said Barnabus, staring about critically. 'Now where is everybody?'

'Eh?' said Dodd.

'Nobody here,' Barnabus said over his shoulder as he threaded across the circling stream of haberdashery to one of the huge round pillars near the high altar screen with its blaze of gold and silver and red silk banners. There were a number of men in jerkins or buff leather standing around the pillar, looking hopeful, pieces of paper pinned to a noticeboard behind them. Barnabus went straight to it, stole two pins from one of the older notices, and stuck up his own paper.

'There,' he said. 'I'll be sorry to leave 'im, but what can you do?'

'You're resigning from the Courtier's service?'

'I've had enough,' sniffed Barnabus. 'Carlisle don't suit me, what with nuffing to do and nearly getting hanged in the summer. I'll leave 'im when I've found a new master.'

'Hmf,' said Dodd. He'd never thought much of Barnabus, who rode like a sack of meal and half the time made no sense at all. Mind you, he had good skills at knife-throwing and the Courtier seemed to rate him, but that was all you could say in his favour really.

Barnabus squared his shoulders and looked round at the competition, some of which seemed large and ugly enough.

'Don't know what I'll find though,' said the little man gloomily. 'What with nobody being here.'

'But . . . look at 'em all.'

'Nah,' said Barnabus, folding his arms and leaning against another pillar to glare disapprovingly down the aisle. 'The Mediterranean's half-empty for the time of year. Must all be up at Oxford, arse-licking the Queen.'

How did they all fit in when they were here, Dodd wondered. He craned his neck to look up at the roof which seemed very new, the upper walls part burned. St Paul's had no proper spire, only a temporary roof where it should have been. Barnabus was beckoning one of the urchins playing dice by the altar steps.

'Here, you, boy. Show my friend here round Paul's for me and if nobody's nipped his purse by the time he gets back, I'll pay you a penny extra.'

Dodd shrugged and followed the mucky-faced child who pointed self-importantly at a large monument full of moping angels and rampant lions and the like on the south side, with a little chapel next to it. Apparently it was Duke Humphrey's tomb for certain sure and definite though some scurvy buggers said it was some John Beauchamp fellow or other, which it wasn't but Duke Humphrey's, did he understand?

Dodd shrugged again and said it could be Good King Henry's tomb for all he cared, to be told sharply that that one was in Westminster, didn't he know nuffing?

Tomb after tomb was knowledgeably pointed out, one with a lot of reverence as Sir Philip Sidney's, and they made the circuit of the nave where pie-sellers, stationers and the apple-women cried their wares. It all seemed crowded and noisy enough for Dodd.

At least the Londoners seemed to be friendly folk. Overfriendly, perhaps. Twice Dodd was hailed as an old friend by men he had never met before, one of them a southerner from Yorkshire by his speech.

The third time a complete stranger clasped his arm and demanded to know what he was doing in London, bless him, Dodd decided to play along with the game.

'Och, good day,' he said with as big a smile as he could muster. 'If it's no' Wee Colin Elliot himself,' he added, naming his family's bitterest enemy. 'What are ye doing here?'

The man, who was as tall as Dodd and by his speech had never been north of Durham in his life, laughed and bowed.

'I could ask the same of you, friend.'

'It's too long a tale to tell,' said Dodd who couldn't be bothered to make one up. 'How's yer wife and the bairns?'

'Well enough,' said the man. 'Well enough indeed. I thought it was you; I was just saying to my friend here, that's him to the life and it was.'

'Ay,' said Dodd, still smiling unnaturally until his face ached with the exercise. The friend was shorter and darker and both were well-dressed in wool suits trimmed with velvet.

'It does ma heart good to find a fellow Berwick man here in this nest of Southerners,' said the shorter of the two in a passable imitation of the Berwick way of talking. 'Mr Dodd, you must have a cup of wine with us. Will ye do that? Us northerners should stick together, after all.'

'Oh ay, we should. O' course,' said Dodd, glancing across at Barnabus who was deep in obsequious conversation with an elaborately taffeta'd young man. Dodd shrugged. If he wasn't feared of the Bewcastle Waste or the Tarras Moss, why should he be feared of London, strange place though it was?

He went along with his two new friends, smiling and laughing like the Courtier, and making out that he was there to deal wool. Oh and that was lucky, because they happened to dabble in the wool trade themselves, and the one that was calling himself Wee Colin Elliot had a number of sacks in a warehouse near Queen's Hythe just begging for a buyer since they'd missed the fair . . .

Dodd's heart began to beat hard as they went out of a side door he hadn't noticed, through the churchyard. It seemed they were heading for a narrow alleyway. A little bit late it occurred to him that actually, when he was on his own with neither his kin nor the men of the Carlisle guard to back him, he was feared of both the Waste and the Moss because they were normally full of robbers.

'They serve the finest wine in the world just around this corner . . .' said the smaller man, hurrying him into the alley.

Suddenly Dodd decided he'd had enough of the game. He balked just inside the alley, felt a hand clutching at his elbow, ducked instinctively, swung about and caught the arm of the bigger man who was bringing a small cudgel down on where Dodd's head would have been. Dodd snarled. This was something he understood. He headbutted the man so his nose flowered red, bashed the hand holding the cudgel up against the wall until the weapon dropped. There was a metallic flash in the corner of his eye, so he kneed the man to put him down, whirled around sweeping his broadsword from its sheath and caught a rapier on the forte of his sword. The rapier flickered past his ear a couple of times and terrified him by nearly taking out his eye. Dodd knew that a rapier which could thrust had all the advantage over a broadsword, especially when he wasn't wearing a jack, so he pulled out his dagger and went properly into the attack, crowding the smaller man up against the opposite wall and raining blows down on him so he had no chance to pull any fancy moves.

Something grabbed his leg and bit his calf and Dodd glared down to see that the larger man had crawled over, still sobbing, and had caught him. He stamped down with his other boot to get the teeth off and went after the one with the rapier again. Unfortunately the bastard southerner was running away, so Dodd shook his foot free again and gave chase.

Barnabus appeared in the mouth of the alley and thoughtfully tripped the man up. Dodd was onto him, kicked the dropped rapier away, hauled him up by a fistful of doublet and slammed him against the wall.

'Careful, mate,' said Barnabus confidentially over his shoulder from where he was robbing the man on the ground. 'Don't kill 'im; Sir Robert's right about juries round here.'

Dodd was snarling at his prize. 'If ye ken who I am, ye'd ken that Wee Colin Elliot's dad killed mine, ye soft wet southern fart. Wis it robbery ye were after, eh? Eh?!'

The man's eyes were swivelling in his head and he was gobbling. Dodd slammed him again. 'By Christ, did ye think I wear ma sword for a fucking decoration, ye long slimy toad's pizzle, who the hell d'ye think . . .'

'Well, 'e wasn't to know, was he?' said Barnabus reasonably. 'He just thought you was some farmer up for the law-term, what with yer homespun suit and funny talk. Poor bugger, look at 'im, he's gone to pieces.'

Dodd realised to his disgust that the man was actually crying now, and dropped him in a convenient pile of dung. Barnabus rolled him expertly, tutted and led the way out of the alley back to Ave Maria Lane, with a quick glance either side at the turning for further ambushes. Dodd, whose blood was up, rather hoped there would be someone, but put his sword away again when Barnabus hissed at him.

Feeling witty, Dodd paused, went back, found the rapier and broke it in two with his boot. Barnabus shook his head at the waste.

'Nasty foreign weapon,' Dodd explained. 'When d'ye think they'll come after us wi' their kin?'

Barnabus laughed. 'Never,' he said. 'Not the way you think. Though I'd keep a weather eye out for coney-catchers – they'll want your purse one way or the other, believe me.'

'What's a coney-catcher, for God's sake?'

Barnabus rolled his eyes at this display of ignorance. 'Someone what wants to help you rob yourself, someone what fools you and draws you in with your own greed and fear. It's philosophical, really. They say nobody can coney-catch an honest man. Mind you, I shouldn't think there's ever been one come to London before.'

Dodd grunted, suspicious of compliments, however back-handed. Not that it mattered. With luck, once the Lord Chamberlain and Vice had satisfied themselves that Carey wasn't working for Spanish spies nor likely to become King James's new catamite, the lot of them could go north again.

A scurrying down by the entrance to the crypt caught his eye. There were black rats on the steps, crawling over and under each other brazenly in daylight. Two rat corpses lay close by, swollen out of shape by death.

'Good God, look at that,' he said in horror. 'Look at the size o' them.'

Barnabus glanced over and shrugged. 'Oh yes,' he said off-handedly. 'They say the biggest rats in the world prance up and down Paul's aisle.'

'Ah hadnae thought they meant real rats.'

'Well both, it's one of them witty comments, innit. You coming in again?'

Suddenly he felt choked by all the buildings rising up around him, hemmed in and trapped. Your eyes were always coming up short against a wall, and he was trammelled and crowded with people, the stink would fell an ox. And he had always hated rats.

He stopped at the side door of the church, unable to bear the thought of entering the high solemnity of the place with its faded paintings too high up to be whitewashed and the human trash prancing to and fro nibbling meatpies beneath the hard-faced old-fashioned angels. And God knew what horrors were underneath, in the crypt where no-one went.

'I'll take a turn round about the churchyard,' he said, hoping Barnabus wouldn't notice how pale he felt. 'Take the air.'

Barnabus nodded. 'You'll be safe enough, I should think. It'll take them a day to work out what to do about you. You could buy yourself a book.'

'Good God, what would I want to do that for?' said Dodd. Barnabus grinned and winked at him, before disappearing into the gloom.

Dodd glowered around but found no more would-be friends. He ambled past the stalls of the churchyard, looking with growing astonishment at all the different books, just casually lying there, higgledy-piggledy in piles with the first pages pinned up on the support posts of the awnings and the brightly coloured signs over the stalls – there was a cock, a pig, a blackamoor, a mermaid, all different like inns.

He stopped under one awning, picked up a small volume and opened it, squinted to spell out the words under his breath. It was poetry – some tale about foreigners, he thought, from the funny names. Dodd couldn't be doing with such nonsense.

Suddenly he caught sight of a familiar face, Mistress Bassano's servant, the balding young man called Will. He was not in livery but wearing a dark green woollen suit trimmed with brocade and a funny-looking collar that wasn't a ruff, but looked like a falling band starched so it stood up by itself. He was standing with his hat off in front of another of the men with inky aprons, though skinny this time, under the sign of a black swan. Will was proffering a sheaf of closely-written paper. The printer shook his head, arms folded, legs astride.

'Nobody's interested in rehashes of Ovid,' grumbled the printer.

'I've told you before, there's no demand for that kind of thing.'

Will's response was too soft for Dodd to hear it, though he caught a whining note. The printer rolled his eyes patiently.

'I know the market, see,' he said. 'It's my business. Your stuff wouldn't sell, believe me. I'm always looking for new talent, of course I am, but I've never known trade so slow and I have to be careful what I take on. Now if you could do me a nice chivalrous romance, or a coney-catching pamphlet or two, like Mr Greene's work – there's something that sells like hot cakes.'

Will's answer to that was sharp.

'Oh, did I?' sniffed the printer. 'Well, listen, mate, not everybody can write like Greene or Nashe or Marlowe. Maybe you should just stick to playing, hmm?'

Will turned away, looking dejected, with his papers under his arm. Not wanting to be caught eavesdropping, Dodd slung the book he was holding back amid all the piles of them, and went reluctantly back into St Paul's to find Barnabus. There was no sign of him. Dodd made two circuits of the Cathedral, trying to spot him amongst the throng, then decided he was no wean to be feared of getting lost; he'd go back to Somerset House on his own.

Dodd had never got lost since he was a lad. He always knew instinctively where he was and where his goal was in relation to him. He knew where Somerset House was now, could have pointed to it, but the trouble was, you couldn't just head straight across country to it; you had to walk along the streets, and the streets were unco-operative. They kept starting in roughly the right direction and then twisted round bewilderingly to spit you out heading away from your goal again. The people and the noise from the shopkeepers roaring out their wares and the children and the dogs and the pigs and goats made him feel breathless and confused. In his own country he was a man to respect, people made way for him even in Carlisle. Here they jostled past him and not one face was familiar, face after face, all strange, more people than he had ever met in his life before and he didn't know one of them. Rudely, not one of them so much as acknowledged he was there.

They were so finely dressed, even the streetsellers wore ancient wool trimmed with motheaten fur, not homespun russet. Once or twice Dodd thought he heard people snickering at him for his countryfied clothes. His neck stiffened and his face got longer and sourer by the minute as street after street seemed to conspire to bewilder him and drive him further from Somerset House.

At last he stopped and decided to take the Courtier's advice and head for the river. Once there he could follow the bank westwards, he thought, or even take a boat. That would be the sensible thing to do.

Half an hour later he was wondering in despair where in God's name the Londoners could hide a river. He had just passed the same overdecorated water conduit for the fourth time. Dodd used the little cup chained to it to take a drink, and leaned on the side to think for a bit.

'Excuse me, sir,' said a nasal drone beside him. 'You serve my Lord Hunsdon's son, don't you?'

'Who wants tae know?' growled Dodd, glaring suspiciously at the man. By God, it was the bald-headed manservant that had been trying to sell papers to the printer in Paul's Churchyard.

'Och,' he snarled. 'Were ye following me? Whit the hell d'ye want?'

'N . . . nothing. Nothing, sir. Only . . . er . . . I've seen you pass by here three times now and it occurred . . . er . . . it seemed to me you might . . . er . . .'

'Spit it out, man.'

'. . . be lost?'

Dodd decided to let the little man live, since what he said was true. 'What of it?'

'I . . . I could lead you back to Somerset House.'

Dodd wasn't going to fall for any more scurvy southern tricks. 'Ay, to be sure. If ye dinna take me down some foul wynd and slip a blade in me.'

The man looked shocked and offended. 'Why would I do that? I'm no footpad.'

'Ay, I mind ye. Ye're Mistress Bassano's singing servant, Will.'

He coughed and made a reasonably graceful bow. 'Will Shakespeare, sir, at your service.'

Dodd thought it was a remarkably stupid name for a man with arms no thicker than twigs and sorrowful brown eyes like a spaniel, so he grunted.

'Ay. I'm Sergeant Dodd. What's the way back tae Somerset House, then?'

They walked in silence through dizzying alleys and passageways under houses that actually met over the pavements, until at last they came in sight of the great galleon of St Paul's moored amongst its attendant houses.

'What was it ye were trying to sell tae the bookseller?' Dodd asked. Will flushed and looked even more miserable than usual.

'Only some verses.'

'Poetry, eh? Ballads?'

'Er . . . no. A classical theme, the sorrowful tale of Pyramus and Thisbe.'

'Och,' said Dodd, who had never heard of the story but wasn't inclined to admit it. 'And did the man no' like it?'

'Seemingly not.'

'But ye found someone else to buy it, did ye no'?'

'No.'

'Well, where are the papers then?'

'I threw them in the Thames.'

'What? That's a powerful waste o' paper.'

Will shrugged. 'I was angry.'

'What did he mean about ye should stick to playing?'

'I am – or I was until I lost my job when the theatre was closed – a player.'

'I thocht ye were Mistress Bassano's servingman.'

Brown spaniel eyes stared into the distance and seemed to well with tears. 'At the moment, sir, I am, yes. My Lord Hunsdon was kind enough to take me in when I . . . when everything went wrong.'

'How did ye come to know the Lord Chamberlain?'

Something subtly out of place crossed the would-be poet's expression. 'He had seen me acting with my Lord Strange's troop and he's a good friend to poetry; he said he thought my version of *Henry VI* showed great promise and he would be happy to tide me over until . . . until, well, my problems were solved.'

The ugly flattened vowels had turned down at the end of the sentence, closing the door to more questions. Dodd thought it all sounded odd, a respectable lord like Hunsdon giving house space to a mere player, but then none of the Careys seemed to worry about things like scandal.

They had come down Ludgate Hill and over Fleet Bridge and Dodd was starting to recognise familiar buildings. He could even see the Thames, glinting tantalisingly between the houses.

'I think I can find ma own way now,' he said.

Will nodded, still lost in thought. As Dodd turned to take his leave, Will seemed to come to a decision. 'Sir,' he said. 'Sergeant Dodd.'

'Ay.'

'Would you . . . would you do me a favour?'

Dodd's eyes narrowed. 'Depends.'

Will smiled faintly. 'I was only wondering if you would pass a letter to Mistress Bassano?'

'Why can ye no' do it yerself?'

Pink embarrassment was edging the player's jaw. 'It's my day off, and, well . . . I think it would be better this way.'

'What is it? The letter. And who's it from?'

'It's . . . from me, but . . . er . . . well, really it's only a few lines I've written in her honour.'

'It's nothing scandalous, is it? It willnae make the lady greet and get me intae trouble?'

Will shook his head. 'I'm sure the poems will please her – she likes poetry. And I think these are . . . er . . . quite good. You'd only have to give them to her and . . . er . . . say they're from an admirer too humble to offer them personally.'

Dodd frowned. 'It all sounds verra strange.'

'Oh, believe me, sir, ladies like that kind of thing. They like mystery.'

For a moment it was on the tip of Dodd's tongue to ask if Will had any claim to the babe Mistress Bassano was carrying, but then he stopped himself. Really it was none of his business, fascinating though the doings in the Hunsdon household were.

Will was holding out his precious letter which he had taken out of the front of his doublet, good creamy paper, carefully folded and sealed. Dodd shrugged, took it and put it in the front of his leather jerkin.

At the gate of Somerset House Dodd was carefully inspected and then admitted without argument. Behind him on the Strand, the heavyset men in their buff coats leaned in doorways or stood in alleyways, waiting patiently for their quarry to reappear.

He asked in the yard where Sir Robert was and then headed where the manservant pointed, towards the stables that looked over the garden. Mistress Bassano was sitting under a cherry tree heavy with fruit, her two maidservants sitting prettily disposed around her, all three of them stitching busily at some large embroidery. Best get it over with, thought Dodd, and marched over to her, made the best bow of his life and stood before her with his cap off, trying to get his thoughts in order. The way she was sitting on cushions with her pale green silk skirts spread out around her, you only had to tilt your head to get a full view of those magnificently rich breasts, riding high over the fertile swell of her belly. Dodd had never bedded a pregnant woman, since Janet was yet to fall for a babe, alas. How did you do it? Could you do it? What would it be . . .

'Why, Sergeant Dodd,' said Mistress Bassano. 'Can I help you?'

Dodd cleared his throat. 'Ay. Ah . . . I was given a letter for ye by . . . eh . . . by an admirer.'

Full pink lips curled up in a slow smile, the ends tucking themselves into a pair of dimples, and the heavily-lashed lids came down a little. Dodd knew he was staring at the woman's chest but couldn't stop himself; he felt like a tranced chicken.

'How romantic. And who is he?'

'Ah . . . he asked me not to say on account of it . . . er . . . being better left a mystery.'

'Oh.' The maid on Mistress Bassano's left giggled and Mistress

Bassano pouted her maddening lips at the girl. 'Now, be sensible. These are important matters.'

'Ay,' croaked Dodd, wanting a quart of beer and wishing the sun wasn't so hot. 'Ah . . . here it is.'

He clutched the letter from the inside pocket of his leather jerkin, and held it out to Mistress Bassano who reached up a hand to take it. Her fingers brushed the back of Dodd's hand and made it tingle and prickle.

'How charming to receive a *billet doux* from such an unexpected messenger,' she said. And oh, the curve of her neck as she looked up at him, he could kiss his way all down the side of it, and . . .

Dodd found his breath was coming short. What did the woman do to radiate desire like that? Was she a witch? Had she laid some kind of spell on him? Ay, maybe that was it. God's truth, he was beginning to hate the Courtier and his father both.

'Thank you, Sergeant Dodd,' said Mistress Bassano as she lifted the edge of her kirtle and tucked Shakespeare's letter away in the pocket of her petticoat. Surely it was no accident that she let Dodd have a flash of her ankle and bare foot . . . Scandalous, no stockings, no shoes, a clear line all the way up her bare leg to her . . .

Dodd clutched his cap, jerked a bow and stepped back, nearly tripping on a miniature box hedge surrounding a bed of herbs.

'D'ye ken . . . have ye seen Sir Robert?' he asked, having to whisper because his mouth was so dry.

A tiny frown crossed the creamy brow under its wings of black hair dressed with pale green stones. 'Oh, I think I heard him shouting in the stables,' she said.

'Ay. Thank ye kindly, Mistress.'

Dodd very nearly turned tail and ran across the smooth green lawn to the complex of buildings around the stable yard. Before he got there he heard the unmistakeable sound of Careys having an argument, as Mistress Bassano had said.

'I came here because you ordered me to,' Carey was saying, obviously trying not to shout though his voice was probably audible in Westminster. 'Your letter, sir, ordered me away from my responsibilities in Carlisle where I am still very far from secure, and where the reivers will no doubt be playing merry hell in my absence. *You*, sir, ordered me to London where I have absolutely no wish to be. *Sir*. If you didn't want me to come to Somerset House, you shouldn't have written your bloody letter. SIR!'

Carey was nose to nose with his father, whose face above its ruff was going purple. Behind them in the kennels, hunting dogs barked and whined in alarm.

'Damn your impudence, boy,' roared Hunsdon. 'Why the hell didn't you go to the Liberties like I told you to? What the devil did you think you were at, prancing into this house when I specifically told you the bailiffs were out in force, you stupid boy?'

'Don't call me *boy*,' Carey ground out through his teeth, his fists bunched. 'And your letter said not a damned thing about bailiffs, as you well know, unless you've bloody forgotten it, you senile old goat.'

Hunsdon roared inarticulately and threw a punch at his son, who ducked, backed and put his hand to his sword. Entertaining though the scene certainly was, Dodd decided he had to intervene. Hunsdon had his own sword half-drawn.

'Sir, my lord.' He had stepped between the Careys, his hands up to fend them off.

'Out of my way, Sergeant,' bellowed Hunsdon.

'Dodd, this is none of your business,' growled Carey.

'Ay, it is. If ye kill each other who's gonnae guide me back home? And forebye, I dinnae understand what yer quarrel is.'

'It's simple enough, Sergeant. When I order my son to make sure he doesn't come into Somerset House but should go to one of my properties in the Liberties of Whitefriars, where he can at least move without being hunted by bailiffs, I expect to be obeyed.'

'How the hell can I obey an order I never received?' bellowed Carey. 'You said nothing about Whitefriars in your letter.'

'Of course I didn't, you overdressed halfwit; I sent a verbal message by Michael.'

'What bloody message? I never got it.'

'Nay, sir, he didnae. Who's Michael?'

'Used to be my *valet de chambre*,' Carey said. 'Father, I never saw Michael.'

'What do you mean, you never saw him?' Hunsdon's voice was now modulating down to a shout. 'I sent him out to meet you at Hampstead horsepond.'

Carey's bewilderment was so clear on his face, even his father began calming down. 'He wasn't there. We were jumped by footpads, but . . .'

The thought struck both Carey and Dodd at the same time. Carey paled and sat down on the edge of the horsetrough. 'What was he wearing when you sent him? Livery?'

'No, of course not. I didn't want to advertise who he worked for. He was wearing a brown wool suit. Why?'

'Ay,' said Dodd mournfully. 'That was him, all right. Brown doublet and hose, wi' some fancy work in black velvet ribbons.'

'That's right,' Hunsdon growled.

'Oh,' said Carey, putting his hand over his mouth. 'Poor bastard.'

Hunsdon's bushy eyebrows were meeting over his nose. 'I thought you said you didn't see him.'

Carey seemed too upset to answer so Dodd cleared his throat and did the job.

'Ay, we saw him, but he couldnae tell us yer message, my lord, on account of he wis hanging from the Hampstead Hanging Elm at the time, and nae face on him neither.'

'What? He was dead?'

'Ay. And not long dead, now I come to think of it. The body wasnae rotted.'

'I should have spotted it,' Carey said to himself. 'What was a fresh body doing on the Elm when the Assizes couldn't have sat for a month?'

Lord Hunsdon sat down on the horsetrough edge next to his son.

'Well,' he said as if the breath had been taken out of him too. 'Who could have thought it? Poor Michael. You're sure?'

Carey nodded once then shook his head. 'It's the only explanation. You sent him with a message about the bailiffs and somebody . . . stopped him delivering it.'

'Ay,' added Dodd dolefully, though in fact he didn't know

Michael from Adam and didn't much care that he was dead. 'And they hid his body where naebody would notice it.'

'Very imaginative of them,' said Hunsdon.

There was a short silence. 'Will you tell his wife, or should I do it?' Carey asked.

Hunsdon sighed. 'I'll send some men up to Hampstead first to fetch the body, make absolutely sure. Then I'll tell her myself. Good God. What a bloody mess.'

Carey turned his head and looked consideringly at his father. 'Father, what's going on here?'

'Damned if I know, Robin. It's all a mystery to me. Why the devil did they have to kill him? All they had to do was knock him on the head.'

'That can kill a man by itself,' said Carey. 'Maybe they did it accidentally. Or maybe somebody wanted to make a point, as it were.'

'His father served me, you know, cared for my guns and armour in '72, when we did for Dacre.'

'Yes, I remember.'

'Good man. Died of flux, I seem to recall, a couple of years after. I remember Michael as a page, eager little lad, always willing. Poor Frances.'

'Is she here?'

'No, I've set them up in a house in Holywell Street, near the Cockpit. Two whippersnappers and another on the way. He was acting under-steward here. Only sent him because you'd be sure to know him. Thought he'd gone home to his wife when you arrived last night.'

'And you could hardly ask with Heneage hanging about.'

'No.' Hunsdon's face hardened. 'God rot his bowels.'

'You think it's . . . er . . .'

Hunsdon looked up, though he didn't seem to see the gargoyle waterspout on the stable guttering that he was glaring at.

'Don't know who else it could be. Damn him.'

'Perhaps it might be worth going to Oxford?' Carey asked.

Hunsdon shook his head, then clapped his hand on Carey's shoulder and stood up. 'I'd best organise a party to go up to

Hampstead, fetch the body and give him a decent burial. I'll draft a letter to Mr Recorder Fleetwood, as there'll have to be an inquest, and I want it conducted properly.'

'If the corpse is still there,' Carey said.

'Hmf. Well, what can you do? You have to try.'

'Perhaps it would be better if we didn't make it too public that we know what's happened.' Carey was speaking very quietly and thoughtfully. 'After all, Heneage will have at least one paid man here.'

'Of course he does. What do you . . . ah. I see. Well, I don't like it. Goes against the grain to leave a man of mine hanging on a gibbet. What if Frances went past and saw him?'

'Excuse me, sir,' said Dodd. 'I verra much doubt he'll still be on the Elm. But could ye no' make a song and dance about they footpads we saw off at the Hampstead Cut and, while ye were at it, maybe find out about your man?' Dodd found himself caught in a crossfire of stares and wished he'd kept his mouth shut. 'Only, there'd be nae secret about that, my lord, since we left three kills of our own there.'

'You omitted the detail of the footpads, Robin,' Hunsdon said drily to his son.

Carey waved airy fingers. 'Fairly cack-handed attempt at an ambush in the Cut as we came through, which was foiled by Sergeant Dodd who spotted what was going on well before I did. Nothing much to say, really, since there was no harm done. To us, anyway.'

'Hm. That was why your gun was loaded.'

'Of course.'

'When you discharged it in the Strand I felt certain you were only defying me and had come prepared to bully your way in,' Hunsdon explained, standing up and brushing down his elaborately paned trunk-hose. 'Excellent suggestion of yours, Sergeant; I'll write to Mr Recorder this afternoon about the attempted robbery. With luck we'll be able to find and hang the men who murdered my servant.'

'If not the man who paid them to do it,' murmured Carey, also standing up.

Hunsdon tilted his head cynically. 'It's the way of the world, Robin, you know that. Now would the pair of you care to view the finest pack of hounds this side of Westminster?'

The hounds were very elegant beasts, and included a yellow lymer with a heavy head and a serious expression. One of the dog-pages explained at length about the thorn in his paw, which the dog held up to show the neat bandage. Both Careys examined it carefully, Lord Hunsdon squatting down with his arm across the dog's back. Dodd examined it himself.

'What do you think, Dodd?' Carey asked. 'It looks clean enough to me.'

Dodd felt around the dog's leg, in case there were any lumps in the animal's groin. You could sometimes get early warning of trouble with a wound if you found lumps, but there were none and the dog panted at him in puzzlement.

'Ay,' said Dodd thoughtfully. 'But I wouldnae hunt with him till it's all healed up, of course.'

'No, of course not,' said Lord Hunsdon. 'You're on sick leave, aren't you, Bellman, old fellow?' The dog panted and licked Hunsdon's face and the old lord pummelled his ears.

'Is he any relation of my lord Scrope's lymer bitch that pupped on yer bed?' Dodd asked, thinking he saw a family resemblance.

'Yes,' smiled Carey, who was rubbing the dog's high chest as the animal groaned with pleasure and plopped himself over on his side. 'He's her brother. Father gave Scrope the bitch as a present a couple of years ago.'

'Pupped on your bed?' Hunsdon laughed. 'What did Philadelphia say about it?'

'She wasn't very pleased. I had a great long lecture about the impossibility of cleaning counterpanes properly, as if I'd told the silly animal to do it. But it was a good thing she did, because she had trouble with the last pup of the litter.'

Hunsdon listened to the tale and agreed that a ruined counterpane was a small price to pay for saving a fine gentle bitch like Buttercup. Robin should take care with the pup though, because this particular line of lymers seemed to be even more greedy than the general run of hunting dogs and they got fat very easily. In fact Bellman himself was a bit tubby, and Jimmy the dog-page must remember not to feed him too much while he couldn't run.

As if to confirm this wisdom, Bellman farted extravagantly and all three of them retired coughing to look at the horses. Dodd was greatly impressed with Hunsdon's stable which held bigger and glossier beasts than any he had seen outside the contraband animals that the Grahams had harvested from the Scottish king's stables. The pathetic nags that they had ridden in from the Holly Tree the day before looked as if they knew how useless they were in comparison.

A bell rang, calling the household to dinner, and Dodd found himself borne along to the parlour where the Careys generally ate their meals, seven covers of meat this time and still nothing Dodd rightfully recognised as food. Afterwards Sir Robert, who had drunk far more than he ate and was evidently going mad with boredom at being cooped up in his father's house, announced he would go and talk to the falconer and see if the birds had finished their moult. Hunsdon grunted and told Dodd he wanted his opinion on some arrangements for the Berwick garrison – would he come along to the old lord's study in an hour? He wished to see Robin privately first; he could come to Hunsdon's study in half an hour.

An hour later one of the grooms led Dodd along the corridors. It was astonishing how many rooms there were in the place – you couldn't count them all – and how peculiar to have one for each thing you might do in a day, such as a parlour for eating and a study for reading and writing, and every single one of them painted and decorated with hanging cloths and furnished with carved oak. Surely to God, Hunsdon could afford to pay Sir Robert's debts, even enormous ones?

Hunsdon's study was a room lined with books and cluttered with papers and official dispatch bags hanging on hooks. Dodd knocked on the door, entered at the single bark of 'Come', and stood straight with his cap off in front of the desk. Hunsdon had been leafing dispiritedly through a pile of letters and looked up at him.

'Sergeant Dodd. Good of you to come so promptly. What do you think of the mews?'

'I'm no' a falconer, my lord, and I canna say I've ever hunted with a bird, though I've watched when I was beating. Yer man at the mews says they might fly next week, being cautious, but we'll be back on the road tae Carlisle by then.' Hunsdon wasn't really listening.

'Hm. Dodd,' he said thoughtfully. 'There was a Dodd under my command when we took Dacre's hide – any relation?'

'Ay, sir. Me father, sir.'

Hunsdon beamed. 'That's right, of course he is. You've exactly the look of him. Damned fine soldier, if a bit serious. Scouted for me, as I recall, with his Upper Tynedalers.'

'Ay, sir.'

'Spotted Dacre's cavalry, I think.'

'Did he, sir?' Dodd could feel his ears going pink. He preferred not to think of his father. It brought back the horrible hollow feeling in the pit of his stomach that he'd had all through his teens.

'How is he?'

'Ma father, sir? He's deid.'

Hunsdon sighed. 'I'm sorry to hear it, Sergeant.'

Strangely enough he did genuinely seem sorry though he could hardly have given a thought to Dodd's father between the Revolt of the Northern Earls and this day.

'Ay, sir. Er . . . thank ye, sir.'

'And what's this I hear about my son's behaviour at the Scottish court?'

The ambush was the more deadly for coming from behind a cover of sympathy.

'My lord?' Dodd kept his face carefully blank. Hunsdon made a 'hrmhrm' noise that was obviously where the Courtier had got his throat clearing and leaned back in his carved chair, causing it to creak at the joints.

'Sergeant,' he said gently, 'I like discretion in a man under my command and I've no doubt my son does too, but I must have the full tale.'

'The one Mr Heneage heard?'

Hunsdon chuckled without the least trace of humour. 'Certainly not. The one in which my son becomes somehow sufficiently deranged to deal in armaments with a couple of Italians who had Papist Spy all but branded on their foreheads, as he saw fit to boast in his letter? The one which explains the rumours about him being arrested for high treason, which he did not mention? The one which accounts for the damage to his hands which makes him embarrassed to take his blasted gloves off in my presence? That tale?'

'Och,' said Dodd firmly, resisting any impulse to smile at the exasperation in Hunsdon's voice. 'That one?'

'Yes,' said Hunsdon patiently. 'That one.'

Dodd told him, or at least all of it that he knew. At the end of his story, Hunsdon passed his palm across his eyes.

'Good God,' he said. 'And his hands?'

'What he said to me was they got caught in a door.'

'Oh really?'

'But considering two fingers was broken – which are fine now, my lord, his grip's good enough to fire a dag – and he's lost four fingernails which arenae grown back yet, my guess is someone had at him wi' the pinniwinks.' Hunsdon raised his eyebrows. 'Ah, thumbscrews, sir.'

Carey's dad had the same capacity as his son for instantly radiating compressed fury. His grey eyes had gone cold as ice.

'King James?'

'I doubt it, seeing how much he likes the Cour . . . Sir Robert, and seeing he give us the guns back.'

'Then Lord Spynie.'

'Ay, my lord. And Sir Henry Widdrington.'

There was a short heavy silence. It was noticeable that Carey's father did not ask why Widdrington should want to mistreat his son. Hunsdon was staring into space. Dodd kept his mouth shut because he recognised that look, and if Lord Chamberlain Hunsdon was meditating on ways and means for a startling piece of vengeance, it wasn't Dodd's place to interrupt him. Eventually Hunsdon looked shrewdly at Dodd,

'My youngest son's capacity for getting himself into trouble and then out again has never ceased to astound me,' he said. 'Is that it, the full tale?'

'All I know, my lord.'

'Barnabus claims to be even more ignorant. Is it true Robin left him in Carlisle when he went into Scotland?'

'Ay, my lord. He was . . . ah . . . he was indisposed.'

Hunsdon grinned. 'So I gathered, poor fellow. Clap's the very devil, isn't it?'

Dodd wasn't at all sure how to answer this as he had no personal experience of clap at all, but was saved by the slam of a window being opened and an indistinct shrieking of a woman's voice on the side of the house overlooking the Strand. Hunsdon opened the window of his office himself, and leaned out to look. Dodd peered over his shoulder.

Mistress Bassano was leaning out of an upstairs window, her magnificent hair flying in the breeze, her magnificent breasts bulging over the top of her pale green bodice and two high spots of colour pointing up the hectic flash of her eyes.

'You pathetic bookworm, you *pillock* of a man, how dare you send this trash to me, how *dare* you!'

She was waving a couple of pieces of writing which had the painful regularity of something much laboured over.

'You look at me with your stupid dog's eyes and you whine of love, but do you see *me*? No. Look at this piece of drivel, you pox-blinded bald nincompoop!'

Mistress Bassano was screaming at Will Shakespeare, who stood in the street unaware of the way the passing throngs were pausing to turn and stare, his face full of misery.

With passionate ceremony Mistress Bassano tore up the papers, dug obscenely under her petticoats with them and then dropped them in a jordan held by her giggling maid. Hunsdon was leaning against the window-frame enjoying himself. Shakespeare stood with his mouth open and his hands out in desperation at this sacrilege. Mistress Bassano nodded to her maid who threw the contents of the jordan with deadly aim at his head. The other walkers in the street had scattered away from him as soon as they saw the jordan, but Shakespeare just stood there, with soiled sheets of paper fluttering around him and something horrible stuck to his doublet.

Lord Hunsdon cheered and applauded, his good-humour slightly edged with malice. Mistress Bassano dusted off her fingers fastidiously, turned a satin shoulder and disappeared from the window. The maid impudently added a finger at Will before the shutters banged closed again.

Suddenly Dodd felt very sorry for the little man. Hunsdon was coming away from the window still chuckling.

In case Carey's father thought to ask how Mistress Bassano had come by Shakespeare's letter, Dodd asked hurriedly, 'My lord, when are we heading back to Carlisle?'

Hunsdon was sitting down, picking up a pen, shaking his head and laughing. 'Splendid girl, Mistress Bassano, full of fun,' he was saying contentedly. 'You still there, Sergeant? No, you're not going back yet. Robin's got a job to do for me first.'

'Och,' said Dodd hollowly, suddenly realising how much he hated London town. 'What's that?'

The door opened and Mistress Bassano appeared alone in a rustle of pale green silk. Hunsdon smiled.

'Stupid bastard,' she was muttering. 'My lord, you should have him arrested.' She curtseyed and then glared at Dodd before emphatically ignoring him. Her back view was almost as delectable as the front, the way the gown was cut tight at the waist to flow over her bumroll, and of course that was how you could do it with a pregnant woman, like a horse, which was a wonderful thought and brought a whole new perspective to Dodd's distracted mind.

'On what grounds? Writing you untruthful sonnets?' Hunsdon was still chuckling.

'Plotting against the Queen.'

Hunsdon tutted. 'No need to hang, draw and quarter the silly poet, my dear; it'll only make him think he's important. Sergeant, Sir Robert will tell you what he's up to in his own good time, I'm sure. It boils down to finding another of my bloody sons who has succeeded in losing himself somewhere in London.'

'Who's that, my lord?' Dodd was fighting the urge to groan with disappointment and frustration.

The eyes had gone cold. 'Edmund. He's Robin's elder brother by two years but . . . well, I expect you'll find out.' Mistress Bassano had taken Hunsdon's velvet hat off and was blowing on a bald spot in the rusty grey.

'I cannot have Will serve me any more, my lord,' she said. 'He is impertinent.'

'Oh clearly. Can't have an ex-player making up to you, sweetheart. I'll tell the steward to assign him somewhere else.'

'Kick him out.'

'Now, my darling, there's no need to be vengeful. The poor chap only scribbled some verses for you – which poets do perpetually, my sweet, they can't help it, it's a kind of sickness. You should be kind to the afflicted, no matter how annoying they are.'

Mistress Bassano tossed her head. 'You are such a generous lord,' she said. 'Are you not afraid sneaking little lechers like him will take advantage of your good nature?'

'No, no,' said Hunsdon, putting the pen back in the ink bottle and shaking sand inaccurately. Mistress Bassano had her arms around his waist and her chin on his shoulder and something she was doing was clearly distracting him. 'Not while you are like a tigress in your loyalty, darling, that's the important part. Mmmmm.'

Mistress Bassano glared at Dodd and jerked her head at the door. Dodd gave her stare for stare and stayed put. Lord Hunsdon hadn't dismissed him yet. And besides, he thought, I know more about you than you think, missy. Loyal as a tigress, eh? As a she-cat, more like.

'Oh ah, Dodd,' said Hunsdon with his eyes half-shut. 'Would you . . . ah . . . ask Mr Blaine my steward to attend on me here in about . . . ah . . . half an hour?'

'Ay, my lord,' said Dodd neutrally. He went to the door and made the best bow he could.

'Make that an hour,' Hunsdon called after him.

'Ay, my lord.' Dodd shut the door behind him and left them to it. Outside in the passageway he sighed wistfully, feeling that it was very unfair that he had to watch the Careys, father and son, being happily seduced by beautiful women at every turn. Was it wealth or looks, he wondered, and decided that it must be both. That Bassano woman was a peach, by God, and the scandalous way she had her smock pulled down meant that every time you looked at her there was the mesmerising possibility that one of her breasts would pop out of its prison and you would be able to see her nipple . . . Dodd liked breasts, he liked nipples, particularly pink and pointed ones, he liked the creamy softness of Mistress Bassano's skin, he liked . . . Of course, he also liked counting his wife's freckles. She would hardly ever let him do it because she hated them. Unaccountably she bleached the ones on her face with lemon juice. There were squeaks and deep-voiced chuckles coming through the door now, and an instantly recognisable rhythmic sound.

Dodd scowled. And none of the blasted courtiers had any shame either.

As he hurried off to find Sir Robert, he wondered what the famous London bawdyhouses might be like and how much they might cost. Janet would never hear of it if he paid one a visit, he was sure, there were hundreds of miles between him and her. And dear God, it would be worth it.

In the casual way of a man with a large staff, Lord Chamberlain Hunsdon decided to give a little supper party that night for his son's benefit. Servants were sent running with invitations, the steward hurried fretfully through the house carrying a sheaf of papers and the kitchens seemed to explode into activity.

Dodd took cover in the room he had been given, where Carey ran him to earth a little later, followed by a manservant carrying a bag containing a fine doublet and hose, a cramoisie marvel of fine wool trimmed with black velvet, padded doublet, padded sleeves and a pair of paned trunk hose. These he laid out on the bed.

'Och,' Dodd said, putting down the book he had been lent by the falconer and coming to his feet. 'What's that, sir? Are ye wearing it the night?'

'No,' said Carey, his eyes dancing with mischief. 'You are.'

'What? Ah'm no' a courtier, sir. I cannae wear fancy gear like that; forbye I'm wearin' ma best suit the day an' there's nae reason tae . . .'

'Dodd, shut up and listen to me. Nobody is impugning your wife's honour or her skills at weaving and tailoring. Janet is a gem of a woman and your best suit is the *dernier cri* in Carlisle, I'm sure, but I cannot and will not have you sitting at my father's supper table wearing homespun.'

'That's nae bother, sir. I'm not invited.'

'Yes, you are.'

'Och, sir, but I dinnae want . . .'

'Who asked you what you wanted, Dodd? Not me. Now this is Anthony who is my father's *valet de chambre*, and who has very kindly agreed to help you dress properly.'

'Nay sir, I willna. It's no' fit.'

'You will, Dodd,' snapped Carey. 'With or without a fight.'

Dodd started to lose his temper. 'I dinna think ye mean that, sir,' he said, trying to give the Courtier a chance to back out.

Carey drew a wound and loaded dag from under his arm and pointed it at Dodd.

'I do. Now go quietly, will you, there's a good fellow?'

Surely to God, Carey wouldn't shoot him over clothes? Surely? Was it worth the risk? Dodd shut his mouth firmly and glared at Anthony who was looking down at the rushes.

After an awkward silence in which Carey sat down on the window seat, put his legs up onto a stool and cradled the gun on his arm so it could point at Dodd with the minimum of effort, the door opened and two more servants appeared carrying a large wooden bath tub. Dodd's mouth dropped open again.

'Get your clothes off, Sergeant. I'm afraid we haven't time to go down to the stews and do the job properly, so this will have to suffice.'

The servants opened out a sheet and lined the bath with it. Then they went out again and reappeared staggering under enormous jugs of water.

Dodd was almost gobbling with rage. 'Are ye saying I'm dirty?'

Carey rolled his eyes. 'When was the last time you had

a bath, Sergeant? I mean all over, not just a rinsing at a pump?'

'I . . . I . . .'

'Quite. Come on.' Carey gestured lazily with the dag. 'Clothes off.'

Anthony was arranging the fancy suit on the bed. Water poured and was mixed into the tub. The other two servants left the jugs behind and tiptoed out and Anthony took a dish of soap, a towel and a scrubbing brush and stood beside the tub with a completely blank face, like a statue.

Slowly, heart thumping with fury, Dodd undid his laces, hung his jerkin on a hook on the back of the door, and stripped off to his shirt.

'All the way,' Carey said.

'But it's no' Christmas,' Dodd pleaded. 'Why would I need a bath in August? And I swam in the Esk in June.'

'Humour me, Sergeant. Put it down to a chronic madness instilled by a Queen who bathes every single month, winter or summer.'

'Every month? Ye dinnae do that, d'ye sir? It's no' healthy.'

'No, of course I don't, unless I'm actually at court. Nonetheless. Even when it's not Christmas, if you are going to sit at my father's supper table, you are going to do it in a civilised manner.'

Mad. The Courtier and all his family were clearly as lunatic as they come. Carey in particular should be in Bedlam hospital, not casually pointing a dag at his Sergeant. Setting his jaw, Dodd pulled off his shirt and dipped a toe into the water, which had rosemary leaves in it, by Christ. What did they think he was, some kind of catamite? The water was hot but he decided not to complain about it as he got in and sat down cautiously, put his hand out for the soap.

Half an hour later, skin tingling from the soap and the scrubbing brush, Dodd got out again and resentfully allowed himself to be towelled dry by Anthony, who had also trimmed and nit-combed his hair while he was helpless in the bath.

'Now what?' he growled at Carey who was still sitting at ease by the window, dag beside him on a little table, reading the book about hunting. For answer Carey lifted his eyebrows at Anthony.

The shirt was of the finest linen Dodd had ever seen, and astonishingly clean, though at least it had no fancy embroidery on it. He pulled it on while Anthony carefully toed his own shirt and netherstocks into a pile by the door. The valet then began the ridiculously complicated business of dressing Dodd in a fashionable suit. He even used needle and thread to alter it on Dodd's body, shortening and letting out the waist. The shoulders were tight but when Dodd mentioned it, Carey smiled.

'They're meant to be tight, it's the padding. Now what are you going to wear on your neck? I've brought a ruff and a falling band.'

'Not a ruff, please, sir,' begged Dodd. 'I cannae wear a ruff.'

'Fair enough. The falling band it is, Anthony.'

How the Courtier could bear to wear such tight clothes all the time, Dodd had no idea. His chest felt imprisoned and his shoulders were firmly pulled back by the cut of the doublet. The servants who had brought the bathwater returned, wheeling a large mirror, and Dodd squinted at the stranger standing awkwardly in it, wearing his face.

'There,' said Carey with satisfaction. 'That's much better.'

'Is it, sir?' said Dodd hollowly. 'Ah cannae see it maself.'

Carey stood up. He was already trimly turned out in brocade and tawny satin, Dodd noticed, the width of his ruff just this side of looking daft. But it suited him. Dodd felt he was a laughing stock, all dollied up in clothes he had no business wearing.

Anthony handed him his sword belt which he shrugged over his shoulder.

'I've brought some jewels, if you care to wear them,' offered Carey.

'No, sir,' said Dodd firmly.

'Suit yourself. Now listen to me, Dodd. This is London. Nobody knows who you are or what a Land Sergeant of Gilsland might be, or who your family connections are or anything about you. That means that if you want to be treated right, you have to look the part. What you're wearing is no fancier than what any middling London merchant would wear and that puts you at about the right level.'

'I'm not a gentleman, thank God, sir.'

'Nor is a middling London merchant. You're not wearing anything approaching fashion; what you're wearing is respectable, no more. It's actually one of my own old suits, so please try not to drop anything on it. All right?'

Dodd growled inarticulately. Carey grinned.

'It also ups your price if anyone wants to bribe you. Now if I discharge my dag out the window, will you promise not to hit me?'

Dodd scowled at him. 'I'm no' stupid, sir.'

'No, of course not. You can hit me tomorrow, if you must, but just for tonight bear with me.'

Carey opened the window, peered out at the reddening sky, pointed the dag upwards and fired. 'Come on. The guests are arriving.'

Dodd followed him awkwardly, suddenly understanding where some of Carey's swagger came from – it was the only way you could walk if you were wearing great stupid padded hose round your thighs.

Afterwards, when Dodd tried with all his might to remember the details of that long summer evening, he found it had disintegrated in his mind to a whirl of brilliantly dressed ladies and gentlemen who greeted him politely enough, addressed a few words to him and then slipped away to laugh and talk with Carey.

The Courtier was clearly in his element, flirting extravagantly with all the women, gossiping delightedly with the men about the doings of Sir Walter Raleigh, regretting that the South Bank theatre was shut as punishment for a riot over a glover, and, with total disregard for truth, reprising events at the King of Scotland's court. They sat down to more unrecognisable food, including a swan dressed in a full suit of white feathers and stuffed with a pheasant, and finished playing primero at separate tables under blazing banks of wax candles until the sweat ran down Dodd's back in rivulets.

Will was there, serving at table with the other liverymen, standing with his back to the wall next to the sideboard loaded with a glittering display of Hunsdon's plate, dividing his time between glowering at his shoes and staring like a motherless calf at Mistress Bassano.

She was radiant in black velvet and grass green silk, her neck milky with pearls, her hands dancing on the virginals' keys while the wealthy Londoners played at cards.

Dodd spent most of the evening watching, since he simply could not bring himself to play for entire shillings at a time. Eventually he tired of the heat, noise and sense of being completely out of place and chokingly wrapped in finery that suited neither his body nor his mind. He put down his cards, bowed to Lord Hunsdon who was roaring 'eighty-four' at the other end of the room, and went blindly out into the garden, where the summer air was a strange tapestry of flat salt and dirt from the Thames, overlaid with roses and herbs, and a familiar whiff of horses and dogs from the stables.

He stood on the grass, blinking up at the stars. Though it was a balmy summer night not all of them were visible, but he could make out the North Star right enough and he looked at it with longing. That was the way home. That was where there would be doings tonight; on such a clear night, the reivers' trails would be busy with soft-footed horses and their bridles padded with cloth to stop any jingling. He sighed.

'Mr Dodd,' came a voice in the darkness, and Dodd tensed, dropped his hand to his sword.

'Ay,' he said, noncommittally, taking a quick glance over his shoulder in case anybody was coming up behind him.

'I have a message for you from Mr Heneage.'

Dodd squinted, saw somebody wrapped in a cloak who didn't look very large, and was talking in a hoarse muffled whisper.

'Ay?'

'Please, Mr Dodd, put your hand out.'

Dodd drew his sword. 'Why?'

'I want to put something in it.'

'A dagger-blade?'

'No, no. A purse.'

Carey had said he should accept any bribes from Heneage. 'Hmf,' he said, and did as he was asked.

The purse was soft leather, bulging and heavy.

'I've been bidden to tell you to think about it,' said the whisper. 'That's all.'

Dodd whirled around, sword at the ready, looking for anyone intending to enforce the warning, and when he looked back at where the cloaked man had been, there was nobody there except a bush. Dodd hurried after him, following the traces in the dew-soaked grass and the movement of leaves. The figure whisked in at the kitchen door where the storehouses were and by the time he reached it, all he could see were scullery boys clearing up, scrubbing tables and washing floors, and liverymen whisking past the hatch picking up more plates of Seville orange suckets and rose-water jellies.

'Did ye see a mon wi' a cloak come through?' Dodd asked.

The scullery boys were staring in fright at his sword. Dodd put it away hastily. 'Did ye?'

'What, sir?'

'A man wi' a cloak . . .'

'Sorry, sir?'

'A man wi' . . . Och, never mind.'

Dodd went out into the garden again, stood near one of the windows where the light from all those candles was spilling onto the gravel and emptied the purse. There was gold and silver in it, three pounds three shillings to be exact, and a tightly folded piece of paper.

' "With good wishes and in hopes of future friendship, Thomas Heneage, Vice Chamberlain." '

It was, as Carey would say, quite unexceptionable. A gift, a sweetener, you might say, not exactly a bribe. What was he supposed to do in return? No doubt Heneage would let him know.

Dodd scowled and stared into the velvet darkness. He couldn't give it back and what would be the point of that anyway? But something about this universal assumption that he could be bought grated on him. Still, as Janet would say, what was he complaining about? With the money from the footpads, he had already netted more than a month's pay from this trip. Dodd took out the footpad's spoils, counted the whole lot together. Five pounds and some change. Nearly two months' wages, cash in hand, no stoppages.

He picked out a couple of shillings and put them in the convenient pocket sewn into his puffed-up braid-decorated left sleeve and hid the rest of his money in the hollow of his crotch, where his codpiece would keep it in place. The next day he would buy a proper money-belt.

Dodd was happier than he had been for years. He was surrounded by warm silky naked flesh, by quivering crinkle-tipped breasts, by smooth round buttocks. Mistress Bassano had his head in her arms so he could suckle her. Thunder rumbled through the sky and Janet, clad only in her beautiful suit of golden freckles, was doing something sinfully obscene for him that made him feel he might explode and . . .

A mighty earthquake struck London and hammered through Dodd's head. He opened one eye to see that God-cursed bastard of a Courtier shaking the bed and grinning at him, with a candle next to him turning his face into a nightmare.

'What . . . what . . .' Dodd spluttered, reached guiltily to cover up Mistress Bassano and then realised that she had turned into a pillow. His groin throbbed and he turned over, buried his head in the other pillow.

'Very sorry, Sergeant,' said Carey in a voice which suggested he might have some notion of exactly how good a dream it was he had spoiled. 'Er . . . You have to get up.'

'Why, for Christ's sake?' moaned Dodd.

Carey coughed. 'We're doing a moonlight flit.'

'What?'

'We're moving out. I can't function here, I'm practically a prisoner.'

'But . . .'

'My father's going to pay off my tailor, Mr Bullard, who's the most dangerous of my creditors. If I can keep clear of any others, I should be all right. Anyway, I'm moving into the Liberties which still has the right of sanctuary.'

Tantalising woman-shapes were still fading in Dodd's abused

75

head and he felt very unwell. Had he been visited by succubi, the female demons who sucked out your soul by your privy member at night? Perhaps. London must be full of them.

Groaning he sat up and tried to rub the sleep out of his eyes. 'So ye're movin?' he whined. 'Why do I have to move too? I like it here.'

Carey looked sympathetic. 'I'm sorry. I need your help.'

'Och' whimpered Dodd, giving his face another rub and wishing very much that the Courtier needed more sleep. Above all things, he hated being wakened in the middle of the night. Or the early morning. Or at all. What he hated was being woken. God, how he hated it.

'Are you awake now?' Carey said solicitously. 'I left you till last. We're all ready. Can you get up now, get dressed?'

Dodd groaned again. 'Ay,' he said at last. 'Ay. I'll be with ye in a minute.'

When he came through into the entrance hall, comfortable in his homespun and leather jerkin, the place was lit by wax candles and seemed full of people. As he sorted out who was there, the people turned into Barnabus and Simon, both yawning and looking shattered, carrying bundles. Carey strode through and smiled at them, fresh as a daisy, newly shaved and smartly turned out in black velvet slashed with flame-coloured taffeta and a clean ruff. Dodd burned with hatred for him.

There was a distinct 'hrmhrm' from one of the doorways. Lord Hunsdon was standing there, wrapped in a sable-fur dressing gown with his embroidered nightcap making him look older.

'Father,' said Carey and bowed. Hunsdon beckoned him over. Dodd was just close enough to hear the tail-end of their muttered conversation. 'Find him if you can, Robin, but for God's sake, be careful.'

Carey smiled at his father. 'You don't mean that, my lord?'

Hunsdon scowled back. 'I do, you bloody idiot. Don't get yourself killed.'

Carey kissed his father's hand with affectionate ceremony, but Hunsdon pulled him close and embraced him like a bear.

When Carey had gone ahead, with Barnabus and Simon trailing unhappily in his wake, Hunsdon growled at Dodd.

'Sergeant.'

'Ay, my lord.'

'You know that my son can sometimes be a little rash.'

Dodd remained stony-faced despite this outrageous understatement. 'Ay, my lord.'

'You seem like a man of good sense and intelligence. Try and restrain him.'

Dodd made an unhappy grimace. 'Ay, my lord. I'll try.'

'Every day I thank God that I have such a fine son. Keep him alive for me, and I'll not be ungrateful.'

Dodd's heart sank at the impossibility of the task. 'Ay, my lord,' he said hollowly.

Hunsdon grinned piratically at his dismay. 'Do your best, man. That's all I ask.'

'Ay, my lord.'

To Dodd's private amusement, instead of going through the postern gate like Christian men, Carey led the three of them into the moonlit garden and over a wall into the garden of the next house, which was a grassy mound with some trees down by the river. Then they went over another wall and into a narrow dirty alley that smelled of the salt and dirt in the Thames at the open end of it. They went the other way and came out into the dark early morning Strand just past the conduit. Nobody was there, not even the nightsoil men, because it was so horribly early in the morning, it was still the middle of the night. Dodd yawned again at the thought. They had no torches but didn't need them thanks to the moonlight, and Dodd thought of the uses of moonlight and the dangers. Cats flashed their eyes and ran for cover and more black ugly things scurried away with their naked tails slithering. Except once, Dodd had never seen so many rats in his life as he'd seen in London.

Carey led them briskly through back streets to Temple Bar where a couple of beggars were huddled up against the inner wall of the arch, with carved headless saints watching over them. They passed a church with a square tower, surrounded by a churchyard, and a

77

vast towering midden that looked ready to topple at any minute; they passed the Cock tavern and at last Carey turned right down another tiny alley, ducked through archways that took the street under part of a house and then turned left into a jumble of small ancient houses and up four flights of stairs under a headless figure of a woman standing precariously on a coiled rope. At the top he used a key to unlock the door and they went into a little attic room with a crazily pitched ceiling that smelled musty and damp with emptiness. The floorboards were bare of rushes except for a few scraps in a corner and there was a bed with a truckle under it and a straw palliass under that. The fireplace was empty, there was a table under the window with a candlestick on it, three stools and that was all.

Barnabus bustled straight in with bags over his shoulder, looked around and nodded. 'Not bad,' he said approvingly. 'This one of your father's investments?'

'Yes, I think so. At least we don't have to pay rent.' Carey was busy with a tinderbox and a candle he had taken out of the pocket in his sleeve. It was a wax candle, Dodd noticed, outrageously extravagant. He looked longingly at the bed where Barnabus had put the bags, though he had no expectation at all that Carey would let him rest.

He was right, though at least Simon unpacked one of his bundles and produced clean pewter plates and a large loaf of bread, fresh butter wrapped in waxed paper and some cheese. Barnabus put a large leather jack full of encouraging sloshing sounds on the table and they sat down to breakfast. Dodd was still feeling too queasy with the morning to eat much, though Carey had an excellent appetite. That worried Dodd who had learned that the Courtier tended to go off his fodder when he was bored and to eat heartily when he was anticipating excitement.

'Now then,' said Carey washing down a third hunk of bread and cheese with beer. 'Edmund.'

'Ay, sir,' said Dodd mournfully. 'Who's he?'

'Edmund is my elder brother by two years, and between you and me he's a complete pillock. He was serving in the Netherlands for a while and he did quite well after Roland Yorke sold Deventer to the Spanish; he led the loyal soldiers out of the place and got them home across enemy territory, but he took it hard since Yorke was a friend of his and he's been pretty much drunk ever since.'

Dodd munched slowly on his cheese and forbore to comment. Carey poured himself some more beer.

'Obviously he's the real reason why Father was so anxious for us to come to London – after all, he could have heard our tale at Oxford where he'd be near the Queen and that would have been useful because I could have asked Her Majesty what's happened to the five hundred pounds she's supposed to pay me.'

'And she wouldn't 'ave told you, would she, sir?'

'No, Barnabus, she wouldn't, but she would at least have been reminded of it. Now, I didn't see Edmund when I left for Carlisle in June, but as far as I knew he was planning to go back to the Netherlands again, try and loot some more cash and pay off the moneylenders. His wife had a bit of land when she married him, but of course that's all mortgaged now and the dowry's long spent. Then, according to my father, some time in early August he disappeared. Father didn't worry at first, he thought perhaps Edmund might be doing a job for Mr Vice Chamberlain Heneage, though Mr Vice denied it of course. But Edmund still hasn't turned up, Heneage is adamant that he doesn't know where he is, and furthermore my father has heard that Heneage is looking for him as well, which means he may have done something to annoy Mr Vice and that is very unwise.'

'Sir,' said Dodd with an effort. 'What sort of thing would your brother do for the Vice Chamberlain?'

'Ah. Yes. Well, as I told you, Mr Vice is currently Her Majesty's spymaster. So it was probably something shady and difficult, not to say treasonous if viewed in the wrong light.'

'Och. But I thocht your family didnae take to Heneage?'

'Edmund is a bloody idiot. He'll do almost anything for money. Walsingham would never have let him near intelligence work, so Heneage must have been desperate. He has some Catholic contacts through his friend Yorke, of course, but still . . . God knows what he was up to. My guess is he made a complete balls up of it, whatever it was, and has gone into hiding, but my father's worried and so we've got to find him. Which is a blasted nuisance.'

Dodd thought about London and the huge number of people in it. How could you find one man amongst all that lot, especially if he didn't want to be found? It was impossible. Dolefully he asked, 'But where will we start, sir?'

'Well, my father was paying a poet to make some enquiries, but he hasn't heard from that man either.'

'Will, d'ye mean?'

'Who?'

'The little bald-headed man that was . . . er . . . Mistress Bassano's servant. He . . . er . . . he helped me find ma way back to Somerset House yesterday and had me carry some rhymes to Mistress Bassano, the ones that annoyed her so badly, damn him.'

Carey wrinkled his brows in puzzlement for a moment and then laughed. 'Oh, him. Skinny, nervous, Wiltshire accent?'

'Ay, sir.'

'No.' Carey laughed at the thought. 'Not that little mouse of a man. Anyway, he's a player not a poet. Didn't do badly with his first try at play-making though – I saw his *Henry VI* at the Theatre in Shoreditch; can't remember which number – there were three of them . . .'

'What, three Henries?'

'*Henry VI*, part 1, part 2 and part 3. Same sort of style as *Tamburlain*.'

'Eh, sir?'

'You got to 'ave heard of *Tamburlain*,' put in Barnabus, his face glowing. 'Now that's a proper play. "*Holla, you pampered jades of* . . ." of somewhere, can't remember where. Foreign.'

'Pampered jades of Israel? India?' Carey was trying to remember too, 'It's a wonderful play, plenty of battles . . .'

'And the Persian king pulling a chariot,' said Barnabus reminiscently. 'You remember, they had him done up like the King of Spain. I did laugh.'

'Anyway, if Shakespeare can pull off anything half as good as Marlowe, he'll be doing well,' said Carey judiciously. 'I don't think he will, though; he hasn't got the boldness.'

'So he's not the man your father had looking for your brother,' Dodd prompted, tired of all this discussion of plays he had neither seen nor wanted to.

'No, no,' Carey laughed again at the idea. 'He's been hanging around my father's household for months – before I left he even had me talk Berwick for some character he was thinking about. He wants a patron like any other would-be poet and thinks my father might be mad enough, but also he's desperately in love with Mistress Bassano.'

'She doesn't like him, though?'

'Of course not. She's not stupid and anyway, he's got no money and isn't likely to get any as a common player. Mistress Bassano has a very clear head.'

'Not that clear, sir,' said Barnabus slyly. 'I thought she had a fancy to you, didn't she?'

Carey's eyes chilled suddenly to ice. 'No, she doesn't.'

Thinking of the scene in the parlour on the day they arrived at Somerset House, Dodd regarded Carey with a grave lack of expression.

Carey did his family's explosive throat-clearing and went back to the real topic of conversation.

'My father hired Robert Greene to find Edmund, seeing as Greene's a well-known poet and he also knows his way around London's stews and slums and he has family contacts with the King of London. Greene claimed to be hot on the trail, got five pounds off my father and since then Father's heard nothing, so the first thing we'll do is find Robert Greene and ask him what he's up to.'

Dodd sighed. 'Find another man first, sir.'

'This one's easier than my brother. I know where he lives and more importantly, I know where he drinks. The second line of enquiry is to find out who murdered Michael to stop him talking to me and why.'

Friday, 1st September 1592, early morning

3

All four of them plunged into the roaring smelly chaos of London's back streets, Carey very cautiously avoiding the Strand and the Thames where the bailiffs still waited, Dodd with his hand twitching to his swordhilt every five minutes and thinking sadly of the civilised joys of Carlisle.

They first of all went to Edmund Carey's house, another one of his father's property speculations in the old Blackfriars monastery. Carey explained this system for making gold breed gold. First you found a place that was cheaper and less classy than it should be considering its location. Then using lawyers and intermediaries you quietly bought up the freeholds of all the houses in it, paying as little as you could. Doing only the most basic maintenance work you waited until you owned the whole place, then you used your court contacts to sort out any legal problems, evicted any disreputable tenants, replaced roofs, redug jakes and generally revamped the area, and then you sold off the freeholds again for quintuple what you paid for them.

Dodd shook his head at such amazing longterm planning.

Edmund Carey's house was a tall narrow building looking out over the old monastery courtyard, a wilderness of pigpens, chicken coops, overgrown herb beds, a jakes, a choked pond and a dead walnut tree, with a long wall of rubble along one side, out of which poked occasional pillars still decorated with fragments of tracery, like stone trees. Carey gestured at it while they waited for someone to answer the door.

'You see that? Used to be full of beggars living in the cloister carrells before the roof collapsed a couple of years ago. Now it would take about a month to fill the pond, cut down the walnut tree, tidy up the courtyard and repave it, after which the houses round about would be worth twice what they are now. If you cleared the rubble from the cloisters and built some houses on the site, you'd make even more.'

Dodd nodded, not all that interested. The door was opened by a pretty blonde woman with a velvet cap and little frown lines marking the smooth brow between her eyes. Her face lit up when she saw Carey.

'Robin!' she shouted and flung her arms around her brother-in-law. 'Oh Robin, you're back. Kate, Eddie, come out and see your uncle back from the wild north. Oh Robin, Robin. I don't know where he is. I haven't heard from him for weeks. Have you seen him? He didn't follow you to Berwick, did he?'

Carey shook his head and disentangled her arms. 'Susannah, my dear, that's why I'm back in London. Father wants me to find the silly bastard.'

'Don't swear.'

'Sorry. Hello, Kate, hello, Eddie.'

Two children threw themselves into Carey's arms squealing, demanding presents and asking was it true that Scotsmen had tails. He told them gravely that he rather thought it was, seeing how big their padded breeches were, and introduced Dodd.

The house had two rooms on the ground floor, one a parlour and the other a kitchen where a grim looking woman was trying to relight the fire. Kate was sent out to get some proper beer, since Susannah was quite sure their Uncle Robin didn't like mild ale, bread and meat from the cookshop on the corner if it was open yet and if not come straight back, don't talk to any naughty street children, and when would Kate learn to comb her hair before she put her cap on, for goodness' sake, and why wasn't Eddie properly dressed and ready for school, did he think his clothes would magically climb on his back by themselves? No, and where was his hornbook, this was the third he'd lost in two weeks and she could not afford to keep buying them, he'd just have to share someone else's and if the schoolmaster beat him, then perhaps he'd take better care of his belongings in future . . .?

Carey and Dodd retired from the shouting to sit in the parlour where the benches were carved but padded with old cushions and the hangings clearly came from Lord Hunsdon's house because they were too big for the walls. Eventually Kate came trotting in, red-faced, carrying a jug of beer and two pewter mugs, while Eddie sprinted out of the door with his mother yelling at him that if he lost another cap, he could go bareheaded and catch lungfever and serve him right.

Finally she came into the parlour carrying her own mug, sat down and smiled wanly at them while Carey poured her some beer.

'The children think their father's in the Netherlands again,' she said. 'I know he's silly, but I wish he'd come back. I do worry so much . . .'

Carey fished in the pocket of one of his padded sleeves and produced a purse full of money which he handed to her.

'From Father.'

The frownlines, that had no business on such a pretty face, tightened further. 'Oh no, I shouldn't, really; Edmund gets so cross when I take more money from my lord Hunsdon. He's really too generous.'

'Rubbish,' said Carey easily. 'Doesn't want his grandchildren to lack for anything, no matter how cretinous their father. What was he up to the last time you saw him?'

Susannah Carey leaned forward, put her elbows on the worn velvet of her kirtle and caged her fingers round her nose and mouth.

'He was . . . He was full of plans, full of optimism, quite sure he would sort out our finances once and for all.'

'Oh, God.'

'Yes. I know. He wouldn't tell me what the secret was.'

'Reselling brocades?'

'No, he's learnt his lesson on that one, though he still notionally owes Ingram Frizer a lot of money.'

'Let the little turd sue.'

Susannah shook her head, clearly fighting tears. 'Obviously, I was worried when he was so pleased with himself. But he wouldn't tell me and . . . and . . . I lost my temper. We had a big fight and he stormed out saying he'd be back when he had hundreds of pounds and then he'd . . . he'd take the children away and . . . and . . .'

Silently Carey handed over his handkerchief, and stared at the ceiling for a bit. After a while he patted his sister-in-law's shoulder and said, 'There, there.'

Eventually the sniffling stopped and Susannah blew her nose.

'What was the secret, Susannah?'

She rolled her eyes and sighed. 'I think it might have been alchemy,' she said tragically.

Carey barked with laughter. 'Oh, bloody hell. I suppose it's one thing he hasn't tried.'

'You see he was talking about how he needed seed-gold.'

'Oh, yes?'

'He sold the last of his rings and my pearls that I had from the Queen when we married, and off he went. He was buying a gold plate off a sailor, he said, before we started fighting, then that gold would be the seed and he'd harvest ten times as much gold from it.'

'Let me guess. The alchemist took the seed-gold, started the reaction, some disaster happened and it didn't work and Edmund needed more money to pay for more seed-gold. Yes?'

Susannah shook her head. 'Well, no. He did come back, drunk, one night in early August and he showed me a big purse full of gold angels. He said he'd bred ten gold angels for each angel of gold he started with. He was very happy, said we'd soon be out of hock, we made up our quarrel and off he went again. That was the last time I saw him.'

Carey rubbed his chin slowly. 'It *worked*?'

'I was surprised myself. I never heard of alchemy working before.'

'Nor me. Did he let slip any names?' Susannah shook her head. 'Well, can I go upstairs and have a look round, see if he left any bits of paper or anything else?'

Susannah gestured at the stairs and finished her beer. Carey went up the stairs and jerked his head for Dodd to follow him.

The main bedchamber was on the next floor, overlooking

the courtyard, smelling musty and much used. The enormous fourposter bed hadn't been made yet and the two clothes chests were open and higgledy piggledy. Carey looked around.

'Poor Susannah. She never was any good as a housekeeper, any more than Edmund has ever been worth a farthing as a provider.'

'Why do they not live wi' yer father?'

Carey shrugged. 'Edmund doesn't get on with Father at all, mainly because Father keeps trying to stop him drinking and gambling and Edmund resents it. They had a really bad fight in May after the Frizer business when Father had to pay the man off, and after the surgeon had reset Edmund's nose, he said he'd rather die in gaol than speak to Father again. All very stupid. Now then, let's have a look here.'

Carey pawed through Susannah's clothes and then did the same with the other chest which was rather more full of fashionable men's clothes, rich black velvet sprinkled with pearls, pale creamy satin. When the chest was empty he thumped the bottom of it in case there were any secret compartments. Dodd narrowed his eyes.

'What's that, sir?'

'What? Oh, yes. How odd.'

Little tiny beads of silver were clinging to the padded leather lining of the chest. Dodd prodded one with his finger and it bounced back, rolled down a seam and joined another bead like two raindrops on a windowpane. Carey tore off a little piece of paper from the small notebook he kept in a pouch in his belt, chased and caught a couple of the little beads, then twisted the paper closed and put it in the pouch.

There was nothing else in the room except for a couple of books of sermons, an empty jewel box and some dirty pewter plates which Dodd brought down with them.

Susannah had a bit more colour in her cheeks from the beer.

'Did you find anything.'

Carey shook his head. 'I'll ask Father to send a woman and a boy to you until Edmund turns up again. When he does you can send the boy to tell us. By the way, did you . . . er . . . did you check the gaols?'

Susannah nodded vigorously. 'Of course I did, it was the first thing I thought of. I went to all of them, the Clink, the Fleet, all of them, but nobody had heard of him. Oh, it's so worrying. What if he's dead?'

She was dry-washing her hands helplessly, her mouth wrung sideways with anxiety. 'What shall I do if he's dead?'

Carey put his arm across her shoulders and kissed her forehead. 'Darling, you know my father won't let you and the children starve. At least if my idiot brother is dead, you'll be able to find someone better to marry, won't you?'

'But I don't want anybody better, I want Edmund.'

'I can't imagine why, he's never treated you properly.'

'Well, you know, he is a bit silly with drinking and card-playing and money-making schemes, but he's a very good man, he's a good father, he's never beaten me once, not even when I've called him names, he . . . he . . . He's not so bad, really.'

'He doesn't deserve you,' said Carey firmly, kissing her again. 'Never has. Now dry your eyes. If the fool isn't at the bottom of the Thames, I'm going to find him. All right?'

Susannah nodded anxiously, blinking up at Carey.

Dodd felt dispirited as Carey bade goodbye to Kate and tipped her sixpence. If folk as rich as the Careys could have money troubles, what hope was there for him?

'Where now?' asked Dodd as they stood in Blackfriars' courtyard.

'We're finding Robert Greene,' said Carey as he struck off eastwards along St Peter and Thames Street. Carey tried Greene's lodgings first, over a cobbler's shop, but found a locked door at the top of the narrow ill-smelling stairs and nothing else. Barnabus and Simon were waiting dutifully outside as they'd been ordered to earlier that morning.

Carey went out into the smoke-dimmed sunlight and rubbed his gloved hands. Over the next two hours they quartered London for Robert Greene and it turned out that knowing the places where the poet liked to drink didn't narrow the field very much since there were so many of them.

After a while Barnabus got restless and asked if he could go off to St Paul's with Simon to see if he could find a new master. Carey told him sharply he could wait until they'd found Greene, and Barnabus lapsed into a sulk.

'If he could just wait a month or two, I could guarantee him a place with George Clifford, who'd employ him like a shot,' Carey said to Dodd.

'Don't want to risk no more northern wastelands,' muttered Barnabus.

'Clifford?' asked Dodd, not surprised that Barnabus had no appreciation for decent places. 'Is that any relation of the Earl of Cumberland, sir?'

'No, it *is* the Earl of Cumberland.'

Every so often Carey would do or say something that completely took the wind out of Dodd's chest. 'The Earl, sir?'

'Yes. Old friend of mine, we ran off from Court in 1588 to serve against the Armada, which we did on the old *Elizabeth Bonaventure*. He saved my life when I managed to catch gaol-fever that nearly did for me.'

'Sir?'

'Very embarrassing, you know. I'd risked the Queen's displeasure in the hopes of killing me a few Spaniards and getting enough loot to pay off the moneylenders. We certainly fought the Spaniards but it was all done with cannonfire and scurrying the ships around the big galleons and of course the fireships at Calais, so I never saw a penny of any treasure. Somewhere around Flamborough Head I lost ten shillings playing dice with the Ship's Master and the Surgeon, got a blinding headache and then went completely off my head with the fever. Apparently I spotted some likely looking cattle and a chest of gold in the crow's nest – you know, the look-out place on the top of the mast – climbed up the rigging in a storm and had a damned good battle with some sails. George was the one who led the sailors up to get me and knocked me out cold so they could bring me down. The Spanish ships had turned tail by then and were well on their way to Scotland, so as soon as the ship docked at Tilbury, he strapped me to a litter and sent me back to Philadelphia and Lady Widdrington in Westminster. Nice chap. Very good friend.'

'Ay, sir.' Dodd was unwillingly fascinated.

'He was the one said I should take up Scrope's offer, said I'd enjoy myself in Carlisle and he was absolutely right.'

Unwillingly, Dodd warmed to the Earl. He wasn't quite sure how much back rent he owed the Cumberland estate for some of the land he ran cattle on, but he was certain he couldn't pay it. He supposed it wasn't the Earl of Cumberland's fault. Maybe if Carey was his friend, he could put a good word in some time.

He looked around. The aggravating man had disappeared again. Dodd blinked at a tiny hovel with brightly painted red lattices and followed Carey inside.

There was no doubt that London was a drinking man's heaven. From the big coaching inns, with their great yards where the carriers' wagons were hitched ready for their long journeys to strange places like Bristol or Exeter, to tiny sheds where widows sold the ale and mead they brewed themselves, it was clear a man need never be thirsty in London. Provided he had money. Even river water cost a penny a quart if you bought it off a water-seller and was as brown as the beer and much less pleasant tasting.

Dodd stuck with beer. Carey's guts at last seemed to have settled down and his were fine, but he didn't want to spend another week sitting on the jakes with his bowels exploding and everyone knew it was diluting your humours with too much water that gave it to you.

At last, as the morning drew on, Carey went into yet another tiny boozing ken, peered around in the choking fumes of tobacco smoke, and cried, 'Ahah!' He shoved his way over to the corner where a man built like a beer barrel was propped up on a bench, mouth open and snoring, his hat drawn down over his eyes and a beard exactly the colour of carrots rising and falling with his snores.

Carey sat down next to him and grinned happily, just like a sleuthdog next to his quarry. Dodd put his hands on his hips.

'That's him,' he said.

'It certainly is,' said Carey. 'Nobody else in London has a beard exactly that shade.'

'I should 'ope not,' said Barnabus, bustling back from the woman next to the barrels with a large jug of ale and some greasy horn cups. 'Let's celebrate. Oh, she says his slate's up to ten shillings and if we want 'im, we've got to pay it.'

Carey shook his head in admiration. 'How the devil did you manage to drink five pounds in two weeks and have a slate?' he asked the snoring poet, who didn't answer and probably couldn't have explained anyway. Dodd thought he looked exactly the way anyone would after drinking five pounds in two weeks, which was to say, unhealthy, red-nosed, stertorous but happy.

'Could we not wake him up, sir?' Dodd asked as he sipped cautiously at the brown liquid in his cup. Carey had finished his.

'We could,' he said. 'Possibly.'

Dodd thought that would probably be a good idea, seeing as the man looked as if he weighed at least sixteen stone.

In the end they lurched out of the ken with one of the poet's arms over Carey's shoulder and one over Dodd's and his legs making occasional stabs at finding the floor.

'Why in God's name did yer dad use a drunk to find your brother?'

'You set a drunk to find a drunk,' said Carey with some edge in his voice. 'I expect that's what he was thinking. Also he doesn't know Greene as well as I do.'

'How d'ye know a poet, sir?'

'I know a lot of poets. Good company.'

'Yarrargh warra gerk . . .' said the poet, and puked over Dodd's boots.

They dropped him while he got it over with and Dodd found some grass growing out of a yard wall and used it to wipe the worst off. Barnabus cleaned up Greene's jerkin as best he could, they slung his arms over their shoulders again and set off once more.

'Where are we going with him sir?' Dodd puffed, trying to breathe sideways so as not to catch anything from Greene's breath.

'Down to the river.'

'Mrrrghh . . .'

'Och, Christ.'

It took two further sessions of unspeakable noises and effort from Greene before they emerged onto one of the little boatlandings that studded Thames bank. Carey set Greene down on the planks with his back against the riverwall, took his hat off and mopped his face. He looked critically at his black velvet suit but had miraculously managed to avoid any spattering. Not for the first time, Dodd wondered how he did it and borrowed Barnabus's handkerchief to have a scrub at his best clothes.

'Robert Greene,' roared Carey in the man's ear. 'If you don't wake up, I'm going to dunk you in the river.'

'Horrrargh . . . grr,' said Greene, sliding down comfortably and starting to snore. Carey shook his shoulder and one large paw swiped his hand away. 'Fuck off,' said Greene quite distinctly, before settling back into snores.

Carey's lips tightened at this defiance. 'Right,' he said. 'You can't say I didn't warn you.'

One fist in the scruff of Greene's doublet, he hauled the drunk over to the edge of the boatlanding, where the Thames water at high tide flowed as dark as beer. Dodd helped him and then Carey judiciously ducked the poet's head into the water.

'I suppose if it don't kill him, it might wake him,' Barnabus commented thoughtfully.

Dodd watched Greene flailing in Carey's grip. 'Ye could let him breathe, sir,' he said after a moment.

Carey lifted Greene's head, listened to his whooping and gasping, then dunked him again.

There was nothing wrong with Carey's hands now, Dodd thought, as he watched the poet start to fight. Carey let him up again.

'. . . I'll kill you, I'll rip your head off and shit . . . blrggggle ggrrrg . . .'

Carey lifted the head out of the water again. 'You awake yet, Greene?' he asked conversationally.

'Herrrck, herccck . . .' said Greene, eyes popping and water streaming down his beard which still managed to glow like a beacon. He sat on the edge of the planks and whooped and spat for several minutes and then grabbed for his sword hilt.

Carey dunked him once more. 'Get his sword, Dodd,' he said.

Dodd got his sword, which was another of those nasty foreign

rapiers the Londoners seemed to like so well, though the blade
was dull and didn't look like it had been sharpened or oiled for
a long time. He tutted at such carelessness, collected the man's
poignard dagger as well and waited for Carey to let Greene
breathe again.

'Huyuhhhh . . . herrrr . . . huyhhhh . . .'

'Are you awake?' bellowed Carey right in Greene's horribly
stinking face. 'Do you know me?'

'Huuuuyuuh . . . I'll . . . herrrgh. . . . I'll kill you. Where's my
sword . . . hugggh . . .'

'I'll fight you any time, Greene, but first I want to talk to you.
Do you understand me?'

Greene pushed him away and lurched to his feet, wiping his eyes
and coughing fit to crack his chest. 'You shit . . .' he gasped. 'You
fucking bastard . . .'

Carey was standing too, with Dodd at his back. 'My father gave
you five pounds for information about my brother Edmund. Now
I want to know what you've discovered . . .'

Greene flailed a fist at Carey, which he ducked, shouldered
Dodd into the riverwall and stumbled up the alleyway. They went
after him and caught up quickly because he was rolling from side
to side so much.

'Tell me what you've learned,' demanded Carey.

'Go to hell, you bastard.'

'No,' said Carey with a dangerous glint in his eye. 'My father's
the bastard, I'm the bastard's get.'

Greene blinked at him cross-eyed for a second. 'Oh yes,' he
slurred. 'So you are. Well, you can go to hell, you cocksucking
bastard's get and your whore of a mother with . . .'

Carey punched Greene in the face. He stood swaying like a
maypole for fully thirty seconds, then said something that sounded
like 'Whuffle' and collapsed.

'Och, sir,' said Dodd wearily. 'Now we'll have tae carry
him.'

'Sir, sir,' Barnabus was calling from the boatlanding behind
them. Dodd looked over his shoulder and saw that Barnabus had
had the sense to call a boat. The boatman was backing his oars

against the tide's ebb and Barnabus had the painter in his hand, was wrapping it round one of the posts.

'Our friend's been taken sick,' said Barnabus and the boatman nodded understandingly.

Carey shook his hand from the wrist and flexed his fingers, rubbing at his knuckles in their elegant kid gloves. He had the grace to look embarrassed, though not very.

Between them they hauled Greene back down the alley and got him into the boat, where the boatman solicitously arranged his head so it flopped over the gunwale. He was at least still breathing. At a nod from Barnabus, Simon jumped out and collected Greene's ironmongery.

'Mermaid Steps,' said Carey.

'That'll be a shilling then, sirs, to include the baggage.'

Dodd opened his mouth to protest at this wicked overcharging but Carey just nodded. Well, it was his money but you could see how he got through so much of it.

Mermaid Steps were slippery and dangerous. It took all four of them including Simon to haul Greene up, and when they stood at the top, Carey growled, 'Bugger this for a game of soldiers, we'll take him in there.'

It looked like a reasonably respectable place, despite having a scandalous bare-breasted mermaid in pink and green on its sign, so Dodd bent his back to the burden again and they managed to get Greene through the door and lay him down on one of the benches just inside.

The innkeeper came bustling over. 'I'm sorry, sir, he can't come in. He's banned.'

'What?' said Carey, who was looking frazzled by now and had a small smear of blood and snot from Greene on his shoulder.

'On account of the damage what he hasn't paid for.'

'He's a poet. You let poets drink in here, don't you?'

'I do, sir,' allowed the innkeeper. 'When they behave in a respectable fashion. Which he don't. So he's banned.'

'Well, he's not going to do any damage now, he's been cold-cocked.'

'That's as may be, sir. But he's banned.'

'How much was the damage?'

'Two pounds, one shilling and eightpence. Sir.'

Carey handed it over, while Dodd shook his head and Barnabus sighed.

'I'll get us all a drink and a bite to eat, shall I, sir?' he said after a suitable pause.

Carey nodded and sat down next to Greene who had rolled on his side and started to snore.

'I suppose we'll just have to wait for him to recover again,' he said. 'Damn it, Greene, you're a bloody nuisance.'

Dodd rested his weary frame on the opposite bench, peered around the gloom. It seemed like a nice place, this time, fresh sawdust on the floor and some tallow candles in sconces on the walls to light up the dim places. Even the tables were clean. Barnabus came over with two trays laden with a light second breakfast of bacon, sausage, fried onions, cheese and pease pudding, beer and some bread.

They ate in tactful silence while Carey cracked his joints and rubbed his knuckles every so often. Dodd hoped his hand was really hurting him. At last Barnabus belched softly, wiped his mouth on a napkin and coughed.

'Well, sir, since you've found him, I was wondering if you could excuse me for the rest of the day, like you said, sir?'

Carey shrugged. 'Well, I shouldn't think Greene's going to wake for a while yet, so why not? I can't give you the whole day, I'll probably need you later, but you can have the rest of the morning off until dinnertime. Will that do?'

'Thank you, sir.'

Barnabus and Simon finished their beer and bustled out of the Mermaid. Five minutes after they had gone, Will Shakespeare came hurrying in, looking around him and waved when he saw Dodd and Carey, who had started a game of primero.

'Sir Robert,' he gasped nasally. 'I've got a message for you from your father, sir. He says he's going down to Hampstead with Mr Recorder Fleetwood to investigate the footpads who tried to ambush you there. He said he'd be grateful if you and Sergeant

Dodd could join him, identify them perhaps, and I've brought two horses for you.'

Carey sighed and put away his cards, which Dodd felt only showed that the man had the luck of the devil since Dodd had a flush.

'That's an infernal nuisance,' he said, looking down at the body of Greene, prone on the bench beside him and snoring a fanfare. 'What am I going to do with this? I daren't leave it behind in case it bloody wanders off again.'

Shakespeare blinked at the man on the bench, caught sight of the carroty beard and twitched. Then he said thoughtfully, 'Well, I could look after him for you, sir.'

Carey smiled. 'Would you do that? I'd be most grateful.'

'Certainly I could do it.'

'If he wakes up and starts causing trouble, don't mess about. Just call the innkeeper to help, all right?'

Shakespeare went pink at this patronage but he only nodded humbly. 'Yes, sir.'

'Splendid. Where did you say the horses were?'

'Hitched outside.'

'Come on then, Sergeant. You'll have to beggar me some other time.'

'Ay, sir.'

Friday, 1st September 1952, morning

4

Carey led the way through the clutter and crowding of the London streets, through the City wall at Ludgate and up the Old Bailey, across the wide expanse of Smithfield which was full of men practising horsemanship and swordplay, some of whom shouted drunken challenges at Dodd and Carey, up Turnmill Street to the little village of Clerkenwell which seemed to be amazingly full of dazzlingly fine women, and then westwards along country lanes until they joined the Gray's Inn Road again. There at last Carey put his heels in and went to a canter and Dodd followed, instantly feeling happy to be away from the constant press of humanity. With fresh horses out of Lord Hunsdon's stables they were there well within the hour, and found Carey's father, the Recorder of London and a large number of buff-coated men. Hunsdon was leaning on his saddlehorn as Carey and Dodd came up, their horses blowing and panting after the long hill. Carey flourished off his hat in a splendid bow from the saddle taking in his father and the Recorder while Dodd touched his cap.

'Ah, there you are,' said Hunsdon. 'About time. Where have you been? I sent Shakespeare out to find you this morning.'

'Talking to Susannah.'

'Hmf. How are the children?'

'Kate forgot to comb her hair this morning and Eddie lost his third hornbook in a month, otherwise they're well.'

Hunsdon smiled. 'Mr Recorder Fleetwood and I have been considering, and we've decided not to interview the locals yet. We're going to start by searching for fresh graves.'

'Good idea, my lord,' said Carey. 'Who have you brought?'

'Who do you think? Here he is. His paw shouldn't take any harm from a little light sniffing around, eh boy?'

Jimmy the dog-page was holding Hunsdon's yellow lymer on a long leash and the dog went sniffing delightedly up to Carey's horse, who put down his head and snorted in welcome.

'Hasn't been fed this morning so he should be fairly sharp.'

'Oh, poor fellow,' said Carey sympathetically to the dog, who panted and looked hopeful for a while. 'Well, let's see what you can find.'

Watched warily by the Hampstead villagers, they left most of the buff-coated men by the horsepond and went into the Cut so that Bellman could sniff the traces left by the deaths of the footpads. Dodd and Carey both went to look for any other traces and found hoofprints and dragmarks in the dust. Then Dodd took Bellman's leash and went up the little path that led up to the Hanging Elm and had the dog sniff around its base for a while. As expected, the body was no longer there.

'Why do you think they bothered to put poor old Michael up on the Elm in the first place?' asked Hunsdon.

Dodd shrugged. 'They knew our nags might smell the corpse and hid him in plain view. And to give a reason for them spooking if they smelled the ambush too.'

'That's what I thought. Barbarous. All right, Bellman. Find. There's a good boy. Find.'

Wagging his tail happily the lymer pottered around the Elm, snorting rhythmically through his large blunt yellow nose. He found a trail, followed it enthusiastically and eventually stood barking in triumph by a large sandy bank full of rabbitholes.

'No, Bellman,' said Hunsdon patiently, and produced a blue velvet cap from a bag by his saddle, handed it down to Dodd to show the dog. 'Find.'

It took several tries but eventually the lymer found another trail and went off down into the village, snorting and sniffing as he went. Out the other side, the southern flank of Hampstead Hill was covered with market gardens being worked by more of the villagers, who stopped and leaned on their hoes as Dodd trotted by, pulled by the lymer, followed by the dog-page and then Carey, his father, the Recorder and two of the Recorder's men. Halfway down, a thick wood began and the lymer bounded into its eaves and stopped in a clearing.

There was an unmistakeable bank of newly disturbed earth where Bellman started digging and barking, so Dodd pulled the dog off in case he ate something he shouldn't. Lord Hunsdon patted the lymer and praised him extravagantly, then produced a large marrowbone from another bag hanging behind his saddle and gave it to the dog who wagged his tail ecstatically, took the bone and lay down with his paws over it, growling if one of the horses or men came too near his treasure. The Recorder sent up the hill for more men and his attendants began working with their spades. After a while they struck something that thudded.

'Four bodies,' announced the Recorder eventually. 'Sirs, would you care to identify them . . .?'

It wasn't difficult and not even very smelly – the bodies had been in the earth for only a day and their bellies were just beginning to swell. Looked at closely, you could tell that Michael's face had been destroyed by a gun put close to it and fired, though whether that was what had killed him was anybody's guess. He was stripped down to his shirt, as were the dead footpads.

Recorder Fleetwood was talking to his men. Dodd thought it was all very orderly and efficient. Michael was put on a horselitter, decently covered, while the footpads' bodies were loaded on packponies to go back up to the Hanging Elm for display.

'Could we search the village houses for that suit of Michael's?' Carey asked.

Hunsdon and Fleetwood exchanged cynical looks. 'I'm afraid I would need search warrants for each house,' said the Recorder.

'Why?' asked Carey. 'Her Majesty's pursuivants regularly tear London apart looking for priests.'

'Ah yes, but that is a matter of high policy and treason. This is only a murder.'

'Besides, they'll have sold the suit, I should think,' said Hunsdon. 'Surely even Hampstead peasants would have more sense than to wear a suit from a murdered man. Never mind, Robin. I'm going to try something else. Mr Fleetwood, would you and your men kindly assemble the villagers by the horsepond?'

Hunsdon addressed the assembled people from horseback.

'Now, as you know, goodmen and goodwives of Hampstead, three wicked footpads were killed by my son and his followers the day before yesterday when they tried an ambush at the Cut. I would not dream of suggesting that any of you would be concealing such criminals, which is of course a crime in itself.'

Some of the villagers shifted their feet. Dodd wondered if he recognised a couple of them.

'However, earlier that day, those same wicked footpads had probably killed my servant, Michael Lang, a good decent married man, that leaves a wife and three children. He had served me since he was a boy.' Hunsdon paused impressively. 'I will pay three pounds sterling for any genuine information about that murder. Three pounds in gold. No questions asked. Understand? You may find me at Somerset House in the Strand and I will receive any such informer personally.'

Carey seemed subdued as they rode back down Haverstock Hill and followed a roundabout route to return to the Mermaid Inn while avoiding the dangers of the Strand. They found Shakespeare sitting quietly next to Greene, reading a book. He had covered Greene with a solicitous if rancid blanket and put his head on a greasy bench cushion and Greene looked comfortable and happy. Carey tipped Shakespeare and sent him back to Somerset House with the horses.

After they had eaten, Dodd had no further luck with the cards and was led into a couple of very rash bets by sheer irritation with the Courtier's breeziness – as Carey sternly lectured him after each game.

Carey resorted to tossing a coin over and over.

'All right,' he said. 'Now we've had two heads in a row. What are the chances the next time it will be tails?'

'A bit higher, I'd say, sir,' Dodd opined.

'No, no, no!' said Carey, who had not been intended by Nature for a schoolmaster. 'The chances are exactly the same.'

'Why?' Dodd was frowning at the offending coin, lying inno-
cently on the blackened table. Barnabus and Simon had come
in while Carey was at his tutoring and now Barnabus gave a
delicate cough.

'Only there's nothing doing in the Mediterranean, sir, and I was
wondering if you'd mind if I took Simon off to see his mum, see
if she's got any news, you know.'

'Of course, it doesn't work if the coins are heavier one side
than the other. What's that, Barnabus? Is that the woman with
the fighting cock?'

'Tamburlain the Great, sir. Yes. I wouldn't mind seeing how
he's shaping now he's finished his moult.'

Dodd, who was desperate to get away from Carey and his
notions about cards and the like, stared hard at Barnabus.

'Sergeant Dodd could come too. I could teach him 'ow to
navigate 'is way around a city.'

'Ay, sir,' said Dodd quickly, heartily sick of card-playing. 'I
wouldnae mind a breath of fresh air.'

It was certainly true that Greene had been farting with the
creativity of the very drunk, but mainly Dodd's head was hurting
from adding up his points and then comparing the score with
Carey's numbers.

Carey looked disappointed. 'Oh, very well.'

'Ye willnae have any trouble wi' bailiffs, sitting here alone,
sir?'

'No, no. The Mermaid's in the Blackfriars Liberty, I should be
safe enough. I might meet some old friends here as well if I stay
long enough for them to wake up and venture out of their pits.'

Barnabus led the way up Water Lane, under the Blackfriars
Gateway and into the broadest street Dodd had seen in the
city, where the cobbles were worn with deep ruts. They walked
eastwards along it with St Paul's looming over the houses north
of them and Barnabus dinning Dodd's ears with a continuous
stream of reminiscence, anecdote and the occasional history lesson
attached to some landmark or other that they passed. It seemed
that navigating in the city was less a matter of knowing where
you were going, than remembering landmarks and turning left or

right at them. Barnabus took them up a long narrow street and out at a big old-fashioned market cross that he claimed was called Eleanor Cross after some Queen or other. Dodd blinked around himself. They were in a dazzlingly wealthy shopping street lined with barred windows where gold and silver plate and magnificent jewels studded with pearls, rubies, sapphires, emeralds glinted tantalisingly. Large buff-coated men with swords stood at every door, giving Dodd considering looks when he went up to gawp at the displays. He knew he was gawping and it annoyed him, but he couldn't help it. Never in all his life had he seen so much money laid out before him, so many vast golden cups and bowls, so much wrought jewellery. It made your mouth water, truly it did.

'This is Cheapside,' said Simon Barnet at Dodd's elbow. 'Good, innit?'

Dodd nodded, speechless.

'Up that way,' Barnabus added, waving an arm to the north, 'that's where the big guildhalls are and Gresham's Exchange is that way on Cornhill.'

'Does yer sister live here?'

'Nah. It's too pricey round here, I just thought I'd show you Cheapside, seeing it's your first visit. I mean, you couldn't come to London and miss the Cheapside jewellers, could you?'

Dodd shook his head. They wandered along for a while and came to a row of stalls selling ruffs of astonishing width, embroidered shirts, women's wigs sparkling with gold chains and pearls, and some extraordinary hats. Dodd's mouth fell open again before he shut it with an irritated click of his teeth. Never in his life had he felt such a yokel, but this made Edinburgh look like Longtown by comparison. Where in God's name did folk get the money to spend on such things?

'Here,' nudged Barnabus. 'Why don't you buy somefing for your wife. Eh?'

'What, for Janet?'

'Yeh. She's your wife, in't she?'

'Well, but . . . These are fer fine court ladies, not Janet.'

'She may not be a fine lady, though she's always seemed pretty fine to me, but you're a man of importance in Carlisle and she should show it, shouldn't she? Here, look, why don't you buy her a hat?'

'What, one of them?'

'Yeh. Why not? You got Heneage's bribe money on you and nobody's nipped it out of yer crotch yet.'

'How did ye ken . . .' Barnabus rolled knowing eyeballs at Dodd and darted forwards to speak confidentially to the woman behind the stall. She looked hard at Dodd.

'A hat for your wife, sir?' she said. 'A French hood, perhaps?'

'Nay,' said Dodd looking at the thing she was pointing at. 'She's got one of them, there's plenty of wear in it yet. What about that one?' He pointed at a high-crowned confection of green velvet with a pheasant's feather in it. 'That would look well wi' her bright hair.'

'And what colour is your wife's hair, sir?'

'Red.'

'How charming,' said the woman with a smile. 'Just like the Queen. Well, I think you've made a very good choice, sir. That will be twenty five shillings exactly, sir, and cheap at the price.'

Dodd gobbled. He heard himself do it, but couldn't stop. *Twenty-five shillings*, for a *hat*? 'Barnabus . . .' he growled and Barnabus took his elbow and whisked him round the side of the stall.

'Look, Sergeant, it sounds a lot, but it'll be worf it, believe me. There's nuffing ladies like better than 'ats and she'd never ever get one this good nor this fashionable anywhere norf of York.'

'But . . . but I could buy a field for that.'

'No doubt you could, round Carlisle, where land's so cheap, but would Mrs Dodd like that so much?'

'Ay, she would, she's a sensible woman.'

'Look, mate. You've treated me right and I'm giving you some good advice 'ere. You give her the hat, and every time she looks at it, she'll forgive you for whatever it is you've done.'

Dodd shook his head to clear it. 'Ah've niver heard of such a thing.'

'Look, let's see what I can do for you, eh? I know Mrs Bridger . . .'

'Och, so that's it . . .'

'Come on. You've got to get her somefing while you're in London or she'll never speak to you again.'

This was incontrovertibly true. Dodd hesitated.

'So you might as well give your money to somebody I know, right? Anyway, let me see what I can do.'

Barnabus trotted round the back of the stall and had a long chat with Mrs Bridger, while Dodd got his breath back and resignedly pulled out his purse.

Barnabus beckoned him close again. 'Mrs Bridger has very kindly on account of our friendship agreed to cut her price by a fifth, which pretty much wipes out her profit, so this is quite a favour . . .'

Dodd counted out two of the golden angels Heneage had given him and handed them over. Mrs Bridger looked at them sharply, and bit both of them. Then she handed one back with an ugly look on her face and glared at Barnabus.

'Are you up to your tricks again, Cooke?'

'What's wrong?'

'That one's false. If your gentleman's got no gold in 'is purse, he shouldn't come buying things at my stall.'

'False?' echoed Dodd, looking at the coin.

'It's pewter with gold on the outside. Look at it.'

Dodd squinted closely at it and had to admit he could see grey metal in the pits made by her teeth. Simon stood on tiptoe to peer at it too, shook his head and tut-tutted.

'You could be hanged for uttering false coin, you know that, Cooke.'

'On my soul, Mrs Bridger, I'd no idea. Look at the other ones, Sergeant, see if they're all right.'

Dodd fished out another angel and bit it himself and it seemed right enough. Mrs Bridger took it suspiciously, bit it, then weighed it on a pair of little scales she had under the counter. At last she nodded. 'That one's all right too.'

With a meaningful sniff and another scowl at Barnabus she took the magnificent hat, wrapped it in a linen cloth, stuffed the inside with hay and put it in a round bandbox with a handle which she gave to Simon to hold.

A horrible idea occurred to Dodd. He poured all the angels onto his palm, bit the three remaining and found one other was the same as the false one. On Barnabus's advice he put the two false angels in his jerkin and the rest of his money back in his crotch and they walked on. Dodd felt he had been robbed, even though he was still carrying more money than he ever did except on rent day.

'We'll 'ave to talk to Sir Robert about that,' said Barnabus. 'I wonder if it was Heneage's bribe or the footpad's money?'

'Have ye got any bad ones?'

'Dunno. I left mine at Somerset House.' His small eyes narrowed with suspicion. 'Hem. Let's go see my sister first, then we'll take a boat.'

They finally came to New Fish Street and ducked down a little alley. 'Of course, there's always a bit of coining going on, but they don't generally bother with gold coins, it's too hard to spend what you make . . . Now, you mind that box, Simon, if anybody swipes it or sits on it, I'll sell you to the Falcon's Chick to pay for it. You should be worth that much, what d'yer reckon?'

Barnabus was still talking as he bustled up to a narrow fronted house with the shutters on the two lower windows still closed, and lifted his arm to bang on the door.

He stopped stock still, frozen in mid-move, made a little short grunt in his throat as if he'd been stabbed. Dodd saw the thing a moment after and felt the blood drain down from his face in horror and fear.

There was a cross branded into the wood of the door, red paint daubed into the burnt furrows which had dripped down the door as it dried. The latch had been nailed shut, and so had the shutters. Below the cross was pinned a piece of printed paper.

Barnabus ripped it down and his lips moved as he read it.

' "May the Lord have mercy on us." '

Dodd had backed away from the door, looked up and down the street which he now realised was suspiciously empty for London. There were other red crosses on other doors.

'Nah, nah,' Barnabus croaked. 'It's a mistake. Easily done. Just a mistake, Simon, don't you worry.'

Simon had his face screwed up and tears in his eyes as he looked up at the cross. 'Mum?' he shouted, 'Mum?'

'Margery!' bellowed Barnabus, hammering on the door. 'MARGERY! It's me, it's Barnabus. Where are you?'

One of the windows opened on the upper storey and a girl poked her head out. She was very pale and she had bandages round her neck.

'That you, Uncle Barney?' she called.

'Letty! Letty, what's happened? What's all this?'

Letty was crying and looked as if she'd done a lot of it, lately. 'Oh, Uncle Barney. It was Sam got it first, and then Mary, and then George and me, and then dad got it and mum's got it, and dad's dead and they took him off yesterday and now mum's all black and she won't wake up and . . . and . . .' She made her hands into fists and howled into them.

Barnabus was panting as he looked up while Simon had placed the bandbox carefully on the step, sat down beside it and was weeping into his sleeve.

'I . . . I don't believe it. She's too good for this. She never done nuffing. She's the best of the lot of us. Letty, are you sure . . .?'

For answer the girl pulled down the bandage under her chin and they could see the scabbed pit under her ear where a buboe had burst. Dodd had looked coolly at the pointed end of all manner of weapons, but this nearly made him lose his water. 'I'm getting better now and so's George, but . . . but Mary's looking poorly and the baby's . . . Well, the baby's dead, of course, but me mam . . . It's me mam I'm feared for, she's all black, all black spots all over and she smells horrible. I think she's still breathing but . . . Oh, Uncle Barney.'

For fully five minutes Barnabus stared up at his niece, breathing hard through his mouth and his hands opening and closing into fists. Dodd was rooted to the spot and the hair on the back of his neck standing up like a hedgehog. He had seen plague. Years ago, back when he was a little wean still in skirts, there had been plague in Upper Tynedale and his cousin Mary had died of it and his uncle had staggered through the village roaring, his face turned into a monster's by the huge lumps on his neck and the black blotches and he'd collapsed over by the stream and none of the grown-ups had dared go near, except poor mad Peter . . . Big strong grown-ups, men that had forayed hundreds of times into Scotland and come back triumphantly with Elliot cattle and sheep, they had smelled of fear and some of them had disappeared forever. Dodd's memory was confused but he knew that one of his sisters, the one he hated because she was littler than him, she had turned black and become a stiff doll-like thing and they had buried her . . .

He found he hadn't been breathing and he took in a deep harsh breath. Simon was still howling on his doorstep. My legs'll move soon, Dodd told himself, and then I'm off, I'm going, I'm out of London and I'm going north whether the Courtier likes it or not . . .

'All right, Letty. You got any food in the house?' How was it Barnabus's voice was so calm. He wasn't even shouting.

Letty shook her head. 'We ate the last hen two days ago,' she sniffled. 'And the bread yesterday.'

'We'll get you some. What happened to Margery's fighting cock? Did you eat him?'

Letty shook her head again and winced. 'No, Uncle Barney, mum wouldn't let us. She said he could make our fortunes if we got through this. But she's gone all black and she won't wake up . . .'

'Now you calm down, Letty, you hear me? You've got to be a good girl and look after the others. Me and Sergeant Dodd 'ere, we'll go get you some food. Have you got a basket and some rope?'

She nodded.

'Good. Now, Simon, you stay here and look after Sergeant Dodd's hatbox and don't you move, you hear me? You stay there. You can get plague just by going in the house, so don't you move!'

'B . . . but me mam . . .'

Barnabus's face crumpled and there were tears in his eyes too. He stroked Simon's hair. 'Son, your mum's dead. If she in't now, she will be soon. If all you've got is buboes, there's some chance

111

for you, but if you get the black spots all over you, that's it, you're done for. And don't forget, you can take the plague just from the bad smell of it, so don't you set foot in that house.'

Dodd nodded at this sense. Barnabus jerked his head at him, and they went back up the silent little street. Dodd knew he was shaking all over, but he wasn't sure enough of his legs to start running yet.

Barnabus's shifty little ferret-face was grim and cold. 'Now we know what's going on 'ere,' he said. 'That's why there's hardly anybody about and the Queen's still in Oxford when the lawterm should be starting soon. Good Christ Almighty.'

'Are we going back to Sir Robert?' Dodd asked, knowing his voice sounded funny because of his mouth being dry.

Barnabus looked straight up at him. 'You can, mate, I'm not asking you to stick around. This is family business.'

'Ay.' Dodd wanted to explain that he was afraid of getting lost again and maybe stumbling into some other plague spot, but couldn't because it sounded so weak. Him, Sergeant Dodd, afraid? But he was, afraid of the plague and afraid of this huge city full of people, any one of whom might be sick to death and not even show it yet.

'Why didn't anybody say what was happening?'

Barnabus sucked his teeth judiciously. 'Well, there's always a bit of plague about in London, but it's usually only brats and babies that get it. They don't start shutting the playhouses and having days of penance and preaching and so on until the parishes are showing more than thirty deaths a week from plague.'

'Thirty deaths a week!' Dodd echoed, horrified again at the numbers.

'Plus of course there's plenty of rich people that want to keep it quiet because of the damage to business.'

'Ay.'

They were in New Fish Street again, according to a dirty sign up on one of the houses. Barnabus looked thoughtfully at the various fishmongers' shops, several of them shut up tight, and carried on down the street until he came to a little grocer's just under a magnificent clock hanging over the street like an inn sign.

They ranged about the nearby streets, buying bread and salt fish and cheese and finished with two big leather bottles of beer that Dodd carried. And that was amazing by itself, not having to wait for market day, being able to just go to shops and buy all that food whenever you wanted. When Barnabus ran out of money, Dodd handed over one of his false angels which made Barnabus grin cynically at him.

The afternoon was sliding away by the time they came back and found no Simon on the doorstep, but Dodd's hatbox sitting there still. That sight made Dodd feel queasy all over again. A twenty-shilling hat, left unattended in the middle of London, and nobody had stolen it.

'Where's that boy?' growled Barnabus. 'If he's gone in, 'e can stop there.'

They shouted up at the window again, until Letty put her head out and let down a basket on a rope. First the bread, then the cheese, then the salt fish, then the beer. They did it in silence, nobody having anything to say.

'We'll go to the river and fetch you some water, Letty,' said Barnabus, still quite calmly. 'You got any water barrels?'

'Simon's bringing it round from the yard,' said Letty.

'You didn't let him in the house, did you?'

She shook her head. Simon appeared in one of the tiny passageways between the houses rolling the barrel in front of him in a little handcart.

'Did you go in?'

'No, Uncle,' said Simon glibly, tears still shining on his cheeks. ' 'Course I didn't.'

'Not to say goodbye to your mum or nuffing?'

'No, Uncle, I wouldn't.'

'Where'd you get the barrel?'

'Well, I went in the yard, I 'ad to, see if Tamburlain the Great was all right.'

'And is he?'

'Well, he's still alive, but he don't look very well, he's huddled up in his cage looking all sad and bedraggled 'cos his hens is dead.'

Barnabus grunted. 'Come on.'

They threaded through little alleys down to some worn riversteps where Barnabus heaved the barrel on its rope into the oily water, waited until it sank and then with Dodd's help, hauled it back up again and heaved it onto the cart. Dodd pushed the barrel up New Fish Street into the alley. Letty still had her head out the window.

'Can you get it in our yard, Uncle Barney?' she called, looking a little bit more cheerful and munching on some of the bread.

'No problem, Letty.'

They manoeuvred the cart up the passageway and found the passage-gate nailed shut as well. Simon showed them where he'd climbed over the yardwall.

'I'll get in and you heft the barrel to me, Sergeant.'

'Ay.'

It was a gut-busting business hauling the heavy sloshing barrel up over the wall and into the yard. Barnabus disappeared for a minute and Dodd's neck hairs stood up again with the suspicion that he'd been mad enough to go into the house himself, but then he was lifting a wooden cage full of squawking red and bronze feathers up to the brow of the wall. Dodd took it from him, nearly getting his fingers pecked by the wild-eyed fighting cock inside, and then Barnabus climbed back into the passage, dusting himself down and shaking his head.

'The cat's dead of it too. I don't believe it.'

Dodd stared at him suspiciously. 'Ye didnae go in yerself?'

Barnabus sighed. 'No, mate, I'm not stupid. The yard should be safe enough, no bad airs there. Come on, Simon, I need a drink.'

They trailed round to the front of the house again and Dodd gingerly picked his hatbox up off the doorstep.

'You all right for the moment, Letty?'

She nodded and licked her fingers. 'Thanks, Uncle Barney. I'll tell mum when she wakes up.'

'All right, sweetheart. I'll come back tomorrow if I can, or the next day.'

'Bye, Uncle Barney. See yer.'

Barnabus nodded and swallowed hard. Dodd heard him mutter, 'Bye, Margery, God keep you, girl.'

They went back into New Fish Street again and looked at each other, exhausted. Barnabus was as grey as a man who had been badly wounded.

'Ay,' said Dodd. 'Ye do need a drink. Where's the nearest boozing ken?'

Barnabus scrubbed his sleeve along his face and coughed. 'That'll be Mother Smith's, up that way.'

Mother Smith's had a red cross on the door and the shutters nailed together. They stared at it dully and carried on up to Eastcheap and along to another little house with red lattices. Dodd bought three large horn cups of aqua vitae and some beer with the change from his false angel, and they sat by the window drinking in silence.

'What'll we tell the Courtier?'

Barnabus thought carefully about this. 'Nuffing,' he said decisively at last. 'Don't want to worry him and I'll have trouble finding a new master if they think I've got plague.'

But you could have it, yammered the scared wean inside Dodd's head, you could and not know it, the death marks could be growing on you out of sight right now, they could . . . He shook his head and swallowed the rest of his aqua vitae.

None of them felt like hefting a clumsy heavy cage full of outraged fowl all the way back to the western suburbs, so they took a boat. Simon sat in the back on the cushions and trailed his fingers in the water and wouldn't look at either of them. Barnabus stared at him the whole way, until Dodd was unnerved just watching.

'Take us past Mermaid Steps, boatman,' Barnabus said. 'I want Whitefriars.'

The boatman nodded, and when they landed Dodd paid him, including a tip after Barnabus elbowed him. He thought he had never ever spent so much money in one day in his life before. He couldn't even bring himself to count it up, it came to so much, and some of it was false and the plague on top of it all.

'We'll take Tamburlain the Great back to the room so he can rest and keep his strength up. Now you've looked after him before, haven't you, Simon?'

Simon nodded and perked up a little with enthusiasm. 'Me dad was teaching me to handle 'im, how to feed him up before a match and make sure he wasn't got at and how to put the spurs on. Dad says . . .' His voice trailed off. Then he shrugged and went back to staring at the water.

'Well, you look tired,' Barnabus said. 'How do you feel? Peaky? Got a headache?'

Simon shook his head.

'Well, you can go to bed so you can keep an eye on Tamburlain. If I know Sir Robert he's playing primero by now and we're in for a late night.' Gloomily Dodd thought he was probably right. London was a den of iniquity and no mistake, full of evil greedy folks just plotting to take your money by any way they could, and no wonder it was being visited by the Sword of God's Wrath.

But would God's vengeance hit Dodd as well, even though he hadn't done anything bad? Well, nothing iniquitous, anyway, just the routine normal sins that everybody committed. But the Reverend Gilpin had said that there wasn't any such thing as a normal sin, a venial sin like the Papists said, they were all sins and that was bad enough to draw down God's wrath. God had good reason to be angry with every man or woman. Dodd shook his head and tried to stop thinking about it. If he let his mind go down that road he'd be a gibbering wreck by the next morning (or dead of plague, if God was angry enough with him). What could you do? If you got the plague, you got it, there wasn't anything you could do to stop it except stay out of plague houses and away from sick people and repent of your sins. And even that wouldn't necessarily help you. Barnabus had said his sister was a good woman, she'd done nothing to deserve such a visitation. Deep in the recesses of his soul, Dodd found it terrifying that God was so much less reasonable than Richie Graham of Brackenhill. At least if you paid your blackrent on time and didn't kill any Grahams, Richie Graham wouldn't burn you out.

On the way to the river they had bought grain to feed the fighting cock. It seemed tame enough when they cautiously let it out of its cage in the attic room, fed it grain on the bare floorboards which magnified every footstep and peck, every creak. It glared at Dodd and Barnabus suspiciously, but it seemed to know Simon and even let him smooth down some long feathers that had been disarranged by being in the cage. At last they left the cock roosting on the head of the bed and Simon curled up in his blankets on the pallet by the wall. Barnabus called him to get up and bolt the door from the inside, which he did.

They clattered down the stairs and hurried to Fleet Street to get back into the City before the gates shut. By the time they arrived at the Mermaid, the sun was drowning in a brilliant red blaze that set light to the water and gilded the little boats scurrying across it. All Dodd wanted was to go to bed and sleep.

Barnabus caught his arm just as they went in. 'Keep quiet for me, Sergeant.'

Dodd sighed. 'He willnae like it when he finds out.'

'He won't find out.'

'All right, if ye want.'

'You're a prince, Sergeant. I owe you one. Not many would have stuck around like that for people that weren't even related.'

Dodd ducked his head in embarrassment, not able to explain that he had stuck around because he was afraid of getting lost in London again.

Carey was happily calling his point score as they came in, putting down more money on a terrifyingly large pile. Beside him was bundled the still unconscious mound of Robert Greene. When he saw Dodd and Barnabus, Carey closed up his cards and smiled.

'Oh, there you are. Greene's no better, as you can see, though I think it's now the booze not the blow that's made him so sleepy. Pull up a stool, Sergeant, I'll introduce you.'

Dodd nodded politely as Carey went round the circle of cardplayers, firing off names like a bowman in a battle. Unfortunately not one of them hit the mark and all were instantly lost from his overtaxed brain. Dodd recognised one man, Shakespeare, his fuzzy dome glinting in the candlelight above him. He had already folded. From the look of concentration on his face and the sideways manner he sat on his stool it was clear he was magnificently drunk. Next to him sat a short rotund man in a grey wool suit with a confiding way to him; Dodd couldn't remember his name. Another one, directly opposite the Courtier had a handsome slightly smug

face, the kind of face that believes itself to be cleverer than any
company, and very annoyingly often is, and a fine doublet of black
velvet slashed in peach taffeta, almost as good as the Courtier's.
Next to him was a pale man with a nose that had been broken once
who Dodd vaguely thought was called Poley or Pool or something,
and that took you to Robert Greene and the Courtier again. Dodd
narrowed his eyes and sat down on a stool deferentially brought
for him by Barnabus and decided that he could throw any one of
them a lot further than he was prepared to trust them, and would
on the whole prefer to throw them anyway.

'Will you join us, Sergeant?'

'Ah'd prefer to watch for a while, Sir Robert. I'm no' so well
in practice with gleek.'

As Dodd knew perfectly well, they were playing primero and
in fact he was in razor-sharp form for primero, for him.

The self-satisfied man in the pretty doublet raised his eyebrows
at Dodd. 'Sergeant?' he asked. 'Are you a lawyer, sir?'

Was the man deliberately trying to insult him? 'Nay, sir, I'm a
Land Sergeant.'

'Very important man, in Carlisle,' said the Courtier helpfully.
'Keeps an eye on some of the most important reivers' trails from
Scotland into England. He has land and a tower in Gilsland.'

The reaction to this was glazed-over politeness.

'Fancy,' said pretty doublet, distantly.

'And ye, sir?' Dodd asked pretty doublet. 'What are ye
yerself?'

Pretty doublet laughed. 'Oh, I'm a poet, a playwright, a scholar, a
striver for the incomprehensible crystal reaches of the heavens.'

Dodd gave him a glazed look right back. 'Och, fancy.'

To his surprise pretty doublet grinned at him. 'Well, it's a more
interesting trade than hammering shoes for a living.'

Carey coughed. 'Marlowe's being modest, which is extremely
unusual for him. Also he hasn't declared his points and I'm waiting
to find out by how much I've beaten him.'

Marlowe leaned back, drank with an unnecessary flourish and
said, 'Eighty-four, of course, like you.'

'I'm out,' said Poley or whatever his name was.

Shakespeare snapped his fingers at the potboy for more drink, which was there with a speed that surprised Dodd. The would-be poet and player looked as if he had a gigantic cloud of black melancholy hanging over his head, so black it was almost visible, and which was deepening by the minute as he drank. Dodd shook his head. Good God, he must be tired, he was coming over all fanciful.

There was a sudden snortle and an earthquake from the huddle on the bench, and Robert Greene lunged upright, his orange beard jutting like a preternatural carrot.

'Beer,' he roared. 'Where's the beer?' Somebody gave him a mug and he lifted it to the company. '*Holla, ye pampered jades of Arsia,*' he bellowed and drank it down. Marlowe rolled his eyes and stretched his lips briefly in a smile that said 'oh how witty, and only the hundredth time this week'. Greene had sunk most of his quart before he seemed to notice the taste of what he was drinking which he then spat out again onto the floor in a stream.

'For Christ's sake, Greene,' drawled Carey. 'It's only mild ale.'

'It's horsepiss,' roared Greene. 'You, boy, get me some proper booze. What the hell are you doing in London, Sir Robert? I thought you'd gone to wap the cows in Newcastle.'

'Carlisle,' said Carey. 'I'll see you, Marlowe.'

'York, Carlisle. Who cares? Somewhere ooop north.' Greene waved an arm expansively. 'I repeat. Why are you here?'

Marlowe put down four fives and Carey shook his head, sighed and threw in his cards. Marlowe smiled in his self-satisfied way and pulled what looked like a very tasty pot towards him.

Dodd tutted sympathetically. 'Your luck out today, sir?'

'I must be on the point of getting married, it's been so bad.' The man called Poley was dealing again and Greene waved a hand to be included.

'Don't waste your sympathy,' Greene slurred at Dodd. 'It's only justice because he won't tell me why he's in London and not up in your part of the world having fun hanging sheep-stealers.'

Carey picked up his cards, raised his eyebrows at Greene. 'You'd have heard about it by now if you hadn't been so stinking drunk when I found you.'

'A slight indisposition,' said Greene, wiggling his fingers generally at Carey. 'Nothing to be concerned about. I've been off colour since I overdid the eels and Rhenish wine last month.'

'No doubt,' said Carey. 'Shocking bad wine the Germans sell, isn't it?'

'On the contrary,' said Greene with dignity. 'I'm certain it was the eels that were off. Very dangerous to the health, bad eels.'

'So why are you back in London so soon, Sir Robert?' asked Marlowe, putting his new cards into a neat pile and laying them face down on the table. 'I thought Mr Bullard was after your blood.'

Greene sucked air in a whistle through his teeth and tutted with bogus sympathy.

'No, no,' said Carey nonchalantly. 'He's being paid off, he's perfectly reasonable.'

Poley laughed quietly at this and so did Greene, only more loudly. Marlowe nodded, grave as a parson.

'You'll be moving home to London then?'

'No, I like Carlisle. I'll be back there as soon as I can.'

'The Queen's in Oxford,' pursued Marlowe. 'Are you going to see her?'

Carey looked at him levelly and Dodd had the sudden feeling that this was a river with hidden whirlpools in it.

'Come on man, out with it,' roared Greene, who seemed unable to talk except in a bellow. 'We never thought we'd see you again, what with the creditors and King James and Lady Wi . . . er, the northern ladies and all.'

'Oh, don't be such an idiot, Greene,' said Carey, in the drawl he used when he was getting annoyed. 'You know perfectly well what I'm doing here, since my father's paying you to do the same.'

Greene opened his eyes wide in a parody of innocence. 'And that is, dear boy?'

'Look for my brother Edmund, who has somehow lost himself in London.'

'Ah yes,' said Greene. 'To be sure. Edmund. Fine chap.' There was a glugging noise as a mug of sherry-sack went down his throat. Dodd called for some himself, on the grounds that if the Courtier had decided to spend the night drinking and losing yet more money, who was he to differ? 'Drawn a blank, though. Nobody's seen him for weeks.'

'Maybe he's caught the plague and died of it,' said Dodd, surprising himself. 'There's plague in London, is there no'?'

'Nothing more than usual, is there?' asked Carey, looking concerned.

'No, no,' soothed Marlowe. 'Just the normal amount. Isn't that so, Will? You'd know if there was plague about?'

Shakespeare had said nothing so far, being more interested in drinking. He blinked owlishly at Marlowe, who was smiling at him. 'Plague?' he asked. 'Er . . . no, I don't . . . No.'

Good God, thought Dodd in disgust, it's true what Barnabus was saying, they're keeping it quiet for fear of losing business. He felt Barnabus staring at him desperately and wasn't sure what he could say next.

Greene had stopped in mid-drink and was scowling pop-eyed across the table at Shakespeare.

'You!' he hissed. 'What are *you* doing here?'

Shakespeare blinked at him. 'Drinking,' he said peaceably. 'Loshing . . . losing money at cards. What are you . . . er . . . doing?'

With an incoherent roar, Greene slammed both fists down on the table in front of him, causing it to jump. Both Marlowe and Carey immediately picked up their tankards, but before Dodd could do the same, Greene had surged to his feet, bellying the table over so that cards and coins and Dodd's full cup of sack went spraying in all directions. Like a charging bull, Greene waded past the table, grabbed Shakespeare round the neck. Momentum carried both of them up against the side of the stairs where Greene started banging Shakespeare's head against the bannisters while he throttled him.

There was a confusion of shouting. Carey tried to grab Greene round the oxlike shoulders and was shrugged off, Marlowe tried a simultaneous blow at the back of Greene's neck with his dagger pommel and was sent flying by a blow from the back of Greene's fist. Shakespeare's face was going purple and he was prodding ineffectually with his fists.

'Somebody had better stop him killing him.' The voice seemed to have only an academic interest in the matter, but Dodd had lost an expensive drink he'd been looking forward to and needed desperately, and he didn't like Greene in any case, while he felt sorry for the player. He picked up the stool he'd been sitting on, prodded the legs into Greene's meaty back, just where his kidneys should be, and heard the satisfying whoop of pain. He slammed the stool sideways into Greene's ribs, dropped it, got his left arm in a lock around Greene's bull neck from behind, leaned back, swivelled his hips and swept Greene's legs out from under him in a Cumbrian wrestling throw.

Greene's weight pulled him down, but he was expecting it and he fell on top of the man, bruising his elbow. Half crouching he got a knee up in the small of Greene's back and then said breathlessly, 'Will I break yer neck for ye?'

Greene heaved and made horrible noises, the cords on his neck expanding. Christ, he was strong, but Dodd was in much better condition and very angry.

'I'll do it, I'll break it and no' think twice. Stop still afore I hurt ye.'

Just to make his point, he levered up his elbow to lift Greene's chin and put more strain on his neck.

'I'd listen to him if I were you,' said Carey conversationally. 'So far Dodd's been quite gentle with you.'

There was that indefinable change of muscle tone beneath him that told Dodd the man was starting to think. He increased the pressure and felt the man surrender.

'Will ye behave yerself if I let ye up?'

'Hhhnnhh.'

After another jerk on his neck to remind him, Dodd let him go and stepped away smartly. Greene lay there whooping and gasping for several minutes before he staggered to his feet. He glowered at Dodd for a while, breathing hard.

'I want satisfaction from you,' he croaked at last.

'Are ye challenging me?' Dodd asked, almost laughing. 'Tae a duel?'

'Name your place and your weapons, sir.'

Behind him Dodd distinctly heard Carey say, 'Oh dear.'

'Ye want to fight *me*? With *weapons*?'

'Don't you speak English? Yes, I am, you northern yokel.'

'Och God, I would ha' thought ye'd want a rest after a' that booze and the battering I gave ye. But well enough. Let's dae it here.' Dodd drew his sword and dagger, crossed the blades in front of him in the *en garde* position and waited expectantly.

To his surprise Greene didn't draw his own blades. His jaw had dropped and he was staring at Dodd as if he didn't know what to do next.

'Come on, man, I havenae got all night. Let's get the mither done wi' and then I can get back tae ma drinkin'.'

In a voice overflowing with amusement, Carey translated this for Greene. Marlowe was standing next to Greene, whispering in his ear. Greene glared about under his bushy red eyebrows, but his hand made no move to his swordhilt.

'Do ye want tae fight, or no'?' Dodd asked, surprised at the delay.

Carey was on the other side of Greene now, whispering in his other ear. Greene was looking at the ground. He coughed.

'I withdraw the challenge.'

'Ay?'

'And the insult about northern yokels?' prompted Carey.

'I withdraw it,' growled Greene.

'Och, Ah dinna care what a drunken southerner wi' nae blood tae his liver thinks o' me,' said Dodd genially.

Carey translated this as acceptance of Greene's withdrawal of the insult.

Behind him Poley was setting the table upright again and arranging the stools round it. The innkeeper was standing nearby with arms folded, eyes narrowed and a large cudgel dangling from his wrist on a cord. The plump little man was sitting Shakespeare wheezing on the bench, dusting him down

and handing him another cup of booze, which the player took
with hands that shook like rivergrass.

'All right,' said Carey. 'Now shake on it, gentlemen.'

Dodd put his sword and dagger away, and held out his hand.
After an almost insulting pause, Greene shook.

There was a universal coughing and the staccato laughs of
released tension.

'Damn,' said Marlowe. 'I had ten shillings to put on Sergeant
Dodd to win.'

'Yes, but nobody was going to take the bet, were they?' said
Carey drily.

Greene slammed his bulky arse down on a stool and glowered.
Dodd sat back down on the bench next to Shakespeare and accepted
the drink brought for him by Poley. The primero circle reformed
itself and the innkeeper stood watching for a few minutes more
before he and two other large men with cudgels melted back into
the loud shadows.

They were piss-poor, these southerners, Dodd thought to himself;
if he could only get the remounts and a sufficiency of right reivers
together, he could run the raid of all time down here.

Poley and the plump man, whose name was apparently Munday,
were both down on the floor, scooping coins and cards out of the
sawdust and complaining at Greene while they did it. Carey was
watching Greene with narrow eyes and a very suspicious expression,
making no move to help. Marlowe was watching as well. Greene
seemed slightly deflated, though he was still knocking back the
booze at a fearsome rate. Now Carey was talking to him quietly,
to a response of shrugs and growls. Poley put the pack of cards
on the table and bent again to pick up the coins. Some of them
were gold crowns and angels, Dodd noted to his horror; it wasn't
any wonder the Courtier was in hock to his eyeballs.

Shakespeare cleared his throat painfully next to Dodd.

'Um . . . thank you, Sergeant,' he whispered. 'Er . . . if you
don't mind my asking, why did you . . . ?'

'Och,' said Dodd, embarrassed. 'He knocked ma drink over
when he sent the table flying.'

'Oh.'

'And he puked on ma boots earlier the day. I dinna take to loud drunks either. And I've had a long day.'

Shakespeare had a wide expanse of brow to wrinkle. 'Ah,' he said, evidently only understanding half of this, though Dodd tried to make his speech sound more like the Courtier's, which wasn't at all easy against the effects of the booze. You had to say this for London town, you could find good drink here. Even the aqua vitae tasted quite smooth, if fiery. He tasted some more of it.

'Ye've not had a good couple of days either, have ye?' Dodd said sympathetically. 'And what was it ye had me give to Mistress Bassano yesterday that made her so wild with ye?'

Shakespeare blinked gloomily at the sherry-dregs in the bottom of his mug. 'Sh . . . sonnets.'

'Ay,' said Dodd cautiously, not willing to reveal that he didn't know what a sonnet was.

The little bald player smiled wanly. 'Poems. Rhymes. In praise . . . in praise of Mistress Bassano.'

'They werenae lewd?'

'No, of course not. They were classical. I compared her to Helen of Troy, Aphrodite, Aurora goddess of the dawn, likened her hair to gold poured from an alchemist's flask, her eyes to sapphires . . .'

'But her hair's black and her eyes are brown.'

'It's poetic symbolism.'

'Ay. Does she ken that or does she think ye werenae thinking of her at all?' This produced an odd effect. Shakespeare stared at him for several minutes together with his mouth open, looking a complete simpleton. 'Only,' Dodd added, making a real effort to help the man, 'if I told my wife I loved her for her yellow hair, she'd hit me with a rolling pin in the certainty I was playing her false wi' a blonde. She's a redhead,' he added, for completeness. 'An' I bought her a fine green velvet hat the day for twenty shillings.' He was now feeling quite proud of himself for spending so much money on a frippery for his woman, though Shakespeare either hadn't heard or was used to the stupid London prices. The player was now nodding to himself, seemingly oblivious to Dodd.

Across the table the Courtier appeared to have won a little of his money back, since he was pulling in a reasonable pot. He raised his eyebrows.

'Dodd?'

Dodd shook his head. 'Yer stakes are too high fer me. I'm no' a rich man.'

Marlowe leaned over, smiling. 'I thought Sir Robert said you owned land.'

'I do. I'm rich in land and kin and kine, but no' in money,' Dodd explained. And yon Courtier's rich in nowt but kin, though that's never stopped him, he thought but didn't say.

'Come on, Sergeant,' said Poley with a little edge to his voice. 'Aren't you going to take the chance to enrich yourself? We could teach you if you don't know how to play.'

Just for a moment, Dodd was sorely tempted. He liked playing cards and he was a lot better at it than he had been.

In that moment, Barnabus brought another tray of drinks, leaned over the table to give them out and while his body was in the way, looked directly at Dodd and shook his head, mouthing a word silently several times. For a moment Dodd was annoyed and then realised that Barnabus was telling him the game was crooked.

'Nay, I willnae. Thank ye for the invitation,' he said politely, when Barnabus was out of the way again.

Greene belched disparagingly. 'Northerners,' he said. 'Mean as Scotsmen and not so friendly. You can't have spent all of Heneage's gold, surely?'

Through his instant anger at the fat drunk daring to compare him with a Scot, Dodd caught an infinitesimal twitch in Carey's expressive eyebrows and cooled immediately to ice. Yes, it was very interesting that Poley wanted him to play and Greene knew about Heneage's bribe, and now Poley was hiding what looked like fury at Greene blurting that out. It was even more interesting in view of the fact that Heneage's bribe or the Hampstead footpads' loot might have contained two forged angels. You could hang for uttering false coin, if you were caught.

'Nay, Mr Greene,' he said. 'It's no' meanness. It's only that I ken verra well ye're all fine card players with far more experience than me at such high stakes. I'm nobbut a fighting man, me.'

Greene tutted, then jumped and glared at Poley who had probably kicked him under the table. Marlowe smiled caressingly at Dodd.

'How quaint,' he said.

'Marlowe,' said Carey warningly.

Marlowe put his hands up placatingly. 'I only meant, how unusual to find someone who knows their limitations.'

Now he knew why these card-sharps wanted him to join the game, Dodd found he could watch their attempts to needle him into it with objectivity. It was even quite funny. 'Ay,' he said. 'What are yours, for instance?'

The cocky smile grew wider. 'Me? I have none. There is no limit on what a man may achieve, if his heart be bold and his spirit enterprising enough.'

'And he's ruthless enough,' said someone, who turned out unexpectedly to be Shakespeare, looking up from where he had been scribbling in a little notebook.

Marlowe nodded at him. 'Yes,' he agreed. 'It's important not to have any scruples.'

'Ha!' said Greene, in a shower of spit. 'Then why aren't you up in Scotland buggering King James?'

There was that tiny gap in the conversation while everyone waited to see how Marlowe would react.

'What a good idea,' he said silkily at last. 'I think I'll go. What do you think, Sir Robert? Do I stand a chance?'

Even Dodd knew that this was very dangerous talk, right here in London. As far as the Queen was concerned, making up to the King of Scots was tantamount to treason, even if he was her likely successor. And never mind that buggery was a deadly sin and officially a hanging crime.

Carey's eyes hooded themselves. 'Hm,' he said, coolly judicial. 'Classically educated. Playwright – His Majesty loves plays. Not too tall or broad – His Majesty doesn't like being towered over . . . Hmm. Yes, I think it's a good match.'

'Such a pity you don't like boys, isn't it, Sir Robert?' said Marlowe with sweet sympathy. 'You'd be running Scotland by now.'

Carey smiled lazily. 'Yes, I know. Her Majesty the Queen said the same. But I think Scotland might be very profitable for you, Kit. Why don't you go?'

Marlowe sighed and waved a tankard. 'So many entanglements in the south. Too many. Eh, Poley? What do you think Heneage would say if I went north?'

Poley's expression was peculiar. It combined knowingness and alertness with a kind of bewilderment. Before he could answer, Robert Greene butted in again.

'And what's Heneage up to, eh? What's all this I hear about alchemists? You know, Poley, don't you, you close-mouthed bastard, why don't you give us the gossip?'

Now Poley was looking worried. 'Isn't anybody going to play cards any more?' he asked. 'Or are you too busy talking treason?'

Marlowe clapped him on the shoulder. 'Come on, my dear,' he smiled sarcastically. 'Get your notebook out, write it all down before you forget, or Heneage will be cross with you.'

'You spell my name G R E E N with an E,' bellowed Greene, dealing cards at expert speed.

Poley looked uneasy. 'I don't report private conversations,' he said unconvincingly and Marlowe put his arm over his shoulders.

'Sweetheart,' he said in a stage whisper. 'This *isn't* a private conversation.'

'Bloody Christ,' roared Greene, bug-eyed again at Marlowe. 'You're not a bugger too, are you, Poley?' Poley was concentrating on his cards and pretended not to hear. Greene shook his head. 'I don't know. What's the point? Once the Scotch king comes in all the buggers'll be dukes.'

Dodd wanted to escape from this horrible outrageous talk. He wanted to melt into the panelling and did the next best thing by sitting back as far as he could into the booth and sipping his drink quietly. The talk puttered along over the cards though it now seemed to be ranging across a vast range of classical allusion as Marlowe shamelessly explained that there was nothing whatever wrong with buggery.

Explain that to the hangman, Dodd thought. Greene thought the same and said so, loudly, incoherently and at length. Shakespeare had put away his little notebook, wiped his pen, stoppered his ink bottle and put them away neatly in a small leather case he had in his doublet-front. Now he smiled uncertainly at Dodd who finally asked the question he'd wanted to put all night.

'Why does yer man Greene hate ye so?'

Shakespeare looked depressed again. 'It's a long story.' His voice was hoarse and he rubbed his neck where the bruises were starting to show.

'Ay. Well, I'm no' playing primero wi' that bunch of perverts and card-sharps, so I've got time on ma hands.'

'None of them are cheating, are they?'

'Sir Robert only cheats when he thinks somebody else is at it.'

'Is he cheating?'

'Nay, did I say that?'

Shakespeare shook his head, evidently too drunk to deal with complexity.

'What's yer feud with Greene, then?'

Shakespeare sighed. 'A year ago he wrote a play for the troop of players I work for. The . . . the idea was good, about Henry VI, but the writing . . .' He shook his head.

'Bad, was it?'

'Hamfisted, cloth-eared. His prose is good – you should read his coney-catching pamphlets, but . . . er . . . his dialogue is terrible. Maybe it's the drink.'

'Ay?' Dodd looked over at Greene to see if he was eavesdropping any of this demolition, but he was in the middle of totting up his points again, one eye shut and breathing hard.

'Well, I'd been badgering Mr Burbage to let me try writing for them, but I was only a hired man, so . . . They said I'd be wasting my time. They said, what would a glover's son know about writing poetry?'

Will's mouth had turned down bitterly. Dodd felt sorry for him. Mistress Bassano hadn't liked his verse much either.

'But we needed a new play and the other ones we had were worse, so Mr Burbage said I could try my fist at reworking Greene's attempt. He's a very popular writer, very well-known, all the printers like him and they pay him . . . oh, several pounds a time for one of his books.'

'That much?' Dodd was shocked. Hats for twenty shillings was bad enough, but several pounds for mere words . . . ? The Londoners were all mad. 'So did ye do it?'

'I did. I . . . er . . . sold up my horse-holding business, took three months off from playing and worked on it like a Trojan. I had it ready by March, and we put it on at the playhouse.' He sighed again and finished his drink, looked around blearily for more. Against his better judgement, but wanting to comfort the little man, Dodd poured him some.

'What happened? Did the groundlings no' like it?' Barnabus had told Dodd some of the things fellow-groundlings might do to plays they didn't like, in which eggs, rotten apples and stones featured largely.

'No, they loved it,' said Shakespeare gloomily. 'They cheered it. Burbage was cock-a-hoop, said I was nearly as good as Marlowe.'

Somewhere, he knew, Dodd had missed something important. Where was the problem?

'But, if they liked it . . . what's Greene got against ye?'

'He says he's an educated man, been to university, an experienced writer, he says the play was perfect before I meddled with it and ruined it.'

'But ye didnae?'

'No, of course I didn't. He's jealous because I've never been to university and I'm nothing but a common player and I can write a hundred times better than him.'

Dodd shook his head. Fighting over stolen sheep or a woman or even a drunken argument, that he could understand. But fighting over words? Why?

'So why do ye care what he thinks?'

'I don't. I care that he . . . er . . . he tries to kill me whenever we meet and he's told all the printers and booksellers to have nothing to do with me and he's half-convinced Burbage that the good bits in the play were his, not mine. The City shut our theatre the month before last and it's not opening until Michaelmas; Burbage fired me

130

at the same time and I haven't been able to get another place as a hired man, not on any terms. Greene's making trouble for me any way he can. He knows the King of London, too. He keeps saying he'll arrange a little accident for me.'

'All because ye fixed up his play?'

'No,' said Shakespeare bitterly. 'Because I'm better than he is and he knows it.'

'Och,' said Dodd and poured them both some more aqua vitae. 'Why d'ye not go to be some rich man's gleeman, his house poet? Then ye'd be away fra London and Greene couldnae harm ye.'

Shakespeare nodded. 'I'd like that, I think. But the problem is . . . Every penniless university man who can string a couple of lines together wants the same and I've got no degree, no contacts, no . . . no nothing. I'd put out one of the poems I've written, dedicate it to someone likely, try getting a place that way, but the printers won't take it because they're scared of Greene, even Richard Field who I went to school with . . . he says he daren't.'

'Would ma Lord Hunsdon no' have ye?'

Will had an unfortunate propensity to blush. 'Not any more, I shouldn't think. It's only a matter of time before Mistress Bassano persuades him to fire me.'

'So ye're stuck.'

Shakespeare nodded dolefully. 'Stuck. I'll be in the Fleet by Christmas.'

Dodd nodded with him, full of oiled sympathy. You couldn't blame the man for wanting to break away from playing, it was no right work for a man.

'But could ye no' do some other line o' work? Like . . . er . . . ye said yer father's a glover? Could ye no' go back to that?'

To Dodd's horror, Shakespeare's eyes filled with tears. 'I'd like that,' he said. 'All I ever wanted to do when I was a boy was make beautiful gloves, but . . . I'm too clumsy. My fingers won't . . . You see the gloves Sir Robert's wearing, fine kid, embroidered in silk? It's very . . . very intricate, making top class gloves like them . . . My father did his best, but . . . It was no good. That's why he turned to drink, you see, because . . . because I was such a disappointment.'

Och, God, thought Dodd, he's turned maudlin.

'And I tried schoolmastering, and Christ, that's an awful job. No money in it. The children . . . I hate them. Ink down your gown. Nails in your seat. Crab apples through your windows. I've never been any good at anything, really . . .'

Dodd couldn't help it, his attention wandered. Marlowe had won again and the buggery argument was still rumbling on. Greene was quoting Leviticus on the subject and Marlowe laughed at him.

'Why should I live my life according to the notions of a starveling band of desert wanderers that were slaves in Egypt, slaves of the Assyrians, slaves of the Persians, slaves of the Macedonians and slaves of the Romans?' he asked.

'Because they were God's Chosen People,' said Poley sententiously and Marlowe laughed again.

'So they say. Which must have been a comfort to them. Surely God's Chosen would be a little more successful.'

Well, there it was, thought Dodd in an icy moment of clarity while Shakespeare droned on about his children and multiple failures beside him, if you wanted a reason for the plague hitting London, that was all you needed. Almighty God, they were doomed. They were drinking with an atheist and a pervert.

'That's enough, Kit,' said Carey very quietly. 'You've shocked us all, now be quiet.'

For a moment Dodd thought he might do as he was told, but then Greene had to stick his purple nose into the brew. 'God will repay,' he roared, wagging a finger. 'God repays the atheist and blasphemer. In the end, He repays!'

'*Your* God may rule by tyranny and injustice,' hissed Marlowe, leaning over the pile of gold on the table. 'You make a fat roaring idol in your own fat roaring image and you bow down before it and then you plume yourself on your stern Protestant virtue and nobility. God preserve me from such a god.'

'Playing I'm not bad at, but I'll never touch Alleyn or Richard Burbage,' Shakespeare was still talking, locked in the drunk's miserable obliviousness. 'I haven't got the size or the looks for it, though I'm not bad at character roles . . .'

'At least I'm no atheist,' spat Greene.

'I'm not an atheist, I'm a pagan,' said Marlowe composedly. 'The God who made the stars, the God who built the crystal spheres, the God of fire and ice and stone and wind, that God is worthy of my worship. But why should I bow down to books of gathered words from hundreds of years ago when with my own pen *I* can write such words *and better.*'

He's mad, thought Dodd in the horrified silence, clearly insane, not with the burbling drooling madness of men that talked with their shadows and shook their fists at the clouds, but a stranger more limpid madness that hid itself in elegance and urbanity. Even Shakespeare had stopped drivelling to gape at the speaker of such blasphemy.

To his surprise, it was Carey who answered Marlowe; not even Greene seemed to be able to find the words.

'Yes,' said Carey, still quietly. 'It's attractive to decide on what God is and worship that. How is what you do different from what you accuse Greene of doing?'

'If I must have a religion, what's wrong with rationality, science, justice?' said Marlowe in general, still leaning forwards as if he genuinely were trying to convert Carey to his strange brand of atheism. 'I could believe in those, not some fairytale designed to keep the people in awe.'

'No doubt,' said Carey. 'And kindness, wisdom, mercy? Where are these? Have you ever seen what happens in a land where the people are *not* in awe? Bloody feud and robbery, the strong against the weak, the children starving. Not everyone is as brilliant and powerful as you. Oh, and I'll raise you an angel.'

'And I'll see you, Sir Robert,' Marlowe didn't seem much abashed and nor was he ruffled when Carey proved to have a flush. He waved the gold coins farewell and called for a pipe of tobacco. Poley and Greene did the same.

'But poetry. I can do that.' Shakespeare was off again as the air around them filled with clouds of foul-smelling smoke. 'Maybe not the way Marlowe does it, but my way. My own way.' He caught Dodd's sleeve and breathed earnest booze-fumes in his face. 'I can *do* it. Do you understand?'

'Ay, ay, I understand.' Give him more aqua vitae, Dodd

thought to himself, maybe he'll pass out and stop blathering at me.

'No, you don't, you couldn't. Plays, poems, anything. I looked at that pile of dung Greene produced, and I knew how to fix it, what it needed. And I sat down with as much paper as I could afford – it's awfully expensive you know, penny a sheet – and I started . . . It was as if something huge, God, something picked me up and carried me, like a spate-tide of words . . . You just open the tap and out it all flows, like . . . like there's this huge barrel of words inside you and you put the tap in and open and . . . whoosh.'

'Whoosh,' said Dodd, who was loosing the will to live, what with mad atheism on one side of him and a barrel of words on the other.

Shakespeare nodded. 'Whoosh. The problem's stopping, really. I can't stop now, not now I've found what I can do, I can't. And that fat bastard, that lily-livered, carrot-bearded, word-mangling, purple-faced, pox-ridden tub of putrescent lard . . . I could kill him.' Shakespeare actually showed his teeth like a dog at Greene who was roaring across the table and betting an angel on whatever new cards he held in his paw.

Dodd patted the player's shoulder and poured some more aqua vitae for him. 'Kill him tomorrow,' he advised sagely. 'Too many wintes . . . witnish . . . people watching.'

Shakespeare drank it down in one and screwed up his eyes. 'Yersh,' he said. 'Tomorrow.' He swayed on the bench.

Quite quietly he folded his arms on the table, put his head on them and went to sleep. Thank God, thought Dodd, whatever that means hereabouts.

Many times in the days that followed Dodd wished he hadn't drunk so much that night so he could remember more of it. Occasional fragments would come back to him, wreathed in tobacco smoke: Carey and Marlowe locked in a crazy betting spiral over the cards, and he could not for the life of him remember who won; Poley coming back from the jakes and smiling; Greene scoffing a large plate of jellied eels; Marlowe trying to convince

Carey that the Ancient Greeks were right and the love of men was far better than that of women and Carey laughing at him and saying he should try women some time, he might like them.

Late in the evening, when Carey had gone out to the jakes, Greene heaved his bulk up, took a gulp from a silver flask he kept in the front pocket of his doublet and then shook it disapprovingly next to his ear. He ordered more aqua vitae and refilled it carefully, breathing hard, one eye shut, stoppered it and put it back. He belched, farted, said something about eels always giving him the squits and went out into the yard.

Dodd wondered owlishly if he should go with the man, to make sure he didn't slip away, but somehow he didn't get round to it. Anyway, he thought, Carey would meet him. And then Carey was back and there was no sign of Greene. The Courtier was very annoyed, went trotting out into the street after him, but came back after a few minutes saying the bloody poet was nowhere to be seen. He glared at Dodd who was too drunk to do anything except shake his head regretfully.

'Oh, don't take on so,' said Marlowe. 'He's only gone home.'

'If you knew the trouble I had finding him and bringing him here . . .' Carey fumed and then sat down again on the bench and scowled. 'I'll see him tomorrow.'

At last they were the only ones left in the common room and the innkeeper came over and said hintingly that he had two rooms spare that night if the gentlemen needed somewhere to sleep.

Dodd had been wondering about that. Marlowe was whispering to Poley, one arm over his shoulder again, and Marlowe announced that since he was lodging in Holywell Street near the Strand and it would be a confounded nuisance to go back there with the city gates shut, he and Poley would take one of the rooms.

Trying to hide his disgust, Dodd tried to shake the player awake to ask him what he wanted to do. Shakespeare only snortled, muttered and slept on.

The innkeeper tried with a splash of water on the balding forehead and got no reaction at all. He sighed.

'Mr Shakespeare's no trouble,' he said. 'He can stop here on the bench until he's feeling better.' He and his son arranged the player on his side and even covered him up with the cloak that had warmed Greene, while Shakespeare slept peacefully through, not even snoring very much.

'Hardly seems worth going to bed,' Carey commented while Marlowe and Poley went upstairs arm in arm. 'It'll be dawn soon.'

'Och, God,' said Dodd, who could feel the father and mother of a hangover waiting for him somewhere in the future and wanted to be asleep when it hit. 'Ye please yerself, Courtier, I'm going tae my rest.'

He remembered the innkeeper giving him the key, he remembered climbing an infinity of stairs, he remembered being vaguely annoyed that Carey had somehow managed to remove and hang up on a nail the fashionable encumbrances of velvet doublet and hose, while Dodd was still struggling with his boots, he remembered being very much annoyed when Carey climbed into the best bed as of right without even tossing for who was going to sleep on the truckle. He hadn't the energy to argue, so he pulled it out from under the main bed and fell onto it full length as the room spun, settled, spun the other way and then stole itself into darkness.

Saturday, 2nd September 1592, early morning

5

The morning came immediately and was as hideous as he had expected. Horrible full sunlight was shining into his eyes because some fool had opened the shutters, his bollocks were itching because he'd gone to sleep in his clothes, his stomach was tied protesting in a knot, his mouth and throat had clearly been roosted in by a fighting cock with the squitters, and his head . . .

'Auwwwgh,' he moaned in agony, rolled and put the pillow over his head.

'Good morning, Dodd,' said Carey's voice from somewhere over to his left. 'I think it's still morning. Or thereabouts.'

'Piss off.'

'Have some mild ale.'

'*Piss off.*'

There was the noise of chewing, swallowing, drinking, echoing as loud as trumpets in the huge beating drum of Dodd's head. I want to die, he thought, please God let me die. Vaguely he remembered treasonous table talk the night before. Fine. You can cut my head off, hang, draw and quarter me, just do it soon.

'Seriously, try and drink something,' said Carey's voice again, inhumanly cheerful and persistent.

Dodd wanted to tell him what he thought of people who were happy in the mornings in general, never mind what he thought of people who seemed immune to hangovers after a night spent drinking and gambling, but the effort was too great.

'Fuck off?' he pleaded.

'Well, Barnabus and I are going for a walk. There's a mug of mild ale next to your bed, don't knock it over. See you in an hour or so.'

Thank Christ, thought Dodd, as the door boomed like cannon fire, and he tried to sink back into beautiful black velvet sleep. But he couldn't because his head was hurting too much and he was dying for a piss.

He put it off for as long as he could and then hauled himself to a sitting position, got up and began searching tremblingly for the jordan.

It was on the windowsill, still full of the Courtier's water. Dodd emptied it out the window and used it which eased his pain somewhat. Some inconsiderate bastard was shouting in the street. Dodd leaned out of the window and screamed, 'Shut up or I'll kill ye.'

Whoever it was obediently shut up and Dodd went looking for something to drink, found the mug of ale just before he kicked it and swallowed it down.

Aggravatingly, the Courtier had been right. It did help a little. Dodd poured himself some more, looked for a moment at the bread and cheese Carey had left on the wooden trencher and dismissed the notion as mad.

Instead he lay down on the main bed, shut his eyes against the disgusting sunlight and went back to sleep.

The next time he woke, it was with the strange feeling that someone small and smooth of hand was delving stealthily in his hose.

She was. When his eyes flicked open he stared full in the face of a pretty little creature with plump pink cheeks, blue eyes and bright golden hair, wearing a smock that had slipped down over her shoulders so that two plump and perky breasts were peering at him over the frills.

'Whuffle?' said Dodd, so stunned at this he almost forgot to feel his headache.

She tilted forwards and kissed him on the nose. 'Now now, my love, you're getting what you paid for.'

Hangover or no, Dodd was sure he hadn't hired anybody the night before. Almost sure. And Carey would ... Maybe Carey had hired her? Yes, that must be it. The Courtier had paid for a woman to come and wake them up and then gone out and forgotten about it or mistaken the time? That made sense.

Or he was dreaming again. No, his headache was too bad. And she was tracking kisses down his chest, unbuckling his belt . . . Oh, what the hell?

Fumbling frantically at the stupid points to his hose, terrified in case the Courtier came back and spoiled everything by laying claim to his whore, Dodd caught the girl by the shoulders, pushed her gently back on the bed and climbed happily aboard.

She made such a squealing, that Dodd actually paused to make sure there hadn't been some terrible mistake, but she reassured him by pulling him down and nibbling his ear before letting out another astonishing yell.

The thunder of Dodd's heart seemed to shake the room they were in, the door bounced against the latch, his mind went white, the girl squealed again, and the whole door crashed open as two men shouldered through it.

Too spent to do anything for a moment except lie on top of the girl's delightfully soft body and pant, while his headache clamped down over his eyeballs like some Papist torture machine, Dodd tried desperately to catch up with what was going on. It was clear he had visitors and that they were strangers. There was a portly man in fine silks and velvets with an expression of pompous and self-righteous rage on his face, and two other men with him in buff-coats, that had 'hired henchmen' all but written on them.

'Sir Robert Carey, what the devil are you doing with my wife, sir?' spluttered the portly gentleman, as if it wasn't perfectly obvious. 'What's your explanation, sir? You have committed fornication and adultery with a married woman, to wit, my wife . . .'

His heart was slowing down to only a triple-hammered pace. Dodd shook his head as the girl started eeling out from under him, her face twisted with fear.

'Oh no, no, my husband,' she gasped. 'I'm done for. All is lost!'

The two henchmen started forwards purposefully with their hands out to grab. Working purely on animal instinct, Dodd rolled the opposite way off the bed onto the floor beside it, landing with a crash that made his skull feel as if it had burst open, yanking desperately at his breeches. Where the hell had he put his weapons last night?

Next to the bed, of course, came the cool answer out of a growing rage. Those two henchmen should have at least cracked a smile at the sight of Dodd, breeches round his knees, draped bare-arsed across their master's wife. Dodd himself would have smiled at it. But neither of them had, their faces were grim and solemn, and that rang false, at least as false as the girl's wails and pleas for mercy.

There was plenty of room under the main bed and the two bullies were coming round it to grab for Dodd once more, so he rolled again until he was underneath, finally got his breeches fastened and belted, then reached out an arm and scooped up his sword belt.

One of them was bending down, flailing about under the tumbled blankets for Dodd. Dodd poked him in the face with the sword still in its scabbard, then emerged volcanically out the other side, kicked the truckle bed on its wheels into the portly gentleman and made for the door. It was locked and he couldn't open it, so he turned at bay with his sword and dagger out and snarled at them all,

'Get the hell oot o' my bed chamber!'

'Don't you realise who I am, Sir Robert?' said the portly gentleman. 'I am Sir Edward Fitzjohn and that's my wife you were attacking.'

Sheer outrage at this ridiculous claim stopped Dodd from roaring and charging at the man.

'What?'

'I am Sir Edward Fitzjohn and I will swear out a warrant against you in the church courts, sir, for fornication and adultery with my wife.'

'*What?*'

'Oh oh,' wailed the girl. 'Don't let them take you, they'll put you in prison, oh oh!'

'WHAT?'

'I have that right, as the offended party,' said Sir Edward Fitzjohn.

'Give him money, anything you've got, only don't let him take you away . . .'

Grinding headache and churning stomach notwithstanding, Dodd was now quite certain there was something very fishy going on here.

'What would it take to settle the matter?' he asked, only glancing at Sir Edward while he made sure he gave no opening for the two henchmen to grab him.

'Are you offering money?' spluttered Sir Edward. 'For my wife's honour? Damn you, sir . . . How much have you got?'

Dodd wanted to laugh, he could feel his mouth turning down with the effort to stay straight-faced.

'Ah dinna ken where ma purse is, Ah think it was lifted last night,' he said, which caused all four of them to wrinkle their brows, including the girl sitting prettily on her knees in front of her alleged husband with her smock still falling off. 'I wis robbed last night,' he explained, trying to speak slowly and clearly. 'I've no money left.'

Sir Edward's face went through a series of expressions – disbelief, disappointment and finally hard ruthlessness. 'We'll have to kill him then,' he said in quite a different voice, and the girl obediently started shrieking. 'Help, murder, oh oh!' while the two henchmen and Sir Edward himself attacked with their swords. The girl scurried on hands and knees under the bed and started pulling on her stays and petticoat, all the while shrieking, 'Murder, blood, help, oh save my husband, sirs, save him!' at the top of her voice.

In the flurry of ducking one sword while he parried desperately at two more, Dodd was never quite sure how soon it was before the door started juddering to somebody else's boot. The bolt ends came out of the door-jamb which was when Dodd realised it wasn't locked, just bolted top and bottom.

Carey appeared in the doorway, sword out, Barnabus next to him on the little landing with a throwing knife in each hand.

'Oh shit!' said the girl under the bed, crawling further under it and starting to pull on her boots. Dodd was in a corner by then, dagger and sword up and crossed, ducking as Sir Edward's rapier flicked for his eyes.

'What the hell is going on here?' demanded Carey's court drawl.

There was a bright glitter in the air and one of the little daggers was growing out of Sir Edward's arm. He yelped, grabbed it out and the henchmen stopped their attack to stare at Dodd's reinforcements. Dodd growled, rage truly flaming in him now for the ruination of one of the few pleasant awakenings of his life, aimed the point of his dagger and charged at Sir Edward's belly.

Sir Edward jumped back, bombast and wool bursting out of the wound in his doublet, the two henchmen exchanged glances, and all three of them suddenly broke for the door. There was a confused scuffle while Carey and Barnabus tried to stop them, but they had momentum and desperation on their side and all three sprinted down the stairs and out through the common room, followed by Dodd, still roaring.

They disappeared into the crowded street and Dodd had to stop chasing at the cross-roads because he couldn't see any of them. Also the Londoners were staring at him and Dodd realised that his shirt was open and his insecurely belted breeches were on the point of falling down.

He sidled back into the inn, up the stairs and found Carey leaning out of the window swiping at something there. Dodd peered over his shoulder to see the girl who had woken him up so well climbing briskly across the thatch, still in only her stays and petticoat. She flipped Carey the finger as she let herself down onto a balcony and he laughed and took his hat off to her.

Dodd slumped on the bed breathing hard, hung his head and moaned at the weight of his hangover.

'Threatened to sue you through the church courts for fornication and adultery, eh?' asked Carey, handing him another mug of mild ale.

'Ay,' said Dodd, rubbing his face. 'And then they tried to kill me when I said I had nae money.'

Barnabus tutted. 'I told you they'd 'ave another go,' he said.

'But you should never let on you're broke, not in London. 'S dangerous.'

Carey laughed. 'Somebody should have warned them about Dodd in the mornings. Bears with sore heads isn't in it.'

'Och. It wasnae so bad afore her husband bust in.'

'Husband!' Barnabus snorted. 'Molly Stone's never been wed in her life, 'cept to a bishop.'

'You couldn't pass the word, could you, Barnabus? Tell 'em to lay off?'

Barnabus shook his head. 'Nah, sorry, sir, I'm out of touch.'

'Give it a try, there's a good fellow. I'd be grateful.'

Barnabus shrugged. He didn't seem himself that morning, though it was hard to say what was wrong. He seemed subdued, depressed. Mind, it wasn't surprising, considering what had happened to his sister and her family.

'At least you're awake now, aren't you, Sergeant?'

'Ay, I suppose I am.'

'Excellent. Make yourself decent and let's go.' Carey had paced restlessly to the window and back again. He looked as spruce and tidy as ever: damn him, he must have gone to a barber's while he was out, his hair was shorter and his face was clean-shaven while he smelled daintily of lavender and spice and he had a new ruff on. It was obscene, that's what it was.

'Where now, sir?' Dodd moaned.

'Greene's lodgings.'

'Och, not him again, sir!'

'Yes, him again. I haven't talked to him properly yet and I'm bloody certain he knows more than he's letting on about my idiot brother Edmund, not to mention the false angels that Heneage slipped you, according to Barnabus.'

'I suppose ye want to catch him when he's sober,' said Dodd, dispiritedly dealing with his points and buttons and wishing there was a more sensible way of fastening your clothes. His head was still pounding and his eyes wouldn't focus properly.

'Good God, no,' said Carey. 'All we'd hear would be rubbish about snakes and spiders and demons attacking him. Catch him when he's only half-drunk, that's the best plan. Come on, Dodd, hurry up or we'll miss the golden moment.'

Dodd found his cap and jerkin and finished buckling on his sword and dagger, followed Carey's long stride out the door.

A thought struck him halfway down. 'Wait, Sir Robert, Ah've lost ma purse.'

'No, you haven't. You left it next to the bed and I took it with me this morning when I saw how dead to the world you were. Here you are. I haven't borrowed anything.'

He hadn't, as Dodd could tell by hefting it. Not for the first time since he met the Courtier, gratitude and annoyance warred in him.

'Not that it's any of my business,' said Carey after a tactful pause, 'but when did you hire yourself a trollop?'

'Me?' Dodd was outraged. 'Ah thocht she was yourn?'

One day Carey would hang for the way his eyebrows performed. One went up by itself and then the other joined it. 'What?'

'I thocht ye hired her, to wake us up like. Did ye no'?'

'No, I didn't.'

'Ye didnae?'

'No.'

Dodd shut his eyes tight and shook his head, trying to clear it, which was a mistake. 'But . . . but when I woke, she was already . . . at ma tackle, ye ken.'

'And so you . . . er . . .'

Dodd could feel himself getting red as a boy caught with his hands down a kitchen maid's stays. 'Ay,' he said truculently. 'Wouldn't ye?'

Carey grinned. 'Yes,' he admitted cheerfully. 'But didn't you wonder how she got there?'

'Ay, I did. Like I said, I thought she wis . . .'

'Mine.'

'So to speak.'

'Ah. So who the hell hired her? Barnabus?'

'No, sir. Why would I? You've never needed any help like that before.'

'Well, did you ask . . . ?'

146

'I woke up with her hand rummaging ma privates and no, I didnae think tae ask her.'

'Hm. Now isn't that interesting. I wonder who the benefactor was?'

Dodd shrugged. 'Sir Edward Fitzjohn hisself?'

'Who?'

'The man in the pretty doublet that wanted all ma money or he'd put me through the church courts for adultery.'

Barnabus snorted. 'Sir Edward Fitzjohn, my arse. That was Nick the Gent.'

'Dodd, could I have a look at that false coin you had?'

'Ay.' Dodd fished it out and handed it over and Carey stopped to hold it up to the light and squint at the bite marks. 'It's very good, you know. It's an excellent forgery. I think it's pewter inside with a thin layer of gold, but the minting's perfect. And you got it where?'

'I think it was in Heneage's bribe. That he give me at yer dad's party.'

'Oh, that's when he did it, is it? Who was the . . . agent?'

'I dinna ken. The man give it me in the garden, all muffled with a cloak.'

'Hmm. Interesting.'

'Ay, well, he could have got me hanged for spending it.'

'So he could. Hmm. Can I keep it?'

'Ay. It's nae worth nothing now.'

'Hmm. You never know,' was all the Courtier would say while Dodd decided that the whyfores of forgery were more than he could handle with his present headache.

Oh God. Maybe it wasn't a hangover. Maybe it was plague. Was that a lump he felt in his armpit? Did he have a fever? He deserved God's wrath after such a sin of adultery and fornication, no matter how desperate the temptation. The Courtier might not be shocked but Dodd was, shocked at himself. Dear God, why had he done it? what if Janet found out? what if he'd taken the pox . . .?

In the common room they passed Shakespeare lying curled up on the bench with a cloak over his narrow shoulders. The only comfort was that Dodd felt quite certain Shakespeare would feel even worse when he woke up than Dodd did. Which served him right.

Carey strolled over to the innkeeper who was just opening and talking to him quietly – got nowhere, to judge by the sorrowful headshakings. And now the bastard Courtier was humming to himself as they walked along yet another stinking street, some tweedly-deedly court tune all prettified with fa-la-las. God, thought Dodd, I hate London and Carey both.

Very slowly, the exercise of walking through the noise and bustle of the London streets in the bright warm sunshine moved from being a torture to a pain to a mere misery. Very slowly the awful pounding in Dodd's head faded down to a mere hammerbeat. Maddened with thirst, he drank a quart of mild ale at a boozing ken's window and felt much better, though still more delicate than one of those fancy glass goblets from Italy the gentry set such store by. If you blew hard on him, he would break.

Greene's lodgings were over a cobbler's shop. Carey asked at the counter which produced hurried whisperings and a small skinny faded-looking woman hurried in from the back of the shop to be introduced as Joan Ball, Mr Greene's . . . ahem . . . common-law wife.

'He's not well, sir,' she explained. 'He's been ill all morning. Very, very ill.'

Carey made a dismissive *tch* noise. 'I know what he's suffering from. I'll see him anyway.'

'Well, I don't know, sir, he's very . . . It's not his usual illness, you know, sir. I'd get the doctor to him if there was any left in London.'

'It's no' plague, is it?' Dodd demanded, with another greasy thrill of horror down his back.

She rubbed her arms anxiously up and down her apron. 'Oh no, no. Nothing like that. Some kind of flux, I think. Or even poison. I don't know, sir. He says he's dying and he keeps calling for paper, says he's got to finish his swansong.'

Carey frowned with suspicion and disbelief. 'What? Let me see him, I'm his patron, damn it.'

'I'll ask,' whispered the woman and scurried upstairs.

'Ye never are,' said Dodd, staggered at this further evidence of financial insanity.

'Yes, I am. Or I was. I paid five pounds for a thing he wrote last year and dedicated to me.'

'What was it?'

'Er . . . can't remember, I only read the dedication.'

The woman came downstairs again, her face drawn and miserable. 'He's not making any sense, sir, and he particularly said he wasn't to be disturbed . . .' Carey slipped a sixpence into her hand and she shrugged. '. . . but you can go up if you want.'

They went up the narrow winding stairs at the back of the shop and into the room under the roof. It was almost filled by a small bed and a little carved and battered table next to it. Papers covered the elderly rushes on the floor, piled up in drifts and held down with leather bottles, plates, rock-hard lumps of bread and, in one instance, a withered half of a meatpie; there were books on the windowsill and books on the floor under the bed. In a nest of unspeakable blankets sat the barrel-like Robert Greene, wearing a shirt and nightcap he might have wiped his arse with, they were so revolting.

His skin was greyish pale under the purple network of burst veins, his face worked in pain. A full jordan teetered on a pile of books. Next to him on the table were a pile of papers covered in a truly villainous scrawl. With a book on his knees and a piece of paper resting on it, an inkpot teetering by his feet and a pen in his fist, Robert Greene was scribbling with the fixity of a madman.

'Mr Greene,' said Carey, marching in and bending over the man on the bed. 'I want to talk to you about my brother.'

Greene ignored him, breathing hoarsely through his mouth and sweat beading his face, the pen whispering across the page at an astonishing rate.

'Mr Greene!' bellowed Carey in his ear. 'My brother, Edmund. What have you found out?'

'I'm busy,' gasped Greene. 'Piss off.'

Carey sat on the bed and removed the ink bottle. The next time Greene tried to dip his pen, he discovered it gone, looked up and finally focused on Carey.

'Give it back,' he said hoarsely. 'Damn you, I'm dying, I must write my swansong . . . Oh, Christ.'

Seeing the man retch, Carey got up hastily and backed away. It was the one of the ugliest sights Dodd had ever seen in his life, to watch anyone vomit blood. There were meaty bits in it. When the paroxysms finished Greene was sweating and shaking.

'Joan,' he roared. 'Get these idiots out of my chamber and bring me another pot of ink.'

He doubled up again and grunted at whatever was going on inside him, a high whining noise through his nose with each return of breath.

'Edmund Carey,' shouted the Courtier mercilessly. 'Tell me what you found out about him?'

'Oh, for God's sake,' gasped Greene. 'Who cares? I'm dying, I know I am, I'm facing Judgement and what have I done, I've wasted my life, I've drunk away my gift, what have I ever done but write worthless plays, books full of obscenity, garbage the lot of it, I must write something good before I die, can't you see that, can't you understand?'

There were tears in the wretched man's eyes. On impulse Dodd took the ink bottle out of Carey's hand and put it back on the bed. With only a grunt of acknowledgement, Greene dipped his pen and started scribbling again. Carey didn't protest.

'Dear, oh dear,' said Barnabus from the stairs as Joan Ball pushed past him. 'What's wrong with him?'

'Why hasn't he seen a doctor?' Carey asked the woman.

'They've all run on account of the plague.' She was wiping sweat off Greene's face as he panted over his page.

'Plague? That's not plague.'

Not as far as you could tell, although Dodd felt it paid to be suspicious. But there was no sign of lumps disfiguring Greene's neck, no black spots. The smell in the room was unspeakably foul but more a muddle of unwashed clothes, old food, drink and an unemptied jordan plus the sour-sweet metallic smell of the splatter in the rushes by the bed. Plague had its own unmistakeable reek.

'No, sir, but there's plague hereabouts, and the doctors are always the first to know and the first to run for the country.'

Carey's eyes were narrowed.

'Have you heard about this, Barnabus?' he asked.

Barnabus coughed. 'There's always plague in London,' he said. 'It's like gaol-fever, comes and goes with the time of year.'

Greene had started whooping and bending over his belly, his face screwed up with pain.

Joan Ball scurried to the window with the disgusting pot, opened it wide, shrieked 'Gardyloo!' and emptied, before running to the bed. 'Get the apothecary.' She hissed, 'Get Mr Cheke.'

'The quality of the angels – there you see the cunning of the plot,' gasped the man in the bed. 'They're all in it, by God, who could doubt angels, . . . urrr . . . And where's Jenkins, eh? Answer me that?' His face contorted.

They tactfully left the room and Carey turned to Dodd. 'Go with Barnabus and see if you can find or kidnap a doctor or the apothecary,' he said. 'I've got to get some sense out of him or I've nowhere to start looking for my brother.'

Dodd was quite glad to get away from the place. As they went down again into the street he tapped Barnabus on the shoulder. 'Where's Simon?'

'Oh, he's back in Whitefriars, looking after Tamburlain the Great.'

'How is he?'

Barnabus didn't look up. 'He's fine. Let's try here.'

It was a barber's shop with its red and white pole outside. There was only one customer and he and the barber glared suspiciously at the two of them.

'What do you want?' demanded the barber.

'We're looking for a doctor.'

'Stay there. Don't come any closer. Why?'

'It's not for plague,' said Barnabus stoutly.

'So you say, mate, so you say.'

'I ain't lying. Will you come?'

'No.'

'Well, is there anyone who will?'

'Certainly not a doctor,' said the barber and sneered.

'What about Mr Cheke?' Dodd asked.

'The apothecary's round the corner. He's mad enough to try it.' The barber was snipping busily again. As he left the shop, Dodd heard one of them sneeze.

They went round the corner and found the right place with its rows of flasks in the windows and a pungent heady smell inside, and a counter with thousands of little drawers all labelled in a foreign language Dodd assumed was Latin. A boy peered over the top of the counter.

'Yes, sirs?'

'Where's the apothecary?'

'Out, in Pudding Lane.'

Philosophically they went back into the street, turned left and then right, and found themselves in a street where every door seemed to be marked with a red cross and a piece of paper, where there were already weeds growing in the silted up drain down the centre of the alley and what looked suspiciously like dead bodies lying in a row down one end.

Both Dodd and Barnabus stopped in their tracks and froze. Down the centre of the street a monster was pacing towards them. It was entirely covered in a thick cape of black canvas and where its face should be was an enormous three foot long beak of brass, perforated with holes. Above were two round eyes that flashed in the sun and from the holes in the beak came plumes of white smoke.

In the unnatural silence of the plague-stricken street, a plague demon paced towards them with a slow weary tread, a bag full of souls in one hand, and its head moved from side to side blindly, looking for more flesh to eat.

'Ahhh,' said Barnabus.

Dodd was already backing away, sword and dagger crossed before him. Would blades kill a plague demon? Maybe. Who cares? It'll not get me without a fight, he promised himself.

'Sirs,' said the demon, its voice muffled and echoing eerily from the beak, as it stopped and put up one white-gloved hand. 'Sirs, don't be afraid. I'm only a man.'

Holy water might stop it, Dodd remembered vaguely, or a crucifix; he'd heard that in the old days you could get crucifixes or little bottles of holy water blessed by the Pope to keep demons off, and neither of those things did he have with him. He had his amulet, but he couldn't touch it because his hands were occupied with weapons that he wasn't even sure could cut a demon and . . .

The demon took its face off and became indeed a tall pale man, with red-rimmed eyes and hollow cheeks. He coughed a couple of times.

'Ah,' said Barnabus. 'Would you be the apothecary for hereabouts?' All credit to him, thought Dodd, still shaking with the remnants of superstitious terror, I couldnae have said anything yet.

'Yes, I am,' said the man, giving a modest little bow before putting the beak and eyes back on and transforming himself into a monster again. 'Excuse me, please, until we are away from the plague miasmas of this place.'

That was sense. Dodd put his blades away and they left the street as fast as they could walk, trying not to breathe in the miasmas, with the demon-apothecary pacing behind them. Nobody else in the next street gave him a glance, though a few stones were thrown by some of the children playing by a midden with dead rats on it. At last they were back in his shop.

'Peter Cheke, sirs,' he said as he took the beak and eyes off again and carefully sprinkled his canvas robe with vinegar and herbs. He wiped his face with a sponge soaked in more vinegar and cleaned the beak with it, then opened one end and took out a posy of wormwood and rue and a small incense burner which had produced the smoke. Dodd watched fascinated.

'Does all that gear stop ye getting the plague?' he asked.

'It has so far, sir,' said Peter Cheke gravely. 'And I have attended many of the poor victims of the pestilence to bleed them and drain their buboes and give them what medicines I have.'

'Did ye cure any?'

Cheke shook his head. 'No, sirs, in all honesty, I think those that live do so by the blessing of God and a strong will.'

Without the sound-distorting beak his voice was unusually deep and rotund, speaking in a slow measured way. He seemed very weary.

'How may I help you, sirs?' he asked, blinking at them as if he was stoically preparing himself for more pleas for his puny help against the Sword of the Wrath of God.

'We don't think it's plague,' said Barnabus quickly. 'It's more like a flux or something. But he's puking blood and getting pains in his belly something awful.'

'Who is?'

'Robert Greene.'

Cheke frowned. 'Greene? When did he take sick?'

'He was well enough when he was playing primero last night,' said Dodd. 'Or he seemed like it. Will ye come look at him, Mr Cheke?'

The apothecary passed a hand over his face. 'Yes,' he said. 'I will, though I was up all night.'

'I dinna doubt it's all the booze,' said Dodd. 'Ye can rest after.'

Cheke smiled thinly. 'I very much doubt it, the way the plague is moving in these parts.'

'Spreading, is it?'

'With the heat, the miasmas are thickening and strengthening at every moment. I was called to three houses last night, and by the time I came to the third, every soul in it had died.'

'Och,' said Dodd. 'But it's plague, man. Why d'ye bother?'

Red-rimmed eyes held his for a moment and Cheke frowned. 'Do you know, I've no idea. I suppose I come in time to comfort some of them. Once I had some notion of finding the answer, of reading the riddle.'

'What riddle?'

'Why does plague happen? Why is one year a plague year and another year not? When London is full of stenches, why does one kind of miasma kill?'

'Och,' said Dodd shaking his head at the overweening madness of Londoners. 'Ye're wasting yer time, man. It's the Sword o' God's Wrath against the wickedness of London.'

'What?' snapped Barnabus. 'What's so wicked about London? Compared to Carlisle?'

'There isnae comparison,' said Dodd, quite shocked. 'London's a den of iniquity, full of cutpurses and trollops that try and blackmail ye oot o' yer hard won cash.'

'Carlisle's full of cattle thieves and blackrenters.'

'That's different. That's making a living.'

'So's cutting purses.'

'Gentlemen, gentlemen,' said the apothecary, putting on a skullcap. 'Shall we go?'

By the time they came back to the cobbler's shop, Joan Ball was back in the kitchen at the rear of the shop and Carey was leaning on the upstairs windowsill peering out.

Greene was putting a chased silver flask back under his revolting pillow, shuddering and coughing. He bent over a new piece of paper, still writing frantically. Next to him was the jordan full of something that looked like black soup. The stench was appalling.

Peter Cheke went in cautiously. Greene surged up in the bed, hands over his belly and started roaring with foam on his lips.

'You!' he shouted. 'You dare come in here . . .'

'Mr Greene, your friends . . .'

'I've got no friends and never you, Jenkins, never you, atheist, alchemist, necromancer . . . Get out, get out . . .!'

A book whizzed through the air and hit Peter Cheke on the head. He turned and walked down the stairs.

'I didna ken that Greene had a feud with ye as well,' said Dodd, hurrying after him. 'Why did ye not say, I wouldnae have wasted yer time.'

'If I had known, I would have mentioned it,' said Cheke. 'But we have never quarrelled before. It is clearly not plague that ails him, but nor does it seem to me a flux. For how long has he been purging blood?'

Dodd shrugged. 'All night according to his woman,' put in Carey as he came clattering down stairs. 'Is there anything you could give him that might bring him to his senses, calm him down? He won't do anything except write, and I need to talk to him.'

Peter Cheke thought for a moment. 'A lenitive might be lettuce juice and a decoction of willow bark. If you can get him to drink it and keep it down, he might sleep and give his body time to recover. Perhaps.'

'Aren't you going to examine him?' said Carey. 'Won't you cast a figure for him or taste his water or feel his pulses?'

'No, sir,' said Cheke gravely. 'I am not a doctor. I know very little of the humours and I have never studied at Padua. I have none of your right doctor's certainty. All I see in the many diseases of men is a great mystery. Besides, Mr Greene seems to think I am his enemy. I doubt he would let me examine him.'

'Try anyway.'

They trailed upstairs again and Dodd and Carey ignored frantic protests and held Greene down so Cheke could examine him. Greene fought like a madman and then stopped suddenly. 'You're not Jenkins,' he whispered like a bewildered child.

'No, you know my name is Cheke. May I use my poor skill to examine you, sir?'

Greene nodded, eyes darting from Carey to Dodd and back. Cheke listened at the chest and breath, felt neck and armpits, poked at Greene's stomach which produced a scream. At last he stepped back.

'It could be a flux, but such violence . . . I would suspect a poison.'

'What kind of poison?'

Cheke shrugged.

'You see!' roared Greene. 'I'm dying, I told you I was, the apothecary thinks so too.'

'Where is Edmund?' demanded Carey as soon as he caught a flicker of Greene's fleeting clarity. 'My father gave you five pounds to find him. Have you found him?'

'Repent or be damned, oh ye atheists of London!' bellowed Greene, picking up his pen and dipping. 'Find him yourself, I'm busy.'

'For God's sake, man . . .' said Carey, holding his shoulders. 'Tell me what you discovered about Edmund.'

Greene spat full in his face. 'I've got to finish,' he panted, shaking his head and swallowing hard. Back he went to his desperate scribbling, for all the world as if enough letters on a page could save him from hell.

Carey let go of him and wiped himself off distastefully with a handkerchief.

The apothecary was fishing in his bag, brought out a leather bottle. 'I have the calming draught here,' he said. 'If he could but take it and keep it down. Goodwife Ball,' he shouted down the stairs, 'will you come up?'

Greene's woman came up again, wiping her hands nervously. She took the little cup of medicine and gently held it to Greene's grey lips. He swallowed, gagged, pushed her away and grabbed his flask from under the pillow to wash it down.

The apothecary put his bottle away, buckled his bag and shrugged the strap over his shoulder. 'I will go to my shop to fetch laudanum since I have none left, and you should fetch a priest, Goodwife,' he said as he left. 'Pray God that that will help the poor gentleman.'

For a while it seemed as if it did. Greene wrote faster and faster, shaking his head as sweat dripped down his face and off his nose, and then at last he seemed to finish for he signed the paper with a flourish, put the last piece on the pile beside him, stoppered his inkpot, wiped his pen on the sheets.

'Now,' said Carey firmly, turning away from the window where he had been getting a breath of fresh air. 'Will you please tell me what you found out about my brother?'

Greene had collapsed back on the pillows and was coughing. He seemed too exhausted even to talk. He whispered something indistinct and Carey bent close to make it out.

'Dying. I heard . . . Don't tell Heneage . . . where . . . Ohhh. Aaahhh!'

Something terrible was happening inside the poet, as if some kind of animal was trapped in Greene's bowels and was rending them, trying to escape. His eyes rolled up in his head and he jacknifed in the tangled blankets. Carey strode to the stairs and shouted for the woman again. Dodd turned his head away from the sight. 'Och, God,' he said, fighting not to vomit himself.

Even in his agony, Greene turned himself so as not to puke on his swansong and the bright red blood flooded amongst the sheets, pooled in the lumpy mattress, endless amounts of it. Dodd heard Barnabus dry-heaving behind him.

'Christ,' croaked Carey. 'Christ have mercy.' Then he did a thing which even Dodd found admirable. He picked his way back to the bed and gripped Robert Greene's shoulder, held onto him while death juddered through him, so he should know he was not alone while his soul battled clear of his flesh.

After several minutes Greene's eyes were staring and Dodd broke the paralysis that had clutched him, went to the window and opened it as wide as it would go, so Greene's ghost could fly free. Joan Ball was in the room, pushing past Carey to fling herself across her lover and wail.

Dodd looked down into the street, as full of people and noise as ever, breathed deep of the slightly less pungent air coming through the window. He heard a long shaky breath beside him and knew that Carey was standing there too.

'Wait . . . wait,' said Joan. 'I'll get it, darling, wait.'

They turned to see her running down the stairs and Barnabus standing by the twisted body on the bed, gingerly turning it on its back, shutting the eyes and putting pennies on them, to keep the demons out.

Will I die like that? Dodd wondered, alone with strangers, in my own blood. I deserve to, came the dispiriting answer, unless I'm lucky enough to hang or get my head blown off in a fight.

Clogs sounded on the stairs as Joan Ball came running back up, incongruously clutching a couple of sprigs of bayleaves from the kitchen. She twisted them together in a rough ring and then took the nightcap off, pushed them onto Greene's balding, carroty brow.

'There,' she said, kissing the bulbous chilling nose and wiping her hands in her apron again. 'That's what you wanted, my love.'

'What the hell . . . ?' Dodd asked.

'It's a wreath of bays,' said Carey remotely. 'What they crowned dead poets with in Ancient Greece.'

There didn't seem anything to be said to that. In unspoken agreement they went down the stairs and out into the sunny street where nothing was any different. Barnabus emerged from the house too, a few moments later, blinking and looking shifty. Carey glanced at him and seemed to come to some decision.

'I need a drink,' he announced which showed he had some sense after all, and he led the way to the nearest house with red lattices.

They sat in a tiny booth and called for beer and aqua vitae. Carey lifted his little horn cup. 'To Robert Greene, may he rest in peace,' he said and knocked it back. Dodd and Barnabus followed suit gratefully.

The drink helped settle Dodd's stomach and scour the stench of sickness out of his nostrils. Before he had quite finished the beer, Carey was up again, heading out the door.

'Where's the apothecary's shop?'

Barnabus led him there, and they met Peter Cheke hurrying into the street holding a bottle. Cheke stopped.

Carey shook his head.

'Dead?' asked the apothecary. 'Poor gentleman.'

'How much do I owe you?' asked Carey with strange politeness and Cheke put his bony hands out in front of him.

'I can hardly charge for such unsuccessful treatment as I attempted,' he said. 'Alas, sir, I am not a doctor.'

'I dinna think a doctor could hae done any mair,' said Dodd. 'There was death on him already.'

Cheke smiled wanly. 'As usual, I shall always be in doubt,' he said.

'Can we come in?' asked Carey and the apothecary ceremoniously ushered them into the pungent dimness of his shop, and then, on Carey's request for somewhere private, through a door into the kitchen at the back of the building. They sat at a scrubbed wooden table standing on painfully scrubbed flagstones; a womanless kitchen for the lack of strings of onions and flitches of bacon hanging from the rafters. Ranged like soldiers on shelves were a vast variety of cups and dishes and strange tortured things made out of glass. There was a bulbous-shaped oven instead of a fireplace.

'You said you thought it might be poison,' Carey asked, suddenly narrowing his eyes and sharpening up. 'Do you know what kind?'

Cheke shrugged. 'There are so many, sir, some masquerading under the name of physic. I only gave him a painkilling dose, but who knows . . . It could have been white arsenic. That attacks the gut although it generally works more slowly. It can make a man who abuses his belly with booze bleed to death.'

'That's Greene, all right. Is there any way you can be sure?'

Cheke shook his head. 'Arsenic has no taste or smell so it is a favourite of those who work with poisons. More than that I cannot say.'

Carey felt in his belt pouch and then produced the little twist of paper in which he had caught the beads of liquid metal in Edmund Carey's clothes chest. Very carefully he opened it.

'Do you know what this is?'

The apothecary looked at the bead of bright silver, his nostrils flaring a little. 'Certainly I do, sir,' he said. 'It is Mercury.'

'What?'

'In the art and science of alchemy we have various materials that partake of certain qualities: there is Venus, Mars, Saturn – and this is Mercury, the messenger and facilitator of the chemical wedding. It is a great mystery, for how can metal be a liquid? Some call it quicksilver. And so indeed it is, for after any reaction concerning it, you may find little dewdrops of it in your clothes, in your pockets, brought there too quickly to see.'

'Could Mercury have anything to do with the Philosopher's Stone?'

'Certainly it is one of the principals in the search. Do you have any understanding of the great quest, sir?'

Carey smiled. 'None at all. What can you tell me?'

'The Philosopher's Stone and also its liquid equivalent, the Elixir of Life, hath the great quality of turning that which is base – such as metal or flesh – into gold, the highest form matter can take. By means of repeatedly wedding Venus to Mars, with the intervention of Mercury, by the transitions through the many stages, it is certain that we shall achieve the transmutation of matter.'

'How d'ye do that then?' asked Dodd with interest. 'How can ye change a thing to gold?'

Cheke's eyes lit up. 'Change is unnatural and stability natural.

Whatever changes is at a lower state than that which always remains the same. Yes? But change is itself not merely unnatural but also wearisome. Therefore, if we force base matter through enough changes it will eventually in exhaustion revert to its natural state, which is gold for metals. The Philosopher's Stone shortens the process much as bone ash aids in lead refining. It is actually a powder, of course, but I have seen such a powder, dissolved in boiling Mercury, change pewter to gold. I myself have seen it, with my own eyes.'

'Where?' asked Carey intently.

Cheke smiled. 'I am sorry, sir, I gave my word not to reveal where and exactly what I saw.'

'Who else was there?'

'The master alchemist that performed the reaction. Also a gentleman that was investing in the process.'

'What did he look like, this gentleman?'

'Reddish brown hair, a little the look of yourself, sir, but stockier.'

'What was his name?'

Cheke shook his head. 'We did not exchange names.'

'Who was the master alchemist?'

'A most worshipful gentleman, a Dr Jenkins, though not previously known to me.'

'How come you were there then?'

'As an assistant, to grind the powder and assist with firing the furnace. I am not one of the *cognoscenti*, you understand, I must study and work a great deal more.'

'No, I meant – who introduced you?'

'Why, a poet, a scholar from Cambridge.'

'Mr Greene?'

'No, a Mr Marlowe.'

Carey compressed his lips and leaned back a little on the bench. 'Hmm,' he said, his eyes narrow. 'How well do you know Marlowe?'

'Not well, but he too is a seeker after truth and the Stone.'

'Oh, is he?' muttered Barnabus. 'Well, fancy.'

'When did you see this demonstration, Mr Cheke?'

'It was a while ago. Last month. I was greatly inspired in my own labours by it – to see base pewter discs smeared with the Stone's matrix, and sealed in the pelican, heated in the furnace and then to see them come out transformed, transmutated into gold – wonderful. Truly wonderful. It seems to me that we are living in a new Golden Age, sir, when the mysteries of God's creation shall be unwound, when we shall truly understand how the world is made, what drives the crystal spheres, the nature of matter itself, all is within our grasp and from that wisdom we shall know the mind of God Himself.'

More mad blasphemy, thought Dodd, full of gloom, no doubt the apothecary would be dead of plague by tomorrow. And me too, perhaps, added the voice of terror inside, I've still got that headache.

'Then the reaction did not take place here?'

Cheke smiled again. 'I promised I would not tell where it happened. I brought some of my equipment, that's all, and some poor skill with the furnace.'

'What was the gentleman wearing?'

'He was very well-dressed, sir, black Lucca velvet embroidered with pearls and slashed with oyster satin.'

'And he looked like me?'

'A little, sir. Redder in the face as well as wider in the body.'

Carey nodded. 'Mr Cheke, you have been very kind and very helpful. Are you sure I cannot ... er ... pay you for your treatment?'

'With the Philosopher's Stone available, why would I need any gold in the world?' asked Cheke rhetorically and smiled like a child. Carey smiled back, rose and went into the shop. Barnabus hesitated and then spoke to the apothecary quietly and urgently.

Dodd came back to fetch him.

'I make no guarantees,' Cheke was saying. 'If I knew of anything that was sovereign against the plague, I would publish a book about it.'

Barnabus actually had hold of the man's sleeve. 'My sister's family got it and half of them are dead,' he hissed. 'Can't you give me anything? You could let my blood, couldn't you?'

'But I don't think it works.'

'Doctors do it against the plague.'

'If the doctors knew of a remedy, why would any of them catch it?'

Dodd thought the man had a good point there, but Barnabus wasn't paying attention.

'Listen,' he said. 'I'll pay you. But you've got to give me something, or do something.'

Cheke sighed. 'Sit down,' he said, digging in his bag again. 'I'll let your blood against infection and give you the best charms I can.'

Dodd waited patiently while Barnabus sat on a stool and proffered his left arm for Cheke to open a vein. The dark blood oozed out into the basin and Dodd wondered about it: men's bodies were filled with blood. When you let some of it out, how did you know which would be the bad stuff and which would be the good? It took only a short time, for Cheke refused to let more than three ounces and he bandaged Barnabus's arm up again and carefully wiped off his knife with a cloth. 'Do you want to be treated too?' he asked Dodd while Barnabus put a silver shilling down on the table which the apothecary ignored.

'Nay,' said Dodd, thinking about it. 'Ah spend too much time trying to avoid losing blood.'

Cheke smiled. 'Both of you should take posies to counteract the miasmas.' He handed them more bunches of wormwood and rue and told them to put them inside their clothes.

'We'd best be getting along,' said Barnabus, rubbing his arm and looking pleased. 'My master was talking about going up to the Theatre or the Curtain to see a play this afternoon.'

'The playhouses should all be closed down until the plague has abated,' said the apothecary, putting his instruments back in his bag.

'What's the point of that?' demanded Barnabus. 'You'll be saying the cockpits and bull-baiting should be shut too, like the Corporation.'

'They should. Wherever men gather closely together the plague miasma forms and strikes.'

It was a horrible picture: Dodd could see it as a demon, now forever in his mind with a long brass beak, hovering over a crowd of men looking for places to strike. The thought made his bowels loosen just by itself.

'Bah,' sniffed Barnabus. 'Never heard such nonsense in my life. If that's true, why don't people get plague from going to church, eh? Or walking up and down St Paul's, eh? Come on, Sergeant, let's go or we'll be late.'

Perhaps only Dodd heard the alchemist answer Barnabus softly. 'But they do. St Paul's is where the plague always starts.'

Saturday, 2nd September 1592, midday

6

Dodd's head was buzzing as Carey strode through the crowds, heading for the Mermaid tavern again. Carey talked at length with the innkeeper who had no idea how Sir Edward Fitzjohn, alias Nick the Gent, and his wife, alias Molly Stone, had managed to get into their chamber, and further could not tell where Kit Marlowe might be nor any of his cronies. Nobody knew anything, so far as Dodd could see, not even when Carey offered to pay them.

Shakespeare was still there, sitting in one of the booths, white and trembling and sipping mild ale very cautiously.

'Shouldn't you be getting back to Somerset House?' Carey asked him and he shook his head, then clutched it and muttered that my lord had told him to serve Sir Robert.

'Excellent. I want to find Mr Marlowe and ask him some questions. Do you know where he is, Will?'

'No, sir. Sorry, sir.' Shakespeare was staring into his beer, gloom lapping him round like a cloak. Carey sat himself down opposite.

'Did you know Robert Greene is dead, Will?' he asked cheerily.

Shakespeare shut his eyes for a moment. 'Oh,' he said, not seeming very happy at the news.

'That means I've got to start all over again, looking for my brother. Do you know anything about him?'

'No.' With a great effort Shakespeare looked up at Carey. 'I'm sorry, sir,' he croaked.

'Did you ever hear of an alchemist called Jenkins?'

'N . . . no, sir.'

'Are you sure?'

'Yes, sir.' Shakespeare was staring at his beer again. Carey watched him speculatively for a moment.

'I think you're lying to me, Will,' he said without heat. 'I'm not sure why. If you're afraid of anyone, it would be better to tell me so I can protect you.'

A tiny sliver of a smile passed over Shakespeare's face. 'I'm afraid of many things, sir,' he said, adenoidally honest. 'I doubt there's much you can do about any of them.'

Carey paused a moment longer, then clapped his hand on the table.

'Well, how do you feel? Ready for a bit of exercise?'

Shakespeare sighed deeply and sipped some more ale. 'Yes, sir,' he said dolefully.

'All right. You go back to Somerset House, you find my father's *valet de chambre* and ask him to find my second best suit, the one with lilies on the hose, and also the suit Sergeant Dodd here wore the other night for my father's supper party. Then you bring them both back here and we'll all go to see who we can find in Paul's Walk this afternoon.'

Shakespeare nodded, repeated his orders, swallowed his ale and hurried off. Carey watched him go, blue eyes narrow and considering. Barnabus coughed deprecatingly.

'Sir, I was wondering if I could go back to our lodgings, see how Tamburlain is getting on.'

'Who?'

'The cock, sir. My sister's fighting cock.'

'Oh. Yes. Well, it's a confounded nuisance. I want you to come with me to St Paul's.'

'Yes, sir. I could meet you there, sir.'

'Oh, very well. Hurry up.'

'Thank you, sir.'

Barnabus disappeared out the door, blinking and rubbing his forehead while Dodd watched him go doubtfully. Did he have plague? Maybe Dodd had plague too. As well as pox.

Carey was tapping his fingers on the blackened table top and frowning.

'Sir, why do you want to find Marlowe?' Dodd asked, feeling that the over-clever pervert was best left alone.

'Hm? Oh, he's in the middle of this tangle, somewhere. I know he is.'

'Well, but, what's he got to do with yer brother?'

'Look, Dodd, there's some kind of complicated plot going on here, something that Edmund's only incidental to.'

'Papist, d'ye mean, sir?'

'That's only one kind. My inclination is that Heneage is up to something.'

'Ay,' said Dodd, thinking back to the supper party. 'I didnae take to him, meself.'

'Father hates his guts. What the devil was he doing, inviting the bastard to supper?'

'Mebbe yer brother's at Chelsea, wi' Heneage?' suggested Dodd as he tucked into the bacon and pease pottage the boy put in front of him. Carey was staring at him, making him feel uncomfortable. 'Well, but ye said he could do the like to me, sir, could he not to yer brother?' Carey said nothing. Dodd chewed and swallowed, washing down the salty meat with more beer. 'That's how Richie Graham of Brackenhill runs it if ye're too strong to take on directly. Captures one o' yer relatives, puts him in ward somewhere he controls and threatens tae starve him to death if ye dinna pay up.'

'If Heneage tried something like that with my brother, my father would go directly to the Queen. Heneage knows that. The Queen doesn't think much of Edmund either, but she won't have her cousins mistreated.'

'Ay,' said Dodd, following a train of thought that twisted and turned like a hunted stag. 'But what if yer brother was up tae no good? Or what if Heneage knew he was dead or in gaol but wasnae sure where so he just let on to yer father he might have him but kept yer father in doot. Richie Graham does that too.'

Carey was scooping up pease pottage with a piece of bread. 'It's possible. If it's true, then Marlowe is the one who'll know what's really going on; he's one of Heneage's men.'

'He is? I wouldnae have placed him as a serving man.'

Carey laughed. 'No, he's a pursuivant. Been at it for years. Started working for Walsingham years ago, back before the Armada, and then when Walsingham died and Heneage took over, Marlowe went to work for him too.'

'What's a pursuivant?'

'A kind of spy. An intelligencer against the Catholics. An informer, a troublemaker.'

'I thought he was a poet.'

'Well, he's that as well but nobody can really make a living as a poet alone, unless he's got a rich patron, and not even Sir Walter Raleigh will take Marlowe on, he's too dangerous. You never know who he's working for, if he knows himself.'

'Och.' Dodd considered this while he sawed away at a tough bit of meat. 'I wouldnae have thought poets would make good spies.'

'On the contrary, my father says they're excellent. Literate, intelligent, good memory, practised liars.'

Dodd snorted, speared a chunk and started nibbling it off the end of his knife.

'And what's all this with alchemy?'

'Yes.' Carey was staring into space while he chewed at a bit of gristle. 'Just the sort of thing Edmund would get into, the idiot.'

'Ye dinna think it was really working?'

'I'd stake my fortune that it wasn't, if I had one.'

'Why?'

'One of the best pieces of advice I ever had was this: if something looks too good to be true, it probably isn't true. Alchemy as the road to enlightenment, possibly. Alchemy as the road to riches – no.'

'But Cheke said he'd seen it work.'

'I think he was mistaken, and so was my brother if he was the gentleman investing in it. I think he was involved in something a lot simpler and more dangerous.'

'What?'

Carey took the forged angel out of his sleeve pocket and spun it on the table where it glittered to a halt and fell over.

'Forgery. He was coining. That's where his purse of money came from that he showed Susannah.'

'Why would he need alchemy to do that? It's not so hard. The

Graham's got his ain mint going at Brackenhill, making silver Scots shillings. Only, they're not silver, ye follow?'

'Has he? That's interesting. I was wondering why the Scots money was worth so little. Well, it's harder to forge gold coins. They're more carefully minted, you can't get the colour right with anything except gold . . . Hm. There's one way to find out and that's why I want us to look decent.'

'Mebbe Heneage was at the coining with this alchemy and yer brother caught him at it.'

'That's possible. If you look at it from Heneage's point of view, you could even see why he might think there was nothing wrong in it. The Queen never gives him enough money to do what he wants. She never gave Walsingham enough either, but he was willing to spend his own fortune on his intelligencing and Heneage doesn't fancy dying in debt like him. So along comes an alchemist who claims he's found the Philosopher's Stone and Heneage either believes it, or sees that it might work well enough to solve his money problems.'

Dodd shook his head sadly. 'Everyone needs more money,' he muttered. 'Where does it a' go?'

Carey looked irritated. 'We spend it, Dodd, where do you think? Besides, the Queen never likes her servants to be too rich, she thinks it might make us arrogant. That's why Father has to be so mean: if she heard how rich he really is, she'd send him to France as an ambassador or put him in command of the troops in Ireland or something ghastly like that.'

'Why would she hear of it?'

'The Queen is uncanny the way she finds things out. I've never known anybody successfully get something past her, except Walsingham's protégé Davison over the Queen of Scots. Anyway, Edmund's just the sort of man an ambitious alchemist would take his process to and if Heneage got to hear of it, which he would, then Heneage would want in on the deal. I think Edmund's precious alchemist transformed pewter blanks to gold which they then used to strike coins. Or at least that's what Edmund thought.'

Carey was turning the false angel in his long gloved fingers.

'And ye reckon it was all a load of rubbish?'

'Of course it was. Poor old Edmund. Always full of ways to

make money, and each one is always the one that will finally make him richer than Father. He's the easiest mark for a coney-catcher I've ever met. Ingram Frizer took him for a hundred and seventy pounds on the old brocade-reselling trick.'

'Whit's that?'

'Oh, Edmund wanted to borrow more money off Frizer, but you're not supposed to charge interest to cover your risk. So Frizer gets Edmund to sign a bond for a hundred and seventy pounds, but Frizer gives him brocade instead of money, worth a little less than the amount Edmund is supposed to repay – theoretically. Then Edmund is supposed to sell the brocades to all his friends and get his money that way and if he makes more on the deal, he can keep it.'

Dodd screwed up his eyes to follow this. 'And the brocades was bad?' he asked. Carey smiled.

'Precisely. The dye wasn't fixed and the colours ran if you so much as sweated into them. The pile came out in the velvets and the silk weaving was atrocious. Edmund was shocked at it and Father nearly murdered him for being so stupid as to fall for such an ancient trick.'

'Ay.'

Shakespeare appeared in the doorway, still blinking and looking pale and sweaty. Maybe he had plague too. He was carrying two heavy bags over his shoulder and puffing slightly.

Dodd looked in dismay at the bag Shakespeare gave him. 'Och, sir, do I have to fancy up again?'

'Yes.'

Half an hour later, feeling sweaty and uncomfortable in Carey's tight cramoisie suit, Dodd was scouting Cheapside for bailiffs. Every jeweller's shop had at least two large men in buff coats standing guard at the door, but none of them looked like bailiffs so far as Dodd could tell. He nodded to Shakespeare, waiting next to the alley where Carey was skulking and a minute later Carey sauntered out with Shakespeare at his heels, looking every inch the court gallant in his blackberry-coloured velvet suit all crusted with pearls and embroidered lilies.

He went to the biggest and brightest jeweller's shop on the street under the sign of a golden cup and strolled past the heavy-set men on guard who, far from barring his path as they had Dodd's, actually bowed to him. One of them obsequiously opened the iron-bound door for him.

Inside, surrounded by gold and silver plate ranged on shelves all around the room, Dodd found his breath coming short. Look at it, he thought to himself, just look at it all. One gold dish, just one gold dish, that's all I need.

Carey drawled a request for the Master Goldsmith to the slender young man who came bowing and scraping up to them and then hitched his pretty padded hose on the edge of the black velvet covered table and whistled through his teeth. Shakespeare stood blank-faced by the door, with his hands tucked behind his back and Dodd rested his itchy fingers on his sword belt and tried to think of something boring, like sheep-shearing.

'I suppose it's just as well Barnabus isn't here,' said Carey good-humouredly. 'I'd never be able to take my eyes off him.'

'Ay, sir,' croaked Dodd, whose throat had unaccountably gone dry.

The Master Goldsmith swept from his inner sanctum in a long velvet gown of black over a doublet and hose of gold and black brocade.

'Master van Emden?' said Carey with an infinitesimal bow. The goldsmith bowed back.

'Sir Robert. How very kind of you to grace my establishment.'

Was there just the faintest tinge of wariness in Master van Emden's voice?

'How may I help you, sir?'

'To be honest, Master van Emden, I'm not intending to buy today.'

And was that relief flitting across the Master Goldsmith's face? 'Oh?'

'No. I want some information about goldsmithing.'

One eyebrow twitched and the goldsmith's expression chilled further.

'Oh? What sort of information?'

'I'm not quite sure how to put it. Um . . . let's say you have something made of a base metal, such as pewter or silver, and you wanted to make it look like gold. How could you do that?'

'These are mysteries of the goldsmith's trade, Sir Robert. My guild-brothers would be very offended if I . . .'

'I think you can be sure that I have neither the skill nor the inclination to take up the goldsmith's art.'

'Nonetheless.'

'Well, is it possible?'

'Certainly.'

'Might the substance called Mercury or quicksilver have anything to do with it?'

Master van Emden's expression stiffened. 'It might,' he allowed. 'Quicksilver is an essential element in the parcel-gilding process.'

'Which means?'

'May I ask to what this is in reference, Sir Robert?'

Carey hesitated for a moment and then came to a decision. 'Master van Emden, I believe a coney-catcher calling himself an alchemist may have . . .'

'Not again,' sighed the goldsmith. 'I beg you, sir, have nothing to do with alchemists, they are either ignorant fools or thieves. May we be private?'

Carey bowed extravagantly and the goldsmith ushered him through into the room behind the shop. The slender young man moved up smoothly to bar Dodd's path. Dodd looked at him consideringly. It would be simplicity itself to knock the man down and then sweep as much gold as he could into a bag, but you had to reckon that the guards outside the door would hear the commotion and come in and you couldn't know who might be upstairs or in the back room with Carey and the master. No, Dodd thought regretfully, it's not worth it. You'd have all London to get through with a hue and cry behind you, and the long dusty road north. It simply wasn't possible.

The young man never took his eyes off either of them and you could swear he didn't blink either. Twenty minutes later Carey emerged from the back room, followed by the goldsmith, looking delighted with himself.

'Thank you, Master van Emden,' he said. 'You've helped me

immensely. Perhaps I could suggest that my father come to you when he's thinking of Her Majesty's New Year's present?'

Now that pleased the goldsmith, you could see. His wary eyes brightened noticeably.

'My order books are almost full,' he murmured. 'But for your honourable father, naturally I will make the space. I have an excellent designer – possibly my lord Baron Hunsdon would care to see some of his sketches?'

'I'm sure he would. I'll tell him. Good afternoon.'

And Carey ambled out into the sunshine, just as if he had not a care in the world, although he looked round sharply at the passers-by once he was clear of the door.

'Where now, sir?' asked Dodd, sweating almost as hard as Shakespeare while Carey paced briskly westwards.

'St Paul's Walk.'

'Och, no, sir.'

'Why not? Most interesting place in London, best place for gossip, best for scandal and we're going to meet Barnabus there.'

'Och.'

'Don't worry. So long as you don't let anybody inveigle you into any little alleys, nobody is going to coney-catch you.'

'I dinna like the place, sir. It gives me the willies. And what about bailiffs?'

'There shouldn't be too much trouble with them, now Mr Bullard's been paid.'

'Why are ye watching out for yerself so carefully then?'

'Some of them may not have heard yet. Anyway, I'm looking for that clever bugger Marlowe.'

'Find him at St Paul's, will ye, sir? Praying, I expect.'

Carey looked amused. 'No, wandering up and down quoting Juvenal.'

St Paul's was as noisy and crowded as it had been last time, though there was no sign of Barnabus by the serving men's pillar. Carey glanced at the throngs, tutted to himself, bought an apple off a woman with enormous breasts, and slipped into the lurid parade in the aisle. Shakespeare stood still, hands tucked behind him again, staring hard. Dodd leaned against a pillar with his thumbs hitched on his swordbelt and watched, narrow-eyed in the shafts of sun striking down through the holes in the temporary roof. A pigeon strutted past, pecking at discarded piecrusts and trying to overawe its reflection in a brass set in another pillar. The resemblance to the young men at their posing was uncanny, you might even say poetical.

Carey was talking and laughing to people who seemed very anxious to fawn on him. None of them seemed able to help him and Dodd himself could see no sign of Marlowe nor any of his cronies. Carey swaggered all the way to the door by Duke Humphrey's tomb and then turned and swaggered all the way back trailing an eager group of hangers-on.

Just as he turned again to pace pointlessly back the way he had come, there was a stir and a swirl amongst the fashion-afflicted. Two men in buff-coats and green livery came in through the door, followed by a tall and languid exquisite in peach damask, festooned with pearls, and with a lovelock hanging over one shoulder.

The exquisite paused impressively at the first pillar and squinted down the aisle. His face lit up.

'By God, it's Carey!' he sang out. 'What the devil are you doing here, made Berwick too hot for you already?'

Carey stopped in one of the most mannered poses Dodd had ever seen in his life and flourished off a bow.

'My lord Earl,' he responded. 'What a wonderful surprise; my heart is overflowing with delight.'

Dodd stole a glance at Shakespeare to see if the player was as close to puking as he was. Carey was striding down the aisle, such happiness on his face you might think the peach-damask creature was a woman. God, surely he wasn't . . . No, whatever else he might be, Carey was not a pervert. And there was Shakespeare, face intent, hurrying to catch up with him.

Sighing, Dodd stood upright and followed.

Peach-damask was giving Carey a nice warm hug and Carey was returning it. Some of the other fashionable young men were staring at his back with faces twisted with envy. Shakespeare hesitated as they came close, but Carey clapped his back jovially.

'Now this is someone you should talk to, my lord,' he said. 'May I present Mr William Shakespeare, late of the Rose?'

Shakespeare's bow was a tidy model of deference.

Peach-damask put an elegantly gloved hand to his breast. '*Not* Mr Shakespeare who wrote *Henry VI*?'

The player bowed again, more deeply. 'I am more honoured than you can guess, my lord, that you should have remembered my name.'

Peach-damask seemed to like being flattered. 'Of course I do, best plays I've seen in years. *Oh, woman's heart, wrapped in a tiger's hide*. Eh? Eh? Wonderful stuff, Sir Robert, you remember?'

'Oh, indeed, my lord,' said Carey and Shakespeare murmured modestly.

Please don't introduce me to this prinked-up fancy-boy, Dodd was praying silently, I dinna want tae have to do any more bowing and scraping.

Peach-damask was absolutely full of good humour, you'd think he was drunk. He quoted more nonsensical lines that seemed to be from this wonderful play of Shakespeare's, then asked the player where on earth he got his ideas and how long it took him to write a play and then, while Carey and Shakespeare both laid on the flattery with a trowel, insisted that they all come back to Southampton House with him, since he was planning a little card-party for that evening. Carey accepted instantly, and as peach-damask took the time for a quick parade down the aisle and back again so everyone could admire his pretty suit, Dodd muttered desperately,

'I'd best be getting back to ma lodgings, sir, make sure Barnabus is . . . er . . .' not coming down with plague, he nearly said, then stopped himself.

Carey didn't notice his hesitation. 'No, no,' he said at once. 'I'm sorry, Dodd, you've got to come with me. The earl will put us up.'

'Will ye no' be wantin' to be private wi' yer friend?' asked Dodd heavily and Carey drew a breath, stared for a moment, and then laughed.

'By God, you don't know me very well, do you?' he said. 'What the hell do you think you're talking about, private with my friend?

Don't come it the Puritan preacher with me, Dodd, I don't like it. That's the Earl of Southampton, my lord of Essex's best friend, and if you think I'm snubbing him to keep your good opinion of me, you're sadly mistaken.'

'I ken I'm no' in my right company, sir,' said Dodd. 'I dinna care what ye do, but I'm no' a courtier, me, and I . . .'

'Oh, give it a rest, Dodd. Nobody's asking you to take up buggery for a living. Just come along quietly, and give me a bit of back-up, that's all I ask.'

'What about the alchemist and finding Marlowe or yer brother?'

'Marlowe's been paying court to Southampton for months now, he might well be at this supper party. As for the alchemist and my brother, they can wait.'

Arm in arm with the Earl, Carry led the way out of St Paul's to the churchyard where the Earl's horses were waiting, held by yet more men in livery. Carey was given a horse to ride, Dodd and Shakespeare left to walk with the other attendants. They made their own small procession around some fine lady's damask-curtained litter that joined the party at Ludgate. The Earl was on horseback, riding a magnificent chestnut animal that had Dodd sighing with envy, leaning back to chat to Carey occasionally. He wasn't a bad rider, if you liked that showy court-style of horsemanship, with one hand on the reins and one hand on the hip.

Southampton House stood in gardens surrounded by a moat in the fields to the north of Holborn at the top of Drury Lane. As they passed over the little bridge to the north of the house and rode round to the door, Shakespeare stopped in his tracks and went white.

Mistress Bassano was being handed down from her litter with immense ceremony by no less than the Earl himself. Her eyes skidded slightly as Carey made his bow to her, his face printed with naughty comprehension. To do the lady justice, she only checked for a second when she saw him, before curtseying almost as low to him as she had to the Earl.

As they followed the company indoors, Dodd distinctly heard Shakespeare moan softly to himself.

* * *

Supper at Southampton House involved more mysterious meats in pungent sauces, leaves doused in oil and vinegar decorated with orange nasturtium flowers, decorated pies, astonishingly smooth-tasting wines. It all gave Dodd a bellyache just looking at it being laid out on the sideboard by the servants who carried it in, and of course every bite of it was cold after the palaver of serving it up and displaying to the Earl and then passing it around. It seemed courtiers showed their importance by making even the simplest things pointlessly complicated. Did they have three servants to wipe their arse, Dodd wondered, once the wine had started to work on his empty stomach.

Shakespeare seemed to have latched onto him again and was sitting next to him at the second table in the parlour, continuing to explain something about how playing was in the way you moved and spoke, not just in gestures and rhetoric. For instance, if you were playing a learned man, it wasn't enough to wear spectacles, you had to look abstracted as well. Dodd nodded politely to all this unwanted information and tried not to yawn.

The Earl was laughing at something Mistress Bassano was telling him.

'Mr Shakespeare,' he called to them across the room. 'A fair lady has just made a serious complaint against you. What have you to say?'

Shakespeare paused in mid-analysis of the contribution clothes made to a play-part, swallowed what he had in his mouth whole, and stood up.

'What was her complaint, my lord Earl?' His voice had changed. It was clearer, less flat, less dull.

'She alleges that you used the fair muse of poetry to tell lies. I had heard better of you. Can it be true?'

Shakespeare paused, looking narrowly at Mistress Bassano who had a cruel expression on her face, rather like a cat torturing a mouse, and then at the Earl who was half laughing at him. Now that was an interesting sight to see, Dodd thought, because something inside the man shifted, you might almost say hardened. It was as if he came to some decision.

'My lord Earl,' said Shakespeare judiciously, his flat vowels filling the parlour full of overdressed people quite easily. 'I'm sorry to say that it is true, if she means the poor sonnets I sent her the other day.'

'So you admit the crime of corrupting the muse?'

'I do, my lord. The bill is foul. The sonnets I made to her praise should never have been sent.'

Mistress Bassano, who had clearly been expecting a pleasant few minutes of poet-baiting, now looked puzzled.

'Then you apologise to the lady?' pursued the Earl.

'I do, my lord. Unreservedly. I should never have said that her hair outrivalled the dawn nor that her voice put the birds to shame.'

'And what will you do for your penance, Mr Shakespeare?'

'Why, with the lady's permission, I'll read another of my poems.'

Perhaps because he was sitting right next to the man, only Dodd saw the tension in Shakespeare.

'Compounding your crime, Mr Shakespeare?' sneered the Earl.

Shakespeare smiled quite sweetly. 'No, my lord. Telling the truth.'

'A truthful poet. An oxymoron, to be sure?'

'Not necessarily.'

'Mistress Bassano? As Queen of the company, do you allow this?'

Creamy shoulders shrugged expressively. 'He may embarrass himself again, if he wishes,' she said.

The Earl waved a negligent hand to Shakespeare, who fumbled in the front of his doublet for his notebook, brought it out and opened it. The adenoidal voice filled the room.

> 'My mistress' eyes are nothing like the sun,
> Coral is far more red than her lips' red:
> If snow be white, why then her breasts are dun:
> If hairs be wires, black wires grow on her head.'

Carey began by staring in shock, but then he smiled. The Earl laughed. Shakespeare let the titters pass round the room and continued.

'I have seen roses damask'd, red and white.
But no such roses see I in her cheeks:
And in some perfumes is there more delight
Than in the breath that from my mistress reeks.'

The whole room was laughing, except for Mistress Bassano who
had locked her stare on Shakespeare. The player ignored her.

'I love to hear her speak, yet well I know
That music hath a far more pleasing sound;
I grant I never saw a goddess go,—
My mistress when she walks treads on the ground.'

You had to admire what the player was doing. He paused for
long enough to let the laughter die down again. And then for the
first time he looked Mistress Bassano full in the face, like a man
taking aim with a loaded caliver, and gave the last two lines.

'And yet, by heaven, I think my love as rare
As any she belied by false compare.'

Even Dodd applauded with the rest of them. Shakespeare shut his
notebook with a snap, sat down and finished his wine, studiously
ignoring the way Mistress Bassano was staring at him. You could
see she was angry but also that she knew better than to show it.

When the supper was done they walked in the moated garden
amongst lavender and thyme and blossoming roses while page-
boys of remarkable beauty scuttled between them with silver
trays of jellied sweetmeats and wild strawberries dusted with
pepper. Shakespeare was beckoned to the Earl's side, and walked
respectfully amongst the box hedges talking to him, nodding his
head in agreement, occasionally making him laugh.

'Enjoying yourself, Dodd?' Carey asked, his voice a little slurred
with drink, interrupting Dodd's thoughts as he stood beneath a
well-pruned tree and stared into the magnificent copper sunset.

'Nay, sir,' said Dodd. 'Why, are ye?'

Truth was a weapon it seemed these courtiers had no armour
against. Carey blinked and his superior little smile slipped slightly,

but he didn't answer, just strode off amongst the rose bushes, his left hand leaning on his sword hilt to tilt it away from catching on the flowers. Dodd folded his arms and leaned against the tree trunk. Away across the fields you could see the women folding up the linens that had been laid out on the grass and hedges to dry, before the dew came down to wet them again, and those gloriously fat London cows gathering at their gates ready to be brought in for milking. An old church poked its battered tower out of a small wood to the west.

'Whatever have you done to Will Shakespeare, Sergeant Dodd?' asked a throaty voice beside him and Dodd looked because he couldn't help it, to be rendered instantly dry-mouthed again at the soft bulge of woman-flesh against red velvet stays.

'What?' he asked, coughed and took a deep breath. 'I beg pardon, mistress, I dinnae understand ye.'

'Will says you gave him the best advice he ever had.'

Dodd wrinkled his brow and then shook his head. 'I cannae remember it. Might have been the other night when we were drunk.'

'Of course.'

He couldn't help it, he had to ask. 'Are ye no' angry with him, for his new sonnet?'

A maddening smile curved between Mistress Bassano's lightly powdered cheeks and her dark eyes sparkled. 'Oh, I am,' she purred. 'Enraged, infuriated.'

God, who could make head or tail of women? Dodd had no idea what to say.

'I wanted to speak to Robin again,' she continued. 'But I think he has gone to play primero with my lord Earl.'

'Ay, nae doot.'

'You can tell him for me. You can tell him not to trust Will, for he has been taking money from Mr Marlowe and providing information on my Lord Hunsdon in return.'

Dodd stared at her, trying to work out whether she was telling the truth or just trying to make trouble for the player. Both, perhaps? Mistress Bassano smiled again, rather complacently, and met his eyes without a tremor.

'Like many other poets, he has turned to spying to make money. He has a great desire for money, you know, Sergeant, great ambition, great passion. Even in bed he over-reaches himself, exhausts himself. And he is very jealous, consumed by it, I'm afraid. He hates my Lord Hunsdon, who is, of course, my lover, and he hates your master too. You should be very careful of him.'

Dodd felt his jaw drop. 'Ah thocht . . .' he gargled. 'I hadnae thought he was that kind of man.'

Mistress Bassano only smiled again and glided off into the garden. Dodd discovered he was one of the last remaining guests still out in the dusk and hurried back to the house. On the way he thought he glimpsed Mistress Bassano, locked in an embrace with somebody whose balding forehead gleamed in the last light of the west.

Carey was playing primero with the Earl and the other over-dressed men of his affinity, cold and bright as a polished silver plate, calling his usual point-score of 'eighty-four' amid sarcastic groans. Dodd stood just inside the door and watched for a little while, trying not to think about what Shakespeare was getting up to in the shrubbery, nor what Mistress Bassano had said about him, nor the likelihood of Carey losing hundreds of pounds in this kind of company and in the mood he was in.

Christ, what do I care? Dodd demanded of himself; I'm not his mam.

'Are you joining us, Sergeant?' Carey called over to him, to Dodd's surprise, pulling in quite a respectable pot of gold coin.

'Och God, no,' Dodd said. 'Ye're all too good for me. Ye'd have the shirt off ma back, for what guid it would dae ye.'

'You disappoint me, Sergeant Dodd,' said the Earl, as hectic-eyed as Carey and even more drunk. 'I'd heard the men of Cumberland never turn down a challenge.'

'Nor we dinna,' said Dodd, thoroughly tired of being needled. 'Name yer place and yer weapons and I'm yer man.'

There was a moment of silence in the overcrowded, candle-heated room and Carey leaned sideways to whisper in the Earl's ear. The overdressed southern catamite smiled widely.

'Why, Sergeant, I think you misunderstood me. I only meant to challenge you to a card game.'

'Ay,' said Dodd, privately quite amused at this climbdown. 'Well, my lord, in that case there's nae shame in admitting ye'd have the mastery over me in any card game ye care tae mention. I've no' the experience nor the resources to meet ye on that field, eh, my lord?' He swallowed down a yawn. 'Ah'm nobbut a country farmer, me. An' wi' yer permission, my lord, Ah'll gang tae ma rest.'

After translation from Carey, the Earl waved negligently at one of the servants. 'Of course, Sergeant. Goodnight, pleasant dreams.'

'Ay, the same to ye, my lord.'

Dodd followed the servant through the carved and marbled rooms, feeling that if Carey didn't see some sense soon, he'd head north by himself.

Obviously, the Southampton household thought he must be Carey's henchman because the servant led him to a truckle bed in a very magnificent bedroom, painted with pictures that made you think you were looking at the sky filled with angels and fat cherubs and the bed hung around with tapestry curtains. Dodd took one look at it and decided he preferred the truckle bed anyway: how could you sleep with no air at all reaching you? He left the watchlight burning and slowly and carefully negotiated his way through the multiplicity of buttons and laces involved in dressing as befitted his station in London.

He woke already on his feet and his dagger in his hand because somebody was moving around in the room.

'It's only me, Henry,' came Carey's voice. 'Don't kill me.'

'Och,' moaned Dodd. 'What the hell are ye doing?' He scrubbed the heel of his palm in his eyes as Carey, with infinite care, transferred the watchcandle to a nest of candles in a corner next to a mirror and lit the room.

'I was . . . er . . . trying to find the pot,' said Carey in the slow painstaking way of the magnificently drunk. 'But it eluded me.'

Dodd blinked his eyes hard. 'It's in the fireplace. Dinna drop it,' he growled, not trying to hide the fact that he was staring at Carey's face where the clear print of a woman's hand was glowing red like the brand of Cain.

Carey swayed over to the fireplace and obeyed what was evidently a very peremptory call of nature, judging by the time it took him. Dodd sat down on the truckle bed again and rubbed his face with his hands, lay down to try and get some more sleep.

No, the bloody Courtier could not let him rest. Carey was next to the bed, reeking of aqua vitae and tobacco smoke.

'Very sorry, Henry,' he said. 'I'm afraid I'm . . . er . . . stuck.'

'What?'

'Can't get out of this suit without help. Irritating, but there you are. Fashion.'

'Och, Christ.'

'No Barnabus. No helpful woman. You . . . you're . . . you're it.'

Murder in his heart, but not sufficiently annoyed with Carey to make him sleep in his uncomfortable fancy clothes, Dodd got up again and followed his instructions as to which laces to untie. All the back ones were inextricably knotted.

'What happened tae the woman?' Dodd asked as he picked away at them, the curiously neutral intimacy of helping another man undress giving him unwonted freedom to ask.

'Gone back to Father. In a litter. Very cross.'

'Is that so? What happened to your face?'

Carey took off his elegant kid gloves and fingered the weal with a nailless finger. 'All my fault,' he said. 'Tactless. Very.'

'Och, ay?'

'Advice for you, Henry. When you're . . . er . . . when you're making love to a woman, try and . . . er . . . remember who she is.'

With magnificent self-control, Dodd did not laugh. 'Och?'

'Yes. At a . . . sensitive moment. Called her Elizabeth.'

Dodd sucked air through his teeth, contemplating Janet's likely reaction to such a mistake.

'Pity really. Wonderful body.'

'Ay.'

'My . . . er . . . my child, I think. Not sure. Could be Father's.'

'Could be Will Shakespeare's?' Dodd asked, some small devil in him wanting to make trouble for Mistress Bassano.

Carey contemplated this in silence as the last laces finally gave way, releasing the back of his gorgeous doublet from the waistband of his lily-encrusted trunk-hose. He had been fumbling with buttons while Dodd worked on the laces and the doublet finally came off, revealing the padded waistcoat that held up his hose. He moved away, shaking his head.

'Thank you,' he said. 'Manage now.'

Dodd lay down again, properly awake by now but determined to go back to sleep, turned his shoulder on Carey's continued troubles with his clothes. Serve him right for wearing such daft duds.

'Int'resting, what you say.' Carey was still talking, though by the smell he should have sloshed with every step. God, did the man never stop? 'The poet, eh? Thought so, wasn't sure. Said so. She denied it. Couldn't deny calling her Elizabeth. Rude of me. But . . . er . . . she'd no call to sneer at her for being provincial. Isn't. Anyway, what's wrong with provincial?'

'If ye're askin' me,' said Dodd wearily, 'Lady Widdrington is worth a thousand of Mistress Bassano, for all her pretty paps and all her conniving ways.'

'Father likes her. So does Will, it seems.'

'Then they can have her.'

'Yes, but . . . Elizabeth won't let me have her,' said Carey sadly. 'Won't. Tried everything. Won't let me bed her. 'S terrible. Never happened before. Can't think. Can't sleep. Can't bloody fuck another woman without . . . mistaking her. Terrible.'

Och God, thought Dodd in despair, any minute now the bastard'll be weeping on my shoulder. I want to go to sleep. I'm tired. I don't like London. I don't like all these fine houses and fine beds and fine courtiers. I want to go home.

'Go to bed,' he growled unsympathetically.

The magnificent four-poster creaked as Carey collapsed into it, with typical selfishness leaving the candelabrum in the corner still blazing with light. Sighing heavily, Dodd got up once more, snuffed the candles and left the watchlight in case Carey needed to find the pot again.

'Balls're bloody killing me,' moaned Carey as Dodd passed the fourposter. Firmly resisting the impulse to tell the Courtier what he thought of him, Dodd went back to bed.

Sunday 3rd September 1592, early morning

7

It gave Dodd inordinate pleasure, just for once, to be up before the Courtier, fully dressed even if it was in that nuisance of a suit, and having eaten his bread and cheese and drunk his morning small beer. He made no attempt to be quiet when he opened up the window and the shutters to let in the pale dawn and birdsong and nor did he keep his voice down when he told the manservant who brought in their breakfast to do something about the brimming pot by the fireplace.

Getting bored with listening to Carey's sawpit grunting, Dodd went out into the silent morning house, lost himself and ended up in the kitchen where the cook found him a sleepy pageboy to show him around. They inspected the stables and the mews and Dodd took a turn in the dew-soaked garden, marvelling at the trees and bushes there that had never ever been cut for firewood nor trampled over by raiders.

At last he wandered back to his and Carey's chamber where he found the Courtier sitting in his shirt on the bed, shakily drinking mild beer.

'Ah. Good morning, sir,' he said as loudly and cheerfully as he could. 'And how are ye feeling this fine morning?'

'Don't,' said Carey carefully. 'Don't bloody push it, Dodd.'

'Och,' said Dodd, enjoying himself. 'Is the light too bright for ye, sir. Will I shut the shutters for ye?' Perhaps he did bang them a bit hard but it was such fun to watch Carey wince. That'll learn ye to be happy in the morning, Dodd thought savagely.

Carey shut his eyes and sighed. 'All right,' he said. 'I'm not expecting sympathy.'

'That's lucky, sir. Ye never give me any. Now. What are we gonnae do about yer brother? Eh?'

'What do you care about Edmund?'

'Not a damned thing. Only I wantae go home and I can see we willnae leave this bastard city until we find yer brother, so let's get on wi' it.'

He picked up the outrageously pretty suit that Carey had left draped over the clothes chest and tossed it onto the bed beside him.

'Will I help ye dress, sir, or would ye like me to go fetch a manservant that kens how to dae it?'

Carey circled his long fingers in his temples, squeezed his eyes tight shut and opened them again. 'Let's not make a fuss. You help.'

'Ay, sir.'

They went through the stupidly complicated business in silence, except for curt instructions from Carey. At last he put on his hat and they went out into the passageway and down the stairs.

'Where's Shakespeare?' Carey wanted to know.

'I dinna ken. D'ye want him, though? Yon pretty woman said he was spying on yer father.'

Carey's bloodshot eyes opened wide at that. 'Did she say that? Mistress Bassano?'

'Ay, sir, last night in the garden.'

Carey blinked contemplatively at a heraldic blaze of stained glass making pools of coloured light on the floorboards. 'It could be true. Marlowe's not the only poet who doubles as a spy.'

'Ay, sir.'

'On the other hand, she could be spying on my father herself and trying to put suspicion on Will to get back at him.'

'Ay.' The whole thing was too complicated for Dodd. He focused on the important thing. 'But it disnae matter in any case, since we have tae find yer brother. Or his corpse.'

Carey winced again. As they came into the wide marble entrance hall, he paused. 'We'll go and fetch Barnabus from the lodgings. Then we're going after this alchemist, Jenkins.'

That seemed reasonable enough. Carey took leave of Southampton's majordomo with some elaborately grateful phrases that sounded as if he picked them ready-made from the back of his mind, and only shuddered a little as they went out into the full sunlight. Dodd remembered to look round for bailiffs as they went out across the little bridge over the moat and round by country lanes full of dust heading eastwards, parallel to Holborn. There were a few men practising at the butts with their longbows in a field, puny little light bows and they weren't very good either, Dodd noted. Carey turned right down a broad lane that narrowed until it passed between high garden walls. A heavy sweet scent wafted across from the lefthand garden. Carey gestured.

'Ely Place Garden. Hatton makes a fortune from it.'

'Ay?' said Dodd, hefting himself up and peering over the wall at a sea of pink and red. 'Fancy? Fra flowers?'

'Rosewater,' explained Carey. 'Supplies the court.'

'Ay?'

Carey ducked down a little lane that passed by what looked like another monastery courtyard, and then into a wide crossroads by a square-towered church. He paused there and blinked cautiously around. He looked as if the effort of walking in his fancy doublet and padded waistcoat was making him sweat, and he didn't look very well. Could he have plague, perhaps? No, thought Dodd, all that ails him is drink and serve him right.

'That's Shoe Lane,' Carey croaked, swallowing a couple of times. 'You go down first and if you see anything you don't like, come back and tell me. It'll come out by the Fleet Street conduit. If you see a lot of well-dressed women there, not doing very much, come back and tell me. Off you go.'

He leaned elegantly in the shadow of the church porch, took off his hat and mopped his brow, while Dodd wandered down the lane between houses and garden walls, humming a ballad to himself. The conduit was running bright with water, but there were only a couple of maidservants with yokes on their shoulders busily chatting as they slowly filled their buckets. Dodd went back and waved a thumbs-up to Carey, who came upright with noticeable effort and followed.

They crossed Fleet Street at the wide point by the conduit, the girls staring to see a courtier up so early, and Carey nipped into an alley that gave onto a courtyard in front of a large handsome house where the servants were just opening the shutters. Dodd tensed when he saw a couple of men standing negligently in the doorway of one of the other houses. He nudged Carey, who glanced at them and shook his head.

'Heneage's men keeping an eye on the French ambassador.'

'Eh?'

Carey gestured at the big house. 'Salisbury House, French ambassador's lodgings.'

That was interesting, thought Dodd, squinting up at the bright diamond windows. Were there Frenchmen actually inside? What did they look like? He now knew they didn't actually have tails, but it stood to reason they must be different from Englishmen.

Carey was slipping into a narrow little wynd between houses and a garden wall, passed under a roof made of touching upper storeys and emerged onto one of the salty muddy lanes that gave onto the Thames. The tide was in – you could see water gleaming at the end to their left.

Looking at the river, Dodd lost track of Carey for a moment, but saw the small alley he must have gone into, like a rabbit into his hole. London was a warren and no mistake. How did anybody ever keep track of where he was?

Hurrying to the end of it, Dodd came out into a cloister courtyard he recognised, saw Carey's suit slipping into an alleyway at the other side of it, into the stair entrance under the figure of the woman tumbler standing on a rope with her head knocked off, and up the stairs all the way to the top.

On the last flight of stairs Dodd saw a sight that froze him in his tracks. It was a dead rat, black as sin, and swollen, lying out there in the open. Nameless dread filled Dodd and if Carey hadn't been ahead of him, he would have turned tail and run. But he wasn't a wean or a woman to be afeared of rats, though he was afraid of them, and he forced himself to go past, only to bump into Carey, standing stock still on the tiny landing.

Carey was staring, lips slightly parted, face ashen, at the door of their lodgings. There was a red cross branded there, the paint still wet, the latch sealed and a piece of paper nailed beside it. The plague-finders could only have left a few minutes before.

Dodd's legs felt weak and shaky. Simon Barnet and Barnabus Cooke were on the other side of that door, along with Tamburlain the Great, Barnabus's fighting cock. And Simon Barnet's family had been visited by God's wrath, and he must have gone in to say goodbye to his mam, must have done. You couldn't blame the lad, but that's how he had taken it and Barnabus must have taken it from him. Plague wasn't like a knife that you could see, it was mysterious, it struck where it wanted to.

As if there were no danger there, Carey went and hammered on the door. 'Barnabus! Simon!' he roared. For answer the cock crowed, and they could hear it flapping heavily about beyond the door. Nothing else. No sound of humanity at all.

Carey lifted his hand to break the seal on the latch, and that galvanised Dodd into action. He grabbed the Courtier's arm and pulled him back.

'Nay, sir. Ye willnae go in,' he growled.

'But ...' There were tears standing in Carey's eyes. 'I can't leave them there.'

'Ye must. There's naething ye can do, save take the plague yersen.'

For a moment Carey resisted and something cold and calm inside Dodd got ready to hit him. 'I've seen plague, sir, back when I were a wean, when it hit us in Upper Tynedale. There's nothing ye can do, nothing. It gets in the air and if ye breathe near a man with the plague, ye get it yerself. Ye cannae go in.'

For a moment Carey stayed rigid by the door, Dodd still holding his arm, and then he relaxed, turned away and headed blindly down the stairs again.

We might have it already, Dodd thought as he followed, both of us might be just a day away from horrible pain and fever and death, you can never tell and Barnabus was with us yesterday when it might have been on him already, you can't tell with plague, there's no way of knowing until you get a headache or start sneezing and the black marks start rising on your neck and armpits and groin ...

Carey was walking out of the cloister, across a little walled lane, to an elaborate gate. He tested it and found it opened, went through into a large walled garden full of big trees, so it was almost like a forest. Dodd could not get used to the way London ambushed you: five steps away from closepacked tumbled houses squatting in the ruins of a monastery and you came out in a cool green place, with grass and flowers as if you had escaped into the countryside by magic.

Carey didn't sit down under a tree, but leaned against the smooth trunk of an elm and blinked up at the blue sky between the leaves. Dodd hitched up the back of his hose and sat down on one of the roots. Neither of them said anything for a while, but they listened to the birds singing in the trees for all the world as if there were no such things as sickness and death.

'I didn't realise the plague was so bad in London,' Carey said, voice remote. 'Was that Barnabus's little secret?'

Dodd sighed, loath to explain what he knew. Best get on with it, he thought, and weather the storm.

He told Carey what had happened to Simon Barnet's family and Carey simply took in the information.

'Why didn't you tell me, Henry?'

Dodd felt guilty. 'I'm sorry,' he said. 'I should have. But Barnabus begged me and so I didnae.'

'I see now why you're so anxious to leave London.'

'Ay, sir. Will we go and find your brother now?'

'It has got a bit more urgent, hasn't it?' drawled Carey. 'I mean, either one of us or both of us could be dead of plague tomorrow, couldn't we?'

'Ay, sir.'

'I wish you'd told me earlier.'

'Ay, sir. So do I.'

Carey shrugged. 'We'll try Peter Cheke again,' he said, and strode between trees to a small passageway running round the back of a magnificent hall facing a courtyard with a handsome round church in it. He went up the side of the church, past the railings, past some chickens and a small midden heap and came to another gate that gave onto Fleet Street. There he waited for

Dodd to catch up, peered out onto Fleet Street and Dodd scouted ahead. The street was filling with people, handcarts, beggars, pigs going to market driven by children, and the shops opening up on either side. As far as you could tell with so many strangers, it seemed safe enough.

They had passed the conduit at the end of Shoe Lane, heading for Fleet Bridge, when it happened. Dodd was a little ahead of Carey, keeping his eyes peeled for men in buff coats, but unable to stop his mind wandering back to speculating on what was happening in their lodgings.

A man in a wool suit tapped his shoulder. 'Sir Robert Carey?'

'Nay,' said Dodd as loudly as he could. 'I'm not him.'

The man smiled cynically, and held Dodd's left arm above the elbow in a very painful grip. 'No, sir, of course you're not.'

'Will ye let me go?' Dodd demanded belligerently. Two other men smartly dressed in grey wool and lace trimmed falling-bands were suddenly on the other side of him. One of them had a cosh in his hand, the other had his sword drawn.

'Please sir, let's not make a scene,' said the man who had hold of Dodd's arm. 'Sir Robert Carey, I must hereby serve you with a warrant for a debt of four hundred and twenty pounds, five shillings.'

'Ye've made a mistake. Ah'm no' Sir Robert.'

The bailiff smiled kindly. 'Nice try, sir. We was warned you'd let on you was someone else.'

Dodd's hand was on his swordhilt, but a fourth heavyset man had joined the party surrounding him. This one briskly caught his right arm and twisted it up behind his back while the one who had first spoken to him held a knife under Dodd's chin and tucked the piece of paper he had read from into Dodd's doublet.

'I'm not Sir Robert Carey,' shouted Dodd, furiously. 'If ye want him he's over there.'

The bailiff looked casually over his shoulder in the direction Dodd was pointing and smiled again. 'Yes, sir. An old one but a good one. Please come along now. We don't want to 'ave to 'urt you.'

Admittedly there was absolutely no trace of Carey anywhere

on the crowded street. The slimy toad must have run for it as soon as Dodd was surrounded, God damn him for a lily-livered sodomite . . .

Boiling with rage at such betrayal, Dodd let himself be hustled along in the direction he and Carey had been travelling, over Fleet Bridge, under the overgrown houses that made a vault above the alley, and up the lane beside the little stinking river to a large double gatehouse. The postern gate opened at once to the bailiff's knock and Dodd was hustled inside, blinking at the sudden darkness.

'Sir Robert Carey,' announced one of the bailiffs. 'On a warrant for debt, Mr Newton.'

A wide beetle-browed man with a heavily pock-marked face came hurrying out of the gatehouse lodgings, rubbing his hands and bowing lavishly.

'Sir Robert Carey, eh?' he said delightedly. 'Pleased to meet you at last, sir.'

'I tell ye,' growled Dodd, 'I am not Sir Robert Carey. I'm Henry Dodd, Land Sergeant of Gilsland, and I dinna owe onybody a penny.'

Mr Newton tutted gently. 'Dear me, sir, that won't wash 'ere, we know your little game. Now come along and let's do the paperwork, there's a good gentleman.'

'Ye've got the wrong man,' Dodd ground out between his teeth. 'I'm no' the one ye want. There's nae point in putting me in gaol, I'm no' Sir Robert . . .'

'So you say. But we was warned you'd come it the northerner once we caught you, so we know all about that. So why don't you give it up, eh? It's not dignified.'

Dodd gave a mighty heave and tried to trip the bailiff who was still wrenching his arm. Newton moved in close and rammed the end of his cosh into Dodd's stomach a couple of times. Dodd bent and whooped and saw stars for a few seconds. A horny thumb and forefinger gripped his ear.

'I don't want to have to give you a hiding, Sir Robert, I know the proper respect for me betters, but I will have order in my gaol, do you understand me? If I have to, I'll chain you, Queen's cousin or no, so don't make trouble. Now let's go and do the paperwork, eh? Get you settled in.'

Unable to do more than stay on his feet and wheeze, Dodd went where they pushed him into the guardchamber of the gatehouse.

It so happened that Nan was down on her hands and knees polishing one of the brasses, the one with the knight in armour and his lady wearing long flowing robes, when the handsome gentleman in the lily-embroidered trunk hose came sliding quickly and softly into the empty church, breathing a little hard. He paused as he shut the door to squint through the narrow gap for a minute, then let it close. He looked all around him at the brightly coloured tombs, the whitewashed walls that writhed with carved vine-leaves and fat bunches of grapes, the headless saints, and the high altar with its beautiful cloth and its empty candlesticks with no sanctuary lamp burning. He took a long stride to come up the aisle, but then paused as he remembered himself, took his hat off reverently. Nan began to warm to him, despite the lurid high fashion of his clothes, as she peered around one of the box pews, to see him walking up to the altar rails where he knelt, sighed and bent his chestnut head in prayer, although she was disappointed to see he didn't cross himself.

Her sight wasn't good enough to make out his face clearly, though he seemed a well-made gentleman, very tall and long-legged, but Nan felt she approved of him. She finished polishing the lady's face and thought about slipping out the sacristy door to find the vicar.

'Goodwife, I'd be grateful if you didn't fetch anybody. I won't be here long,' said the gentleman, without looking round.

She heaved herself up from the floor, folding her duster, and rubbing her creaking knees, then waddled round the box pew to curtsey to him.

He was standing by the altar rails now, bowed in return, smiled faintly down at her.

'I promise I'm not after the candlesticks, goodwife.'

'And much good they would do you if you were, sir,' she said tartly, 'since they're chained to the wall.'

'Ah.'

She blinked critically at him. He looked pale and there was a sheen of sweat on him which wasn't totally explained by his velvet doublet since the church was cool and dim. 'Can I help you, sir?' she asked, with another little curtsey.

'I very much doubt it.'

Nan shook her head. People always thought that because she was round, short and old, she was useless. 'Well, if you're here for a rest from the sun, which is certainly powerful for September, come into the pew and sit down, sir.'

He hesitated, then shrugged and let her open the door of the churchwarden's pew, usher him into it. His clothes were too fashionable to let him sit comfortably, so he leaned diagonally on the bench.

'Can I fetch you anything, sir?' she asked. 'Would you like some wine?'

'Communion wine?' he asked, sceptically. She grinned at him.

'I always replace it.'

'Ah.' He passed his tongue over his lower lip which did look dry. 'Well, why not?'

She trotted out into the aisle and went into the sacristy where she had a spare key to the locked cupboard where the vicar kept the wine. She came back with two plain silver goblets on a tray which held mixed water and wine since she believed in the curative properties of wine but could not afford to replace too much. 'The water is from St Bride's well itself,' she said, as she gave one of the goblets to the gentleman. 'It's clear and pure as dew, sir, and sovereign against all kinds of troubles: shingles, the falling sickness, leprosy, and scrofula too.'

'A pity I don't suffer from any of those things.'

'Now you never will, sir.'

He toasted her, and drank. 'How does it do against plague, cowardice and debt?'

She sat herself down on the bench with a sigh at the ache in her old bones, and drank from her own goblet.

'Oh, and idiocy,' added the gentleman.

'Who was chasing you, sir?' Nan asked. Well, if an old woman couldn't ask nosy questions, who could?

The gentleman shut his eyes briefly. Up close, Nan could see they were bright blue and also rather bloodshot. Something about his face was familiar, the beak of his nose, the high cheekbones, but she couldn't place it. She was quite sure she had never met him before.

'Bailiffs,' he said. 'Waving warrants for debt.' He sighed again, rubbed elegantly gloved fingers into his eyesockets. 'I let them arrest a friend of mine, one of the most decent and loyal men I've ever met, and I ran like a bloody rabbit to get away. Nice, eh?'

'And the plague?'

'My servants have it and my lodgings have been sealed.'

Nan tutted sympathetically and poured him more of the watered wine from the flagon. 'And the idiocy, sir? You don't look like an idiot.'

He raised winged eyebrows at this cheekiness and smiled shortly. 'I've been acting like a damned idiot ever since I got to London, goodwife. Looks aren't everything.'

'No indeed, sir. What will you do now?'

He puffed out a breath. 'I haven't the faintest bloody idea.'

She leaned forward and patted his arm. 'Please, sir,' she said. 'This is God's house. Don't swear.'

'Sorry.'

Despite her opportunities, Nan drank very little, preferring the life-giving water of the well. The wine was beginning to go to her head slightly and she waved her plump work-hardened hand at the church above and around them. 'I know it doesn't look like it any more,' she confided. 'You should have seen the church before the change in the boy-King's reign, when it was all painted with bright colours and the roof beams were gilded and stars painted there. Oh, it was beautiful, with the light through the glass. Noah's Ark was on that wall, before they whitewashed it, with elephants and striped horses too, and on this wall was the marriage at Cana and St Bride at the well, giving the child Jesus a drink. The same water from this very well, sir, Our Saviour drank from it, almost where we're standing.'

'When did Jesus Christ do that?' asked the gentleman.

'When he flew here as a child and got lost, and St Bride gave him her water and so he could fly back home to Our Lady in Palestine.'

The gentleman blinked a couple of times, but didn't laugh as one over-educated Divine had in the past. 'Oh?' he said.

'And certainly, if he didn't, he could have, so perhaps he did.'

'Ah. It's not mentioned in the Bible, though.'

'No, well, sir, if you read it, you'll find many things not mentioned there.'

The gentleman coughed. 'Er . . . yes.'

'The New World, for instance. Though I heard once that St Bride travelled there herself, in a silver boat.'

'Did she?'

She smiled sunnily at him. 'Perhaps. Perhaps not.'

He nodded abstractedly, clearly humouring her which was at least polite of him. His attention had wandered again, though, his wide shoulders were sagging with worry.

'Let me help, sir,' she coaxed, putting her hand on his velvet clad forearm. 'Tell me your troubles and perhaps you'll see a way through them.'

'I don't really see how you could . . .'

'Not me, sir,' she said simply. 'You. If you give yourself time to think, it's wonderful what notions God will put in your head.'

'He hasn't yet, and I can't say I blame Him, the way I've been behaving.'

She patted the arm, which felt very tense. 'We're all sinners, sir. If Our Saviour was walking in London town today, we would be the first he'd invite to dinner.'

Now that was better. What a charming smile the gentleman had to be sure.

'Well now, mother,' he said. 'That's certainly true.'

He stared at the high altar for a moment, his bright eyes flicking unseeingly between the wonderful painted glass of the workers in the vineyard and the scarred wooden saints of the altar-screen.

'Tell me. If only to pass the time while you wait for your enemies to give up.'

'It doesn't make sense,' he said to himself. 'I know he was wearing one of my old suits, but still . . . Mother, if you were looking for a popinjay courtier and you saw one man in a woollen suit and one man tricked out like me, which would you pick?'

Nan smiled and pointed at him.

'Quite. But I distinctly heard them address him as Sir Robert . . . by my name, and ignore his denials.'

'Perhaps a friend of yours pointed out the wrong man.'

'Yes, but . . . why? Why not have them arrest somebody completely different. Why Dodd? It doesn't make . . .' He stopped and stared at her without seeing her at all. 'I wonder. Would he do that? Why?'

Nan said nothing, only addressed an heretical prayer to St Bride and also St Jude to do something to help the young man. It seemed her prayer was answered for he suddenly smiled at her radiantly.

'I'm a fool. I've treed myself again. He's probably waiting outside with a good force of pursuivants. When is the Sunday Service?'

'In about an hour, at nine of the clock.'

'Excellent. Mother, would you run an errand for me?'

She smiled impishly. 'Walk, certainly. Run – no.'

Kit Marlowe waited for his henchmen, sitting perched languidly on the churchyard wall of St Bride's. He was annoyed with himself and with Carey. He hadn't thought the man so dense, had in fact considered him not far off his own intellectual equal, for all the Courtier's lack of the classics. And you could see what King James of Scotland saw in him; such a pity Carey only liked women.

Marlowe had one man to cover the side door and was himself watching the main door. It was possible of course that the Courtier had found another way of escape, but Marlowe doubted it because his men were scattered strategically around the various alleys and he would have heard the noise if Carey tried to get past them.

Londoners dressed in their best clothes were arriving in the courtyard, the women gathering in bright knots to chatter, the men talking and nodding among themselves. Oh now, that was annoying. He had forgotten that Sunday Service would be starting soon, but it meant he couldn't search the place, even after his men had arrived. He should have gone straight in.

A little old woman came out of the church, trotted past with her hat on, as short and round as a chesspiece. He moved to block her path.

'Goodwife, a word please.'

'Yes, sir?' She curtseyed and smiled at him.

'I am looking for a Papist gentleman, very well dressed in cramoisie velvet, lilies on his hose, dark red hair, blue eyes, a little the look of Her Majesty the Queen. Have you seen such a man?'

Her round wrinkled face blinked up at him. 'A Papist gentleman, sir? Fancy!'

'Yes, a very dangerous man. Did he come into your church?'

'Why would a Papist go into our church?'

'To hide from me.'

'Oh, sir. I've not seen any dangerous Papists.'

'Where are you going?'

'To fetch vestments. Why, sir?' she said. 'Are you waiting for the service to begin?'

'Yes, goodwife,' he said shortly.

She nodded her head inanely. 'Isn't St Bride's beautiful in the sunshine?' she said. 'Isn't it a work of God to see it. We have a well of miraculous water, you know? Did you know that Our Lord drank from the well, our very own well?'

'Did He?'

'Oh, He did sir, it's quite certain.'

Marlowe rolled his eyes. 'Thank you, goodwife.'

'Then I'll see you at prayer, sir.'

'No doubt.'

'Well, God be with you, sir.'

Marlowe didn't give the normal reply, only turned his face and stared pointedly at the beheaded saints on the church wall. 'I very much doubt it,' he muttered, and ignored her curtsey as she trotted past.

The church was definitely filling up fast now, mothers with their children in clean caps, arguing and being threatened with beatings and bribes if they made as much noise as last time, elderly men with long beards and fine gowns . . . All of Fleet Street was there, and Fleet Lane and Ludgate Hill.

'There you are again, sir,' said a perky cracked voice beside him, and the cleaner was simpering up at him again, puffing hard with a heavy cloth bag in her hand. 'Well, would you care to see the vestments? Very beautiful, made of silk, you know, as beautiful as a rainbow.'

'No thank you, goodwife,' said Marlowe impatiently, watching hard for anyone going against the throng. If he was there, Carey would almost certainly wait through the Service and then try to slip out with the crowds of folk as cover – it was the obvious thing to do.

One of Marlowe's men came over for orders as the church cleaner went in at the sacristy door, and Marlowe disposed them as best he could. He was a hunter, and his fox had gone to earth. What he really needed were terriers and an ecclesiastical warrant. Unfortunately, it took at least three days to get one from the argumentative church courts. But Carey had to leave the church at some stage if he was going to do anything now he had no men to his back, and that's when Marlowe would nip him out. Then they could talk.

Marlowe sighed. Somebody had to go into the church, to be ready by the door, but not him. Carey knew his face too well.

Divine Service had never seemed so long before. Marlowe presumed the vicar was preaching the evils of atheism and the essential nature of God's church, with no doubt some lurid and dubious tales of Hell to keep the congregation in awe. It passed his understanding why anyone ever believed anything a priest said: how the Devil could anyone know what happened in Hell, since nobody was ever going to come back and describe it?

The church itself was nothing but a vast playhouse for instructing the people in subjection to their betters. He supposed it was good enough for the general run of men and for all women, of course, but anyone with a real brain must see through the mummery. However, hardly anyone did. They repeated meaningless words and yearned towards the void like the sheep they were.

At last the congregation was coming out. Marlowe stood straight and paid attention as the men took their leave of the vicar and the women started their ceaseless starling chatter again.

He waited, beginning to grow concerned. Leaving one man to watch the main door he went round to the side door but found it still locked. His man confirmed that none had come out.

He hurried back again and asked the man he had left there who had come out. An important family, some country bumpkins visiting London, another family, children, serving men.

'Any courtiers?'

'I'd have stopped him if I'd seen him, sir,' said the man, looking offended. 'I know what we're looking for. Tall, dark red hair, blue eyes, lilies on his hose. Right?'

'Nobody like that has come out?'

'No, sir. Nor anything even similar.'

The crowds were thinning, a few boys were being shouted at by their mother for tightrope-walking along the church wall. Marlowe folded his arms and his lips thinned with anger. Surely Carey hadn't given them the slip. His men weren't bright but their job involved watching carefully for men described to them and they were good at it. Also they were afraid of him and his power from Heneage. They wouldn't have missed Carey. He must still be skulking inside.

'Oh, the hell with this nonsense,' snapped Marlowe. 'We'll search the place.'

With his henchmen to back him, Marlowe went into the church and because he had to maintain some kind of respectability in front of his men, he took his hat off.

'Vicar,' he said to the portly man putting out the candles on the altar. 'I am going to search here for a Papist traitor I am seeking. Please don't put me in the position of having to order my men to lay hands on you.'

The vicar stood stock still, and seemed on the verge of protesting. Then he took a deep breath and gritted his teeth. 'I protest, sir,' he said. 'And I will be writing to the bishop this very afternoon.'

'Do as you like,' said Marlowe and nodded to his men to quarter the church.

They did, very carefully, and then the sacristy and that was when one of them came hurrying out, triumphantly waving a lace with a glittering aiglet.

Marlowe took it between his fingers and held it up to the light. It was a beautiful piece of work: gold, with the sharp point of the aiglet formed in the shape of a stork's beak. Nobody except a courtier would bother with such elaboration. The lace had been snapped by someone in too much of a hurry to untie his doublet points properly.

There had been no naked men in the crowd. 'Devil take it,' growled Marlowe. 'He changed his clothes.'

He spun on his heel and barked at the vicar, still standing at his altar. 'What did he put on?'

'I beg your pardon?'

'Don't pretend to be any stupider than you are. What was he wearing when he slipped out?'

'Who?'

'The man I am looking for, on the Queen's business, Sir Robert Carey. The man who left this on your sacristy floor.'

The vicar looked at the pretty little thing in Marlowe's fist. 'I really don't know what you're talking about.'

'What was he wearing?' Marlowe was pacing across the church up to the altar, advancing on the vicar who shrank back at first and then seemed to find some courage somewhere in his windy fat body and faced him boldly.

'Sir, I was working on my sermon, putting last minute touches to it, in my study. If there was a fugitive here, which I doubt, then to be sure he must have been wearing something. What it was, I have no idea.'

'The vestment bag. The old bitch coney-catched me,' said Marlowe to himself. 'Of course. Where's the old woman? A little short woman who burbled to me about St Bride?'

'Do you mean Nan? I'm sorry sir, she isn't here. She asked for the day off and I gave it to her and she's gone.'

'God damn it.'

'Will you stop taking the Lord's name in vain in my church?'

'No, I won't. It hasn't done me any harm yet and I doubt it will. I shall have words with my master, Mr Vice Chamberlain

Heneage, I shall have you investigated thoroughly for Papistry and loyalty, if it lies within my power I shall have you in Chelsea and question you myself.'

'I'm sure you would,' said the vicar with a patronising smile. 'But my own Lord of Hosts will protect me, quite possibly through the agency of my lord the Earl of Essex who is my temporal good lord.'

Marlowe was outbid and he knew it. In the feverish scheming of the court, Essex was implacably opposed to Heneage and worse, Essex hated Marlowe, whereas the Queen loved Essex and generally did what he asked. And Essex was the ultimate object of all Marlowe's manoeuvring.

Marlowe wrestled with the urge to punch the fatuous old man.

'If the gentleman returns who changed his clothes very hurriedly in your sacristy, tell him that Kit Marlowe wants to speak to him. I'll be at the Mermaid.'

'Certainly sir. Goodbye.' As if trying to rouse Marlowe to an even worse fury, the vicar lifted his hand in the three fingered sign for benediction. 'The Lord bless you and keep you, the Lord make his countenance to shine upon you . . .'

The church door banged behind Marlowe before the old man had finished his superstitious prattling.

For a moment Marlowe stood in the courtyard, irresolute, his thoughts disordered by anger. Carey had somehow managed to give him the slip, probably by changing into his henchman's old homespun clothes. He was loose in London; probably he was already on his way to Somerset House to talk to his father, or possibly he was taking horse in St Giles in the Fields, to ride to Oxford.

He beckoned his men over and gave them orders for the search, then headed towards the Mermaid inn for an early dinner. He needed a drink badly and he needed to sit and consider how to rescue his plan.

Nan stood by the stairwell in Whitefriars over which there had once been a handsome figure of Our Lady standing on the globe, now defaced by Reformers. The young man she had taken rather a liking to came clattering down, now dressed in a well-made homespun russet suit a bit wide for him and short in the breeches, and a leather jerkin, with a blue statute cap on his head. He had done his best to hide the colour of his hair and the excellence of his boots with mud and dust and he had kept his sword which had anyway been an incongruously plain broadsword. There was no question but that he had been a great deal more fine when in his courtly clothes, but she liked him better now. Also he had pawned the whole beautiful suit he had been wearing and got an astonishing price for it, some of which he had given her, without her asking, which had pleased her greatly. And he had told her to call him Robin which also pleased her.

'Are you sure about this, mother?' he asked her with a worried frown on his face. 'When I wished I could find a nurse for my servants, I never . . .'

She tutted at him and pulled down her little ruff to show him the round scars on her neck. 'See?' she said. 'I had the plague years ago, when I was a maid. We all got it but I was spared. You never get it twice. That was why I went to the nunnery, you know, my family was dead, except my uncle and he didn't want me.'

'I didn't know you were a nun.'

She beamed up at him. 'Why should you? And I'm not any more, now I clean St Bride's church.'

'Don't you mind?'

Young men were so sweet, so worried about things that didn't matter. 'No, of course not. I can pray all the Offices whenever I want to.'

'Do you do that?' he sounded impressed.

She laughed. 'Generally I forget.' She took his arm. 'Now help me up all these stairs, I'm not as young as I was.'

The climb left her breathless, so she sat down on the top step just above the dead rat and fanned herself while Robin used his wonderfully enamelled little tinder box and lit the candle she had told him to bring.

As he put it back into the pocket of his jerkin, he paused and frowned, pulled the pocket inside out and looked closely at the seams, as if he was searching for nits. Nan couldn't make out what he had seen, but she saw his lips move. 'Mercury?' he asked and frowned in puzzlement, then shook his head and put the pocket back.

She was recovered by then so she heaved herself up and took her knife, heated it in the flame and carefully prised off the seals on the door, leaving them hanging by their cords.

Cautiously she opened the door while the young man stood back, looking worried, and then she braced herself and went in.

The smell was bad but mainly because of the magnificent fighting cock roosting on the bedhead. It took its head out from under its wing and crowed once, then settled down to watch her with the cold beadiness of all fowl. The place was a mess, the small chest was open and its contents flung on the floor, the main bed had been stripped and the mattress lifted, slashed open. The man in the truckle was obviously dead, but the boy lying on the straw pallet just inside the door was not. He was trussed like a boiling chicken and efficiently gagged and as soon as she came in his tear-swollen eyes flicked open and he started grunting at her frantically.

She put her head round the door. 'There's no plague here,' she said. 'Or not yet. Come and look.'

Carey came in after only a moment's hesitation and stood staring at the scene for one frozen second. His fists bunched and his blue eyes blazed with rage.

'God damn them to hell.'

Seconds later he had his knife out and was carefully cutting the boy free of the ropes, undoing the gag and helping him spit out the wad of cloth in his mouth. The boy was weeping and couldn't talk because his mouth was too dry. After shutting the door to stop the cock getting out, Nan gave him some of the wine posset she had brought with her, mopped it when he dribbled. Carey was rubbing his purple and swollen hands and feet.

'Don't talk for a bit,' he told the desperate boy. 'It's all right, Simon. Don't worry.'

Leaving Nan to give Simon more wine and help him use the pot, Carey went over to the truckle bed and stood looking down at the twisted body there, the sheets filthy with blood and muck. Nan came over to look.

'He died hard, God rest him,' she said objectively. 'Was he stabbed?'

Carey had tears running freely down his face. He checked the body carefully and shook his head. Then he went to the window, opened the shutters and flung them wide so the man's soul could fly. He stood there a while, his head bowed. Nan waddled over to give him her handkerchief so he could blow his nose, and then he went back to the boy who was still weeping, clasped him like a brother and patted his shoulder.

Whatever the little ferret-faced man on the bed had died of, it certainly wasn't plague. There were no swellings at his neck, nor was his face blackened. From the disgusting state of the blankets, she thought he must have died of a flux or bad food. She carefully shut his eyes and put pennies on them to hold them shut, then she drew up the least horrible blanket to cover his face.

'One minute, mother,' said the young man behind her, his voice still choked.

She stepped aside and watched as he gingerly felt about the little man's soiled doublet and then reached under the pillow. He drew out a worn silver flask, that had once been nicely chased and enamelled. He looked at it carefully, then opened it and sniffed what was inside.

'Do you know what he died of?' she asked, seeing the enlightened expression on Carey's face.

'I think so,' he answered her gruffly. 'I saw a man die of the same thing yesterday morning.'

Nan tutted. 'It's no kind of plague I've ever seen. It isn't even the sweating sickness.'

Carey shook his head. 'I think it's not catching either,' he said. 'Except one way.'

He didn't explain any more, only went back to where Simon was sitting, tearing ravenously at the bread and cheese Nan had brought for her own meal. Carey squatted down in front of him.

'All right, Simon, what can you tell me?'

'It was awful, sir, it was terrible.' The boy was rubbing his cheek muscles and jaw hinges and wincing. His face was bruised and his lip was swollen from a cut but he was so desperate to talk that he was almost gabbling. 'Uncle Barney was sick in the night, he was up and down and then he was sick something horrible, and he wouldn't let me help, only said he thought it was something he'd eaten and he'd be better in the morning. So I went back to sleep, like he said, sir, I never meant him to . . . d . . . die . . . I never thought . . .'

'I don't think there was anything you could have done for him, Simon. Did he drink from this flask?'

'Oh, yes. He had it refilled at the boozing ken down the way, and drank that as well, said it was medicine, only it wasn't, it was aqua vitae, but that was before he took sick. He was scared because he had a headache and a fever like me, he was scared he had plague, see.'

'How's your head?'

'It's better, sir,' Simon sounded surprised. 'And me neck isn't stiff or anything. Do you think I won't get it, even though I kissed me mam goodbye?'

'You might not. Nobody knows why some people get it and some people don't.'

Simon was crying again. 'Me mam's dead now, in't she, sir? That's what Uncle Barney said. He said, if she was all covered in black spots, then she's as good as dead.'

Carey sighed. 'I don't know because I haven't seen her, but I'm afraid that is true.'

'Oh, sir. What am I going to do? Everybody's dead. 'Cept my sister and I don't like her.'

'Shh. Everybody has to die sometime.'

'Yes, but not all at once. Not like that.' He gestured at the shape on the truckle bed.

Carey sighed again. 'Tell me what happened. Your Uncle Barney was sick and you went back to sleep.'

'Yes, sir, 'cos I never knew how bad it was, he didn't tell me, he said I should . . .'

'Nobody's blaming you for sleeping. What happened? How did you come to be trussed up?'

'Oh, yes. Well, I went to sleep, like I said, sir. Next thing I knew, it was still night and they was banging on the door.'

'Who was?'

'They was. The men.'

'Who were they?'

'Didn't say, sir. I didn't want them to disturb Uncle Barney what had just dropped off, as I thought, so I went to open the door and tell them to be quiet and they just pushed it open and came in and one of them grabbed me and I tried to fight but he just clipped my ear and held me tighter and they searched the room. One of them looked at Uncle Barney and said, "Jesus", and then another one asked me questions.'

'What did they ask?'

'Where you were, sir, which I didn't know because Uncle Barney didn't tell me, and where your brother was, which I didn't know either and where some money was which I said you had and what we were doing in London which I said was looking for your brother . . .'

'Did they hurt you?'

'They knocked me about a bit, sir.'

'I can see that. Did they do anything . . . er . . . else?'

Simon shook his head. 'No, sir. Only they said they were going to tie me up and gag me because I was a bad boy and then they'd make sure nobody came in here at all until I was dead of thirst only they wouldn't if I'd tell them what they wanted to know, but I didn't know it, so I couldn't and Uncle Barney was dead so they couldn't ask him and they were worried in case it was plague, so they did what they said, they tied me up and . . . and . . . then they left me and then they scorched the cross on the door, I heard them, so I knew nobody would dare to come in and . . . and . . .'

Simon's shoulders hunched over and shook with sobs. Carey sat down next to him and let the boy howl into his shoulder. When the storm had died down a bit, he asked very softly, 'Did you know any of them, Simon? Had you ever seen any of them before?'

'Well, they was four of them, but I couldn't see their faces because they had cloths muffled up to their noses and their hats pulled down.'

'Was there anything at all about them that you can remember?'

'They sounded like courtiers, sir, gents.'

'Hm. What were their hands like? Rough? Smooth? Did they have rings?'

'Well, the one that did the talking had two rings but I don't remember no more, sir, honest I don't, I was so frightened, what with Uncle Barney being dead and the men hissing at me, and I couldn't think what with getting my head slapped and everything . . .'

'It's all right, Simon,' said Carey. 'You did the best you could. None of it was your fault. Do you know what they were looking for?'

'No, only it was small from the way they searched.'

'Hm.' Carey stared straight ahead of himself, at the dented plaster of the wall. 'The men expected me to be here?'

'Oh yes, sir, when they came in they all had their swords drawn and one of them had a dag with the match lit.'

'Hm. Do you think you could walk?'

Simon sniffled and rubbed his hands. 'I dunno, sir. My feet are killing me wiv pins and needles.'

'Try. I want you out of here in case the men come back.'

'But where will I go, sir? What can I do? My Uncle Barney's dead and . . . and . . .'

'Simon, do you think I'm going to put you on the streets because Barnabus is dead? Do you think that's the kind of man I am?'

Simon gulped hard. 'No, sir.'

'You're not thinking straight. We need to get you somewhere safe. Now it'll be a lot easier if you could walk down Fleet Street to Somerset House, but if you really can't manage, I'll get you a litter.'

Simon shook his head and struggled to his feet, biting his lips and leaning on Carey's arm. Then he sat down again.

'It hurts. But I think I can. But I can't do my boots up, my hands is too sore.'

Nan came over with the boy's boots and between them, they got them on. Then Carey took Nan to the window and looked out carefully.

'Mother,' he said looking straight in her eyes, so she found herself smiling and thinking what a pity it was she wasn't forty years younger. 'I want you to do me a great favour. Take this boy to Somerset House and ask to speak to my Lord Hunsdon. Tell him what we found here and what Simon told us and also tell him that Dodd's been arrested in mistake for me, God knows how. Can you do that?'

'My Lord Hunsdon?' she asked, very impressed. 'Is he your lord?'

'In a manner of speaking,' said the young man drily. 'Tell him Robin sent you and if he wants confirmation, you can tell him I said I'm at the reiving again, only for two-legged kine this time.'

'You're at the reiving again, for two-legged kine,' Nan repeated uncertainly.

'Don't be frightened if he laughs or shouts, that's just his way. Tell him Dodd's in the Fleet in mistake for me.'

'Will you not go with us?'

'No. I'll keep an eye on you, but my guess is that the men who did this might be watching the place and as it's me they want, I don't want them seeing me.'

'What if they stop us?'

'Play stupid but don't try anything with them, they're very dangerous.'

'I didn't take to the young man, your enemy.'

'No. I have a bone or two to pick with him.'

'And your servant?'

'Barnabus? He'll come to no harm here. I'll see he gets a decent burial when I can.'

'What about the fighting cock?'

Carey eyed the bird who stared back at him defiantly and decorated the ruined bed again. 'That's Tamburlain the Great. He's got water and he's got grain. I should think he'll be all right for the moment. I'll send someone with food and medicine to Simon's family as soon as I can.'

They helped Simon out onto the tiny landing and Nan used the candle very carefully to restick the seals. Carey had to carry the boy down the narrow winding stairs but once on the level Simon could shuffle along, holding tight to Nan's arm.

She walked down Fleet Street feeling heavy with fright, the boy sniffling beside her as he walked. The street was teeming with people, carts, large dangerous-looking men, women carrying buckets.

They passed the gauntlet of the beggars at Temple Bar and the ballad singer and the rat catcher with his strings of dead black rats slung across his back and onto the wide dusty Strand. When Simon showed her the gate to Somerset House she felt almost too frightened to try it, because it was so grand, but the boy insisted. They had to wait for a long time because the porter sent for the steward and when she said she had a message for my lord from Robin, this caused a flurry, before they were escorted into the magnificent marble entrance hall and then deep into the building. The steward's wife came to fetch Simon to her stillroom to dose him against plague and melancholy, which Nan found left her bereft since at least she had met the boy. This was so rich and brilliant a house, more elaborate than any church she had ever cleaned, it made her feel very small. They told her that my lord Baron Hunsdon was not at home, being out inspecting some properties, but was expected back that afternoon. They asked her if she wished to wait, or pass on her message, and she said conscientiously that she would wait.

Dodd had spent the morning trying to hang onto his temper. He had signed the Prison's logbook at the Deputy Gaoler's office in his own name, causing tuttings and sighings. Deputy Gaoler Newton wrote Sir Robert Carey's name next to it. Then two of Newton's bullyboys had held his arms while Newton personally searched his body, a process of nasty intimacy made worse by Newton's deliberate roughness. Triumphantly, he produced Dodd's purse and took one of the angels from it, biting it cautiously before he put it away. Ten shillings. Almost a week's wages.

'There's my garnish,' sneered Newton. 'Now, sir, the charge for the Knight's Commons is a shilling a night, or sixpence if you share a bed. The Eightpenny ward is eightpence a night or fourpence if you share.'

The charges were iniquitous. When Dodd had spent six months in ward at Jedburgh for one of his wife's relatives, the charge had only been a couple of pennies a day, though admittedly he had had to sleep on a bench instead of a bed and the food had been frightful.

'You'd better go in the Knight's Commons,' said Newton. 'Seeing as you're a knight.'

'I'm not a knight, thank God,' said Dodd. 'I'm the Land Sergeant of Gilsland.'

'Oh, really, sir, give over this nonsense. You'll go where I tell you and I say you're a gentleman, so you go in the Knight's Commons. Will you be wanting a bed on your own, sir?'

'Och, no, I'll share. I wouldna pay a shilling a night for the best inn in London.'

'Well, you would, sir, and more. But never mind. I take it kindly that you're willing to share, makes my job simpler. Now do I have your word as a gentleman that you won't cause trouble?'

'No, ye do not.'

'I'll have to chain you in that case.'

'Och. All right. I willna make trouble.'

'Your word on it, sir?'

'Ma word on it.'

Newton escorted him through the second gate and across the yard which boiled with people, men and women in all states of raggedness, most of them trading or working. There was a group of women gathered in the shade of an awning, sitting on the ground with their skirts spread out around them like brightly coloured pools, every white-capped head bent over some kind of linen stitchery and their fingers flashing.

Newton went over to one of the men playing cards in a doorway, sitting on boxes.

'Sir John,' he said. 'Here is Sir Robert Carey who is to be in your ward tonight.'

Sir John stood and bowed elaborately to Dodd who felt

215

embarrassed at his imposture, despite it not being his fault. He did his best to bow back.

'Sir Robert is amusing himself by pretending to be a northerner,' said Newton sarcastically. 'See if you can bring him to his senses.'

Newton and his henchmen stumped off across the crowded courtyard and Dodd watched them go, wishing he could bring his kin all the way from Upper Tynedale and Gilsland, raid the man's house, lift his kine, take his insight and beat him to a pulp for insolence. He sighed. God, it was hard to be a foreigner.

Sir John was squinting at him curiously.

'Sir Robert,' said the man in charge of the Knight's Commons, whose doublet was velvet and his Venetians brocade but the whole outfit sadly worn. 'I'm sorry to see you in this state. How may I be of assistance, sir?'

Well, that was polite at least. What would Carey have said? Something witty about Sir John helping him by giving him four hundred pounds, no doubt. But that was not Dodd's style.

'Sir,' he said firmly, doing his best to copy the southern way of talking. 'There's been some kind of mistake. I am not Sir Robert. Ma right name is Henry Dodd an' I dinna owe anybody in this town a penny. But I canna persuade Newton of it.'

Sir John nodded noncommittally, evidently not believing him.

'That's all right, sir,' he said respectfully. 'I can see you're incognito.'

'But I'm not incognito, whatever that means. I am what I am. I dinna want tae make any pretence at being what I'm not. D'ye follow me, sir? I'm no mair a gentleman than Newton, thank God.'

Sir John nodded again. 'Well, sir,' he said. 'I myself have never met Sir Robert Carey before now, and so I cannot tell whether what you say is true or not. But Newton seems to think you are Carey and his word is law in this prison. So I suggest you go with what he says and be a gentleman until your friends can come and sort out the muddle.'

Dodd sighed again. It made him feel profoundly uneasy to have a gentleman calling him sir, it felt like he was sitting on top of a mountain and might fall off at any time. He couldn't enjoy being respected for something he was not.

'Is it right Newton can chain me if I make trouble, and me a gentleman an' all?'

'Oh yes, sir. I'm surprised he hasn't done it already; he usually does for the first week to encourage you to pay him garnish to strike them off. Then he chains you again until you run out of money.' Sir John gestured at one of the other primero players, a skinny man with a cavernous cough and an exhausted expression, whose damask doublet hung in folds on him and whose feet were chained.

'What else can he do?'

Sir John pointed at a group of ominous wooden shapes in the other corner of the courtyard; Dodd narrowed his eyes and saw they were a set of stocks, a pillory and a whipping post.

'Or,' added Sir John, 'he can throw you in the Hole which is six inches deep in water from the Fleet and has no light and not much air.'

'Ay,' said Dodd gloomily. 'Well, nae doot he must keep order.'

'He is heavily fined for escapes,' continued Sir John. 'And very vigilant since a notable and dangerous escape five years ago. If you spend a day in the pillory, you must spend a night in the Hole for he will not leave anyone out in the courtyard overnight as he did formerly. I beseech you sir, do not even consider escaping, no matter how unjust your imprisonment may seem; he has flogged gentlemen to the bone on a mere suspicion.'

'Och, Christ. I thought he couldna do that to a man of worship?'

'It is an iniquitous and barbarous tyranny, but as he has pointed out to me, he can see to it that a gentleman dies of ill usage, sickness and want before any suit can go to Star Chamber, and he will.'

'Och,' said Dodd, feeling more depressed by the minute. If being a gentleman couldn't protect you from a flogging, what the hell was the point of all the bowing and scraping involved? At least in Jedburgh there had been no question of that, since the

Armstrongs would have taken any bad treatment against Dodd very personally.

There was a shouting and a bell-clanging, at which the gentlemen sighed and gathered up their cards and winnings.

'What's going on?'

'Sunday Service,' said Sir John. 'An excuse to muster the prisoners, in fact.'

Dodd followed and stood in a little group with the other inmates of the Knight's Ward, answered to the name of Sir Robert Carey with a growled 'If ye say so', and found himself being pointed out and stared at by many of the other prisoners. He scowled back at them.

The sermon was long, read aloud by a sweating little priest with a red bulbous nose, and dwelling on the iniquities of luxurious clothing and the wickedness of starch. Dodd couldn't quarrel with a word of it, but wished heartily it had been Carey listening to it instead of him. He still wasn't used to the way his smart woollen suit constricted his arms and legs and forced him to pull his shoulders back.

At last the priest wound reedily to a close, blessed them and trotted off already drinking from a flask he had in his sleeve pocket. Somebody tentatively touched Dodd's sleeve.

'Sir. There is a little time before dinner.' It was Sir John, smiling very friendlywise at him. 'Would you care to play primero with us?'

What was it with Londoners? Why did they all want him to play cards? Well, there was one obvious answer. Dodd was tempted. He knew he was a lot better than he had ever been before. Also that proved Sir John could not have met Sir Robert Carey, since no one who actually knew the man would think he was a good mark for a primero game.

'Ay. I'll play. Though I'm verra rusty and ye might need to remind me of the rules.'

Sir John exchanged glances with the skinny gentleman, who moved round so that Dodd could squat down in their circle. He looked around him at the four gentlemen who were playing and thought that he could definitely undertake to throw any one of them a great deal further than he would trust them. Carey's words paraded through his mind. 'Play very cautiously with people you don't know. If the odds are consistently wrong – whether you're winning or losing – then you can be absolutely certain somebody is cheating.' The odds were still something of a mystery to Dodd, though he had sweated to learn the numbers Carey told him were important. The Courtier had boiled it down by translating the numbers into fights: two to one against you, and you might fancy your chances, five to one and things were looking bleak, twenty to one and you might as well not bother. It had been a strange distraction against the griping misery of the Scotch flux but endless practice using pebbles for money had driven some of the ideas into his head.

An hour later he was pocketing a little pile of shillings and gloomily resisting the depressing certainty that the fine, if threadbare, gentlemen were clearly cheating, on Carey's definition. Dodd wasn't often lucky with the cards, which he supposed must mean Janet was a better wife than she sometimes seemed, but in that hour he had seen more flushes and choruses than he had seen before in all his adult life.

The bell went for dinner while he was wondering what to do about it and so he filed off with the others and his purse jingling, into the dining hall at one side of the courtyard, where the prisoners were carefully counted in by a gaol servant scowling with concentration.

The food wasn't too bad. Tough, of course, and mostly covered in a sort of brown sauce, but none of it actually stank. Compared to the garrison rations it was really quite tasty. Dodd was too busy filling his belly to look around at first, but after a while he realised that one of the women sitting at the other end of the table was looking at him curiously.

He looked back at her. There was nothing whatever remarkable about her, excepting that she had a child sitting on either side of her, but they weren't the only children in the hall, if a little better behaved than some. She was of middling height and quite slender build, she had brown hair neatly tucked under a cap and pleasant long-lashed brown eyes. Three needles were threaded through her bodice which was doublet-style and made of a dusky rose coloured damask and she was squinting a little short-sightedly. Dodd felt as if Carey's fetch was sitting next to him and jogging his elbow; Carey would have tipped his hat to her and given her one of his most charming smiles, because that was the kind of man Carey was. Dodd, however, was different and proud of it. He preferred not to remember his sin of lust the previous morning, which was no doubt the cause of all his troubles since. Dodd was married. He looked firmly away from the woman and concentrated on his meat.

After they had filed out of the dining hall into the afternoon sunlight, there was Sir John at Dodd's elbow again, nagging him to play cards. This confirmed all Dodd's suspicions.

'Nay, I'll not chance it,' he said. 'I was lucky this morning but I'm not anywhere near as skilful as ye gentlemen.'

'The way to increase your skill is to play, surely?' said Sir John with a tight, rather desperate smile.

Barnabus's voice came to Dodd's memory. 'Wot you do is, you let the barnard win a bit and then you take it off him again and generally speaking, he'll play harder to try and get his winnings back which is when you skin him, so to speak.'

Sir John then suggested a restful game of dice and Dodd shook his head sadly. The card-playing circle were looking annoyed as well, which was a little worrying.

Somebody came up behind Dodd and said, 'Excuse me, sir?' He turned and saw the woman who had been staring at him during dinner. She curtseyed and he made his best bow which caused Sir John's eyes to narrow.

'Ay, mistress,' he said politely. 'Can I help ye?'

'Are you Sir Robert Carey?' Her voice trembled a little.

Dodd sighed. Was this another of Carey's multiplicity of women? How the devil did he find time for such a complicated private life?

'That's what Newton thinks,' he said.

Her brow furrowed and she looked about to burst into tears. 'Well, but do you know him?'

'Ay, I do.' No, of course it couldn't be one of Carey's trollops, what was he thinking of? She would hardly mistake him, would she? 'Though I dinna ken where he is, mind.'

She frowned again, obviously not understanding him.

'I don't know where he is,' Dodd said again, straining to speak in a southern way. 'But I do know him, mistress, ay.'

'Please, sir, will you come with me?'

'Why?' Dodd was suspicious now. Was this some means of inveigling him into a corner so Sir John and his cronies could take his purse?

'It's very important.'

'Nae doot. But what's it about?'

She beckoned him closer and when he bent towards her, stood on tiptoe and whispered in his ear. 'His brother.'

'Och.' Dodd looked severely at her. Was it possible to be so lucky? 'What are ye saying?'

'Will you come?'

'Ay, I will, mistress.'

Newton had taken his sword when he was signed in, of course, but Dodd still had his dagger. He loosened it in its sheath and then followed the woman across the courtyard, past the sewing circle where the woman's children were sitting under the gimlet eye of an older woman, past a cobbler's stall and a general stall covered over with a dizzying array of objects for sale, and into the doorway of one of the oldest parts of the place, stone built and with a swaybacked roof.

They went down worn spiral steps. One of the gaol servants was standing there and after the woman had paid him a penny, he unlocked the heavy door. They went through into a dark stinking cellar, with a broad ribbed roof and small high windows that were barred and had no glass. The stone flags of the floor were slippery and there were puddles in the dips, the place stank of piss and mould and sickness to take your head off. There were still shapes lying huddled in the shadows, some of them in no more than their shirts, and there was no sound of talk, only harsh breathing, echoing coughs and the occasional moan.

'Och, God,' said Dodd, shaken. 'What's this place?'

'Bolton's Ward, sir, where Newton puts those who have no money left, the beggars' ward.'

'Why do they not leave?'

'They are chained, sir.'

'Jesus Christ.'

In his time Dodd had heard some fairly frightening sermons on the subject of Hell, but this was worse than any of them. Jedburgh itself hadn't been half so bad.

The woman went over to one of the huddled shapes in the corner. Dodd followed her, feeling sick with pity.

She bent down to the man who lay there, felt his forehead, and he moved his head restlessly at her touch. For a moment, in the dimness, Dodd's belly clenched with superstitious fright because although the man was far skinnier than Carey, it could have been him, with the beaky nose and the high cheekbones. But the man's greasy hair was receding off his forehead into a widow's peak and there was a difference about the chin and mouth, and also he had a straggling beard. He was lying on a straw pallet with a bag of clothes for a pillow, wearing nothing but his shirt which was fine linen but ragged. The blanket hunched up over his shoulders was a stinking disgrace Dodd wouldn't have put on a horse.

'Do you know him, sir?' asked the woman.

'Is that Edmund Carey?' Dodd asked.

Her face relaxed a little. For the first time she smiled at him. 'Yes, it is.'

'But why did his father not find him?'

'He's in the book under another name, under Edward Morgan. He was kind to my children when he was first brought to the Fleet, in the beginning of August. Then he took a gaol-fever a week later. Newton was enraged with him for he said that all the garnish he had paid was forged and Newton himself was nearly arrested for it. He had no other money by then, and so Newton put him down here.' She looked down at her neatly clasped hands. 'I . . . um . . . I have been trying to nurse him. He told me his real name when he was delirious but then when he was in his right mind he begged me not to tell his family and . . . some other things . . . and so I did not, but I have been in a quandary to know what to do, sir, because I think the poor gentleman is not far off dying and he should be taken out of this place and looked after properly. I'm not even sure if I have done right bringing you here, sir,' added the woman, her voice dropping, 'because he was particularly anxious that his brother not be told; he kept begging me not to let little Robin see him in case he was frightened.'

Dodd kept his face solemn though in fact there was something funny as well as pathetic and idiotic at the idea of Sir Robert being 'little Robin' and at risk of fright at the sight of his brother brought so low. But then, he supposed, if he was in a like case and not quite in his right mind from fever, he might want to stop Red Sandy from seeing him. Old habits die hard and you could never stop being a big brother once you were one.

He squatted down and took the bony wrist which felt hot and dry. 'Och, puir man,' he said. 'How much would it take to move him somewhere better?'

'At least ten shillings, since he's in debt to Newton for the Knight's Ward charges as well. And another couple of shillings' garnish to unchain him.'

Dodd's lips tightened. He was beginning to take a considerable dislike to Newton.

'What's your name, mistress?'

'Julie Granville, sir.'

'Is your husband not about?'

She looked down. 'He was a sharer and officer in a ship bound for Muscovy, sir, and when the ship didn't return, and we had heard nothing of it for a year, our creditors arrested me for his debts.'

'But that's terrible, mistress. What about yer family?'

'I haven't any, sir. And my husband's family are . . . Well, his father was opposed to the voyage in the first place.'

Dodd shook his head. Impulsively he put his hand on her arm. 'I'm not Sir Robert, see ye, but I am his man, and I'm a man o' parts myself in ma ain country. Now dinna ye fret, Mistress Granville, I'll see it sorted.'

She obviously didn't understand much of what he had said, but she understood his tone of voice and she smiled. She took a cloth out of the bucket she had been carrying and began wiping Edmund

Carey's face and hands. He woke a little more and began muttering. She shushed him and began feeding him spoonfuls of some kind of porridge she had brought in a wooden bowl.

Dodd stood, turned on his heel and strode to the door, banged on it and was let out of the hell of Bolton's Ward, up the stairs and into the courtyard. He was scowling with thought; God might move in mysterious ways, but this was a little too pat for his tastes. What a strange coincidence that he should be arrested in mistake for Carey, when Carey had been blazing about the streets with courtier branded on every inch of him, and brought to the one prison in London that also contained Carey's missing brother, for whom Greene had been searching before his death, and Carey as well. It didn't make sense, or rather it did and he didn't like the sense it made.

He was not at all surprised to find a familiar face in the courtyard when he came blinking out into the sunshine, Mistress Bassano's erstwhile servant, the balding poet.

Dodd strode over to the man, took his elbow between thumb and forefinger in a way which forbade argument, and propelled him into the shade of a corner between two buildings.

'Sergeant Dodd,' said Shakespeare, his voice shaking a little. 'I'm . . . er . . . I'm very glad I've found you.'

'Not half sae glad as I am to find you,' said Dodd, deliberately crowding him against the wall. 'Now, I ken ye work for Mr Vice Chamberlain and I dinna give a pig's turd why. But I'm sick and tired of being used as a fucking chesspiece in some fancy game o' yer master's, so now ye're gonnae tell me what the hell's going on here, or I willnae be responsible for what I do to ye. D'ye understand me or will I say it again more southern?'

Shakespeare was white-faced and trembling. 'I . . . er . . . I understand,' he panted.

'So.' Dodd leaned one arm against the wall in front of Shakespeare, blocking him with his body. 'I'm waiting.'

'Er . . . I really don't know . . . very much.'

'Och,' said Dodd with false sympathy. 'That's a terrible pity. I'll have to kill ye on general principles then.'

Dodd hadn't even bothered to draw his blade nor lay hands

on Shakespeare, but for some reason the little poet believed him.

'I . . . I don't know where to start.'

'Ye're the man that told Heneage that Sir Robert was on his way south, ay?'

Shakespeare nodded. 'I told Marlowe, though.'

'When did he warn ye to do that?'

'About August, I think.'

'How did ye tell him? In person?'

'No, in writing, in code. I leave messages with a . . . a trustworthy person who passes them on.'

'Who is the person?'

Shakespeare shook his head. 'I can't tell you.'

Dodd considered beating the name out of him, but decided not to since he didn't want to draw attention to himself.

'What's Heneage's game? What's he trying to do?'

Shakespeare looked at the ground. 'I don't know. Why would he tell me?'

'All right. What's he told ye to find out?'

'He . . . er . . . I think he wants to know anything about my lord Baron Hunsdon that will discredit him with the Queen. He also wants to know where Edmund Carey is. That's quite urgent. He's been quartering London for the man.'

Dodd blinked and looked hard at Shakespeare, who was swallowing and trembling in front of him. He was not a fighting man and although he was a poet and must be good at lying, he didn't look as if he was lying now. In which case, what the hell was going on? Dodd had been convinced that Heneage had put Edmund Carey in the Fleet, possibly into Bolton's Ward as well. But if Heneage didn't know where he was . . . And wanted to find him . . .?

Dodd changed plan. 'What are ye here for?'

'To talk to you, find out if you needed anything.'

Dodd scowled deeper which made Shakespeare shrink back against the wall.

'Who sent ye?'

'I can't . . . er . . . tell you.'

225

'And why not?'

'B . . . because I . . . I'm more frightened of them than I am of you, sir,' said Shakespeare with a desperate glint of humour.

Against his will Dodd let out a short bark of laughter. 'Ay. Well, that's because ye dinna know me sae well.'

'I don't think so.'

'Bide there while I think what to do.'

Dodd looked around him for inspiration and scowled. The complexity of the situation was making his head hurt. His immediate impulse had been to send Shakespeare hotfoot to Somerset House to roust out Lord Hunsdon and bring him to the gaol to fetch his son. But the messenger was tainted. The likelihood was that a verbal message would go straight to Heneage or the mysterious person that scared the poet so much, and a written message the same. For a moment Dodd thought about codes but he didn't know any and besides, it stood to reason that experienced intriguers like Heneage or even Shakespeare would know more about secret writing than he did. He couldn't even tell Shakespeare simply to fetch Lord Hunsdon for the same reasons. He couldn't send the man to fetch Barnabus or Simon Barnet because they had the plague and were probably dead by now.

'I've got naething for ye to do, because I canna trust ye,' he said to Shakespeare, leaning towards him. The poet was trying to burrow backwards into the wall. 'If ye had a particle of decency in ye, ye'd go tell my Lord Hunsdon where I am and why, but as ye dinna, I willnae waste my breath asking ye to.'

'I . . . I'm sorry.'

Dodd drew back disgustedly. 'Och,' he said. 'Piss off. Ye're dirtying my nice clean gaol.'

Shakespeare sidled past him and into the courtyard, then scurried across it looking pinched about the mouth. Dodd spat in his wake.

For a moment Dodd thought of paying the money that would get Edmund Carey moved out of the stinking disgrace of the beggars' ward but then it occurred to him that any action like that would probably be reported to Heneage within the hour and Heneage would want to know why he was so solicitous of a stranger, might well make the connection.

It occurred to him that there was one thing he could do without giving away any secrets, since it would be expected of him. He went back into the courtyard and over to the table covered with a higgledy piggledy array of things, including a lump of rock covered in dust that the dog-eared notice by it claimed to be gold ore. There, after considerable haggling, he bought himself paper, pen and ink and sat down cross-legged with his back to a corner and a stone in front of him for a writing table. He hated paperwork. He knew his ability to write, which was rare among the Borderers, had helped him get his place in the Carlisle garrison as Sergeant, but he still hated it. The effort of making up words and then forming the letters for them always made his head hurt and his hand sweat. He avoided the labour as much as he could but this time there was no help for it.

Peter Cheke had gone to bed after another night of desperate labour against the plague, also ending in failure. He had slept the dreamless headlong sleep of exhaustion and woken very late in full daylight, feeling thirsty and still exhausted. He had even slept through the bells calling him to church. As he went to the window to look out into the street, he saw a tall man in ill-fitting homespun russet jogtrotting purposefully through the crowds, straight to his locked shop door.

The hammering resounded up the stairs and Cheke stood staring down at the statute cap of the man, overwhelmed with helpless misery. Yet another desperate father, begging for something, anything to save his babies, his wife, offering every penny he had for healing Cheke knew he could not give, as if salvation could be bought.

Eventually he put on his gown and hat, went down to open the door and tell the poor fool to begone.

At first he didn't recognise the man because of the conflicting signals of clothes and bearing and the fact that his hair and face were dirty. By the time he had worked it out, Carey had pushed his way into the shop and shut the door behind him.

'What ... er ... what can I do for you, sir?' he asked nervously.

'Mr Cheke,' said Carey. 'I've come to you because I have nowhere else to start. I must know where Dr Jenkins performed his alchemy.'

'Sir, I gave my word ...'

'I know you did. But what if they were coney-catching? What if the process you saw was not alchemy at all, had nothing whatever to do with the Philosopher's Stone, but was a well-known goldsmithing mystery called parcel-gilding?'

'I am sure it was the true art, sir, as sure as my life.'

'Then let's prove it. Have you scales?'

'Yes.'

'Do you have any of the angels that were made?'

'I ... I was given a fee, yes.'

'Excellent. I have here a true angel direct from Mr van Emden on Cheapside.' He took out a small yellow coin and tossed it, snapped it out of the air and showed it to Cheke, the Archangel Michael, battling the dragon, bright and fine upon it.

Angry at this bland certainty that Carey was right and he was wrong, Cheke led the way silently to the kitchen of the house, and brought out his scales. Then from a loose brick by the oven, he took one of the angels he had seen made and struck and brought it over.

Ten seconds later the last bastion of Cheke's world had fallen, for the pan with the true angel on it dipped much lower than the one he had been given by the worshipful Dr Jenkins.

He took the others out, checked them against Carey's coin.

'Yours is full of lead,' he said, desperately.

'No, Mr Cheke,' said Carey wearily. 'Lead weighs less than gold. Look how thin mine is, how much it weighs. You were coney-catched, Mr Cheke, like others before you, and like my brother, who was the gentleman investing in the project.'

'We weighed them at the ... the place.'

'Who supplied the scales?'

'Dr Jenkins.' Cheke looked at the flagstones. 'But ...'

228

'You know yourself it's not so very hard to alter the balance arm of a pair of scales so it's biased one way or the other.'

Cheke put his head in his hands and fought not to weep. Carey paused and then said quite softly, 'I am not claiming that the transmutation of matter, that the goal of alchemy, is impossible. I am only saying that you yourself have not yet seen it done.'

'You have no idea,' said Cheke, his voice muffled. 'You don't know how happy I was. I have spent most of my life seeking out the truth of matter, trying to understand God's mind therein. And to know it had been done, to know that someone had succeeded . . . It didn't matter to me that it was not I that did it, only that it had been done. That God had vouchsafed a little of his mystery . . .'

'Mr Cheke, I'm sorry. I must know. Where did the process take place? Where were the angels made?'

For a moment Cheke burned with rage and hatred for Carey and then the fire died inside him, to be replaced with a grey hopelessness.

'In the Blackfriars monastery, in the old kitchen where there is a fireplace we altered to be a furnace. The gentleman had a key.'

'Of course he did. And with the noise of hemp-beating in the Bridewell prison nobody would hear the sound of the coins being struck.'

'Yes, sir, that's right.'

Carey smiled at him. 'Come on, Mr Cheke. I want to see it.'

He hadn't the energy to resist any more. He stood and went with Carey. They threaded through the back streets of the city, behind Knightrider Street and St Peter's, alleys pockmarked with red painted crosses in some places and utterly normal in others.

Getting into the Blackfriars was made a little complicated by the fact that for some reason, Carey did not want to go through the gatehouse and the cloisters. Instead they went down St Andrew's Hill to Puddle Wharf and round the remains of the monastery walls that way, threading between the newly built houses to a much older, swaybacked stone building separate from the Blackfriar's hall.

Carey tried the door, but it was locked.

'The gentleman had a key to it,' offered Cheke.

Carey nodded. 'Yes, he would. I think my father owns this part too. Well, let's see.'

Carey padded restlessly round the whole building, disturbing a goat in its shed, craning his neck to look at the high windows and the massive chimney.

'Come on, where is it?' he said to himself.

'What?'

'I never saw a kitchen yet that only had one door. Where did the servants collect the food, where's the hatch?'

'Hatch?'

Carey looked across a tiny jakes-cluttered yard at the Blackfriar's hall, jutting above the rooftops with its buttressing, narrowed his eyes as he followed some invisible notional path and came up against the goat shed again.

'Must be,' he said, and barged into the shed where the goat bleated in fright. There were a couple of bangs and crashes. 'Come and give me a hand with this,' he ordered Cheke.

After sidling past the goat who stared with those unnervingly cold slit-eyes of hers, Cheke saw that Carey had managed to wrench two planks from the back wall of the lean-to shed and had uncovered what was obviously a serving hatch. They both tried to lift it, but it was stuck fast and so Carey simply picked up a stone that must have been used for milking and battered through the old wood. It gave in a shower of musty-smelling dust and Carey tutted.

'It's got dry-rot,' he said. 'We'll have to demolish it.' He climbed up onto the sill and pushed through the hole he'd made; Cheke followed him, borne along by Carey's certainty. The goat stuck her head through the gap after them, bleating with interest.

Very little daylight was filtering through the high glassed windows. A huge table stood in the middle of the flagged floor, the vast fireplace was empty except for its rusting fire-irons and spit. They had used the chimney from the smaller charcoal fireplace on the other wall because it was narrower than the great fireplace and the airflow was more easily controlled. Where the monks' food had been sinfully soused with complex spiced sauces, Peter Cheke had built a small closed-in furnace with stones and cement, sealed with clay. His own pair of bellows lay at one of the air-holes.

Carey hunted around until he found what he was looking for, a whole treetrunk made into a block, with a small neat round hole set into it. The mallet lay nearby.

'Now where are they?' he muttered to himself and began digging in the cupboards. In one he found a dusty academic gown and what Cheke at first took for a dead cat, until he picked it up and found it was a false beard such as players used at the theatre.

It was all too ridiculous for words. Cheke remembered his joy and pride at being present when Dr Jenkins produced the scrapings of the Philosopher's Stone, of actually admiring the curly dark beard, streaked with grey, that was now tangled with the noble doctor's gown. He started to snigger helplessly.

'What is it?' asked Carey, emerging from another cubbyhole, covered in dust.

Cheke couldn't stop. 'He . . . I think . . . this is all that's left of Dr Jenkins.'

Carey glanced at the gown and false beard. 'Of course it is.'

'Do you know who played the part?'

'I don't know. I suspect. Was the good doctor bald?'

'Yes.'

'Thought so. Well if the coin dies are here, I don't know where. Do you know?'

'I think that the gentleman had them. He told me he had bought them off a retired mint-master fallen on hard times who had kept a trussel and pile that should have been cancelled as an old design.'

'Hm. Are you convinced?'

'How was it done, sir?'

'Parcel-gilding – you dissolve ground-up gold in boiling mercury to make an amalgam. Then you spread the paste on your pewter rounds, fire it up in a furnace to drive off the mercury and out come your gilded coins.'

'So the Philosopher's Stone was only powdered gold?'

'That's right.'

Cheke shook his head. 'What a fool I've been.'

'Don't blame yourself. My brother was just as much a fool, if not worse.'

'Do you think Marlowe knew?'
'Of course he did. It was probably his idea.'
'What will you do now?'
Carey showed his teeth in an extremely unpleasant expression.
'I'm going to talk to him.'

Sunday, 3rd September 1592, afternoon

8

Marlowe waited at the Mermaid where the innkeeper was afraid of him as well as being an employee of sorts. He ate the ordinary which was a pheasant in a wine sauce with summer peas and a bag pudding to follow, and he drank the best wine they had which was always brought to him. As was only right the innkeeper refused his money.

He watched the people coming in and out of the common room, eating, drinking, talking, kissing their women. How could they think they were important, he wondered, since they lived like cattle in the narrow fields where they were born, according to the rules of their herd, and never looked up to the stars or out to the horizons? His father had lived like that, perfectly happy to make shoes all his life and taking an inordinate stupid pride in the smallness and evenness of his stitches and the good fit he produced. As a boy, Kit Marlowe could remember the boiling of angry boredom under his ribs while his father tried to explain how the strange curved shapes he cut out in leather would bend and be stitched together to form a solid boot. Once the silly man had tried his hand at sermonising: When it's flat, see how strange it looks, he had said, oddly tender, and then when it's made, see what a fit shape it was. Perhaps our lives are like that, Kit: strangely shaped when we are alive and then when we die, we see how the very strangeness made us better fit our Maker.

Even as a child I rebelled at being told I was God's shoe, Marlowe thought, and rightly.

'Sir,' said a low nervous voice beside him. Marlowe woke out of his thoughts and blinked at his man.

'Yes,' he said, not bothering to hide his impatience.

'A woman and a boy went into Somerset House,' said the man, sweating with his run up Fleet Street. 'We thought you'd better know.'

'A boy?'

'Yessir.'

'The same one?'

'Yessir.'

'Well, why didn't you stop them?'

'We weren't sure and anyway you never told us to.'

Marlowe rolled his eyes. 'I assume Carey wasn't with them.'

'Oh, no, sir, we never saw him.'

'You got the message that he's in disguise, wearing home-spun?'

'Yessir. But we never saw him. We'd have stopped any man, just to be sure, but it was just an old woman and a boy.'

'A short old woman, built like a barrel?'

'Er . . . yessir.'

'Well, it's a pity you didn't stop them, but I don't suppose it matters that much. Off you go, keep your eyes open.'

The man pulled his forelock and sidled away. Marlowe tapped his fingers on the table and thought. Carey had evidently gone back to his lodgings despite the plague-cross on the door which Marlowe hadn't thought he would. He couldn't watch every place; he had the main roads out of the city covered; he had Somerset House under watch and the Fleet prison, but even with all the men at his disposal he couldn't cover everywhere. Perhaps he should have kept a man at Carey's lodgings, but then it had never crossed his mind that the Courtier would go into a plague house just for a couple of servants.

Damn him, where was he? Hadn't he worked it out yet? Was even Carey too bovine and stupid to understand what Marlowe was about? He ought to have enough information at his disposal by now, especially with the massive hint of Dodd's arrest. So where was he?

It occurred to Marlowe that perhaps Carey was lunatic enough to go to the Fleet to find his henchman. This was the trouble with real people as opposed to the shadows who danced in his head when he wrote plays: the real thing was so hard to predict.

Marlowe knew he should stay where he was and receive messages, Munday had told him often enough he was too impatient, but he was bored and worried and he could see the structure of his plan crumbling around him because of Carey who didn't know his proper place in it. Shakespeare hadn't come back from the Fleet yet either. He didn't think the ambitious little player had the imagination to know what was happening but he couldn't be sure.

'Damn it,' Marlowe said to himself and pushed away his half-finished ordinary, which was now as cold as a nobleman's dinner. He put on his hat and went and told the innkeeper to hold any messages for him until he came back and then went out into the sunlight, heading up Water Lane towards Ludgate and the Fleet prison.

Just as he passed through the old Blackfriar's Gateway, a tall fellow came up to him and pulled at his cap.

'Ah've a message for ye, sir,' came the guttural northern tones.

Marlowe paused. 'Yes, what is it?'

The tall northerner moved up swiftly, caught his arm and twisted it up behind his back, rammed him bodily through the little door where the monks' porter had sat and into a dusty tiny room full of bits of padding, petticoats and sausages of cloth. Marlowe was shoved into a pile of the things, stinking of women and old linen, the grip on his arm shifted slightly but when he tried to struggle free, it was twisted and lifted so that pain lancing up through his shoulder joint made him gasp. He couldn't see, he could hardly breathe and now somebody's knee was in the small of his back, hurting him there and there was the cold scratch of a knife at the side of his throat.

'The message is,' came a familiar voice behind him, 'don't fucking play silly games with me, Marlowe, I'm tired of it.'

He'd been waiting, Marlowe realised dimly, bucking and gasping in an effort to find a way to breathe, and he's very angry. Half-suffocated and with lights beginning to flash in his eyes, Marlowe tried to say something, only to feel the knee dig harder into his back, the knife moved from his neck and Carey was fumbling for his other hand.

No, thought Marlowe, he's not going to tie me up. He grabbed desperately to move the bumrolls out from under his head, found the end of one and whipped it round as hard as he could left-handed in the direction of Carey's face. If you were willing to hurt yourself more, there was a way out of an armlock. Marlowe heaved convulsively to the left, felt Carey's weight slip, and punched still blind with his left hand for Carey's groin. He hit something, heard a gasp, scrambled out of the pile of underwear and got to a wall where he stood up and drew his sword.

Carey already had his sword and dagger drawn, crossed in front of him. Behind him the door was shut. The room was so small, their swords were already inches from each other's face.

'The Queen's going to be very angry when I get blood on her bumrolls,' said Carey conversationally. 'Why not surrender?'

'Do you really think you can kill me?' Marlowe asked, his heart beating hard with excitement and the fresh air in his lungs.

Carey grinned at him, looking much more like a wild northerner than the Queen's courtier Marlowe had known. 'Oh yes, if I want to.'

'But you don't want to, or you would have, already,' said Marlowe with absolute certainty.

'I want a few answers.'

'I'm sorry. I thought you knew them all.'

Marlowe was deliberately trying to annoy Carey into an attack. In such a small space his primitive broadsword was a positive liability against Marlowe's rapier. The glittering poignard was a much better weapon for close quarters, but that was in Carey's left hand.

To Marlowe's surprise and irritation, Carey laughed. He straightened slightly, though he kept his weapons *en garde*.

'You silly bugger,' he said, almost affectionately. 'You know you wanted to talk to me, tell me how clever you are. That's why you were hanging around in the Mermaid all morning, all on your lonely own. Do you think I don't know bait when I see

it? So talk to me. Tell me your magnificent plan. Watch me gasp
with admiration.'

'This wasn't how I'd intended to do it.'

'No, I'll bet it wasn't. Me in irons, no doubt, and you with the
thumbscrews to aid my concentration.'

'Not quite like that,' murmured Marlowe, inspiration at his
shoulder as it usually was in times like this. 'Is that what happened
to you in Scotland?'

Carey had no gloves on since his own were no doubt far too
fine to go with the baggy homespun he was wearing. Several of
his fingernails were only half grown and Marlowe knew one thing
that did that.

Carey's face tightened and lost some of its good humour. After a
pause he answered, quite softly, 'Yes, it was.' The silence stretched
a little and Marlowe suddenly found the look in Carey's eyes
frightening.

'I didn't plan anything like that,' he said hesitantly. 'I promise you.'

'Oh really?' Carey's voice was still soft and inexplicably terrifying.
'What about Heneage?'

'I'm not working for him at the moment.'

'You're commanding a lot of his men. I recognise them.'

'Well, he doesn't know that yet.'

Carey laughed, still quietly. 'What the devil are you up to,
Marlowe? What do you want?'

Marlowe took a deep breath. 'I want to work for my lord Earl
of Essex. Not Heneage.'

'What? Essex hates your guts.'

'I know that. I was hoping you might . . . er . . . intercede.'

Carey's eyebrows often seemed to have a life of their own. One
went up, almost to his hairline. 'Me?'

'Yes. You're still his man, aren't you?'

'I am. So?'

'He'll listen to you; he has in the past.'

'He might.'

'You could at least get me an audience, so I can put my case.'

Carey barked a laugh. 'You don't know him very well, do you,

Kit? And you haven't given me one reason yet why I should do a damned thing for you.'

'No,' Marlowe sighed, thought for a minute and decided to gamble that Carey hadn't been completely changed by his service in France and the North. He tossed his rapier onto the dusty floor and sat down on a pile of under-petticoats. Carey blinked, then smiled and sheathed his broadsword, squatted down peasant-style with his back against the door. He held his poignard in his right hand though, which Marlowe thought was probably fair enough.

'Heneage wants to be Lord Chamberlain,' Marlowe began. 'He wants the power over the Queen he believes your father has.'

'He's an idiot. The Queen . . .'

'The Queen's a woman and can be influenced.' Carey's eyebrows said he didn't think so, but Marlowe continued. 'In any case, it doesn't matter what's true, it matters what Heneage believes. Heneage has been trying very hard to find a way to discredit your father in her eyes, but it's difficult. Your father's so bloody honest, so far he's just ignored all the attempts Heneage has made.' Carey grinned. 'Or the Queen has. Now this summer Heneage ran some kind of operation involving your brother Edmund – I'm not clear what, since I wasn't involved then – which should have got your brother arrested on a capital charge, probably treason, thus giving Heneage the lever he's always wanted against your father. But just before the net closed, your brother disappeared, and when he did, he had some evidence that would have got Heneage into trouble. So the Vice Chamberlain has been combing London for your brother, just as your father has. When he sent for you to come back from Newcastle . . .'

'Carlisle,' corrected Carey.

'Wherever, Heneage decided that one son was as good as another and besides, if he had you, Edmund might come out of hiding. So he made sure that the bailiffs knew you were coming . . .'

'Did you kill Michael?'

'Who?'

'The servant my father sent to warn me off?'

'Oh, him. No, that was a mistake. Heneage wanted the footpads to stop him, not kill him.'

'He should have been more specific. And perhaps if he hadn't paid them with forged money, they might not have been so anxious to jump us,' said Carey in the soft tone of voice Marlowe found so worrying. 'Michael left a wife and children, you know?'

Marlowe shrugged. What was he supposed to do, weep for the man? 'The next thing Heneage decided was that perhaps we could take your henchman and use him to trap you . . .'

'Who, Dodd?'

'The northerner.'

'*Take* him?' Carey sounded very amused. 'What happened?'

'We didn't succeed.' Marlowe was annoyed. 'He got away from us.'

'Was the trollop and Nick the Gent you as well?'

Marlowe nodded. 'It wasn't a very good idea, but Heneage was getting impatient.'

'Why the hell didn't he just arrest me, Dodd, the lot of us. Why be so complicated?'

'How could he possibly arrest *you* on a charge of treason? The Queen would have hysterics. He wanted you imprisoned, but he didn't want to do it himself.'

'What's Shakespeare's part in all this?'

'Who? Oh, him.' Marlowe waved a dismissive hand, 'He's my informer in your father's house. He was supposed to keep an eye on you and report back. He's not much good.'

'He played the part of Dr Jenkins the alchemist well enough.'

Marlowe eyed Carey unhappily. 'Oh?'

'Come on, Marlowe, don't try doling out your story like bloody ship's rations. You were there at the time, you organised the whole rigmarole with little Mr Shakespeare dressed up in a gown and a false beard to be an alchemist.'

Marlowe smiled reminiscently. 'He was really very convincing. I almost believed it myself.' He caught himself at the expression on Carey's face. 'I'm sorry. It was one of the things that made me decide to quit Heneage's service.'

'Oh, was it, indeed?' Carey's voice was soft. 'I wish I could believe that.'

Marlowe coughed. 'Why would I lie about it?'

'Why? I don't know. I think you've got so used to plotting and making people dance like puppets, you don't know what reality is any more. What about Greene? Did you poison him?'

Marlowe shook his head. 'Of course not, I wanted to know what he'd found out as well. We were sure he'd discovered something but the way he was drinking . . . Well, you saw him yourself. Nobody could get any sense out of him.'

'So how did he come to be poisoned?'

'I've no idea. I'm not the Devil, I'm not responsible for everything bad that happens.' Marlowe was sneering. 'Anyway, by this time, I'd decided that whatever Heneage was up to, I didn't like it. So when the order came to set the bailiffs on you again, I made sure they arrested the wrong man.'

'And put Dodd where?'

'In the Fleet, of course; it's the debtor's prison for this area. Also, I think your brother's there but I haven't been able to find him. He's not in the book and he's not visible.'

'Why do you think Edmund's in the Fleet?'

'Because Newton tried to spend some of the forged angels.'

'Ah.' Carey tossed his poignard from one hand to the other, making the jewels glitter. 'Does Heneage know that yet?'

'No.'

'And my servants?'

Marlowe sighed. 'That was Heneage again. He'd decided to take you himself and see what he could get out of you or . . .'

'Make me confess to?'

'Yes. It's how he thinks. I was with him when we broke into your lodgings, and all we found was your man dead of something that wasn't plague and the boy who was too stupid to tell us anything useful.'

'You left him tied up.'

'Heneage is planning to go back this evening when he's had time to think and . . .'

'And get thirsty and hungry and cramped? And terrified?'

'Well, yes. And then persuade him to tell us where you were and what you were up to, perhaps other things.'

Carey's eyes had become chips of ice. 'Confess to Papistry? Say I've been hiding Jesuits?'

Marlowe shrugged.

'You went along with this?'

'Heneage has done worse,' said Marlowe defensively. 'He's not like Walsingham.'

'No.'

'I've been trying to find you, have a meeting with you, all day . . . All I wanted was to explain . . .'

'You're a fool, Marlowe,' Carey said. 'Why didn't you just go to my father and tell him all this?'

'How could I possibly go into Somerset House with Shakespeare hanging around there?'

'Written him a letter?'

'You don't know much about how Heneage works, do you?'

'The other night, at the Mermaid?'

'With Poley there?'

Carey sighed. 'No,' he said. 'I think you enjoy the play too much, I think you like making people dance.'

Marlowe shrugged. 'I've talked to you now,' he said. 'What are you going to do?'

Carey told him.

Dodd had finished his letter, sealed it, and after careful enquiry among the stallholders, had given it to the gaol servant who normally carried messages, along with a shilling to encourage him to deliver it. Obviously, it would be opened and read before it left the prison, but he had written it with an eye to that fact.

He sat in the sun and watched the activity around him, the children playing games in the dust, the women sewing, some of the men gambling or training rats or trying to press their suit with the women, some of whom were suspiciously well-dressed and vivacious. Apart from the glowering gaol servants and the men who were dragging chains around with them, it could have been a busy marketplace.

Dodd was just thinking wistfully of Janet and what she would make of him in his fine suit when three of the largest gaol servants came up to him, holding clubs. They looked worryingly purposeful and Dodd scrambled to his feet and looked for somewhere to run. Only there wasn't anywhere, of course, that was the whole point of a gaol.

Two of them grabbed him and twisted his arms behind him.

'What the hell is it now?' he growled. 'Why can ye no' leave me alone?'

'Sorry, Sir Robert,' said the third, sounding pleased. 'Orders.'

They started hustling him across the courtyard, causing the other prisoners to stare, into the gatehouse office, through another door and into what were obviously Newton's living quarters. There were four other men standing waiting for him. The one in the middle, dressed in dark brocade and a fur-trimmed velvet gown, looked familiar with his smug moon-face and small pink lips. His expression wasn't smug, however. It had started that way but as soon as it caught sight of Dodd, it changed, ran through puzzlement, incredulity, horror and ended in rage. Then it went blank.

'I told you to fetch Sir Robert Carey,' he snapped.

'Yessir,' said the gaol servant who had spoken before. 'This is him, sir.'

Under the plumpness, jaw-muscles clenched. 'No, it isn't, you fool. It's his henchman, Cod or Pod, or whatever his name is.'

'Dodd, sir. Sergeant Henry Dodd, o' Gilsland. Mr Heneage, is it no'?'

'Where's your master?'

'Och,' said Dodd sadly, his heart thumping hard. 'I wish I knew that maself, sir. Only I don't. I wis arrested in mistake for him and that's the last I saw of him.'

'You? In mistake for him?' Heneage's face was incredulous again.

'Ay, sir,' said Dodd. 'It's a puzzle to me too, sir. I dinna look anything like him, but there it is.'

'Where's Carey gone then?'

'I told ye, sir, I dinna ken.'

'Don't try that half-witted northerner game with me, Dodd, I know you know.'

'I dinna, sir. Sorry.'

The blow when it came was open-handed to the side of Dodd's head, and hard enough to make his teeth rattle. It hurt, but Dodd had been hit much worse than that in his life, many times, and that wasn't what he found frightening: it was the considering expression on Heneage's face, the sort of expression boys wear when they take the wings off flies to see what they do. Heneage hadn't been angry, hadn't lashed out in a rage like most men. He had taken a cold considered decision to strike Dodd, to see how he would react.

If he could, Dodd would have hit him back, beaten him to pulp, Queen's Vice Chamberlain or not, but he was being held too tightly by men who knew how to do it.

'We'll take him anyway,' said Heneage to someone who was standing behind Dodd.

'Would you sign the book, please, sir?' said Newton, his face twisted with deference. 'Only the trustees get . . .'

'This man isn't the one I wanted.'

'Yes, well, would you sign it anyway, sir? Seeing as it's not my fault?'

Heneage tutted and clicked his fingers. Newton brought the logbook over, held the inkpot while Heneage wrote swiftly in the space next to Dodd's name.

'Are you bailing him, sir?'

'No, I'm transferring him.'

'The warrant . . .'

'This is the Queen's business, Newton, don't interfere.'

Dodd knew that phrase, Carey had told it to him. 'I'm no' a Papist,' he said. 'And I'm no' a traitor, neither.'

Heneage looked at him fishily. 'I think you're lying,' he said conversationally. 'We'll go to Chelsea where we can talk, as I suggested a few days ago, remember?'

And Carey had told him what that meant. Dodd felt cold.

'What d'ye want from me?' he asked.

'I want the whereabouts of your master or his brother. It's quite simple. When you've told me, I'll have no further interest in you.'

Dodd drew a long shaky breath and thought quite seriously for several seconds about simply telling him that Edmund Carey was sick near to death a few yards away in Bolton's Ward, in the name of Edward Morgan. He thought about it, part of him wanted desperately to do it, but he couldn't. He couldn't give a sick man to Heneage to save his skin, even if it hadn't been Carey's own brother. Not that he particularly liked the blasted Courtier or his family, it had very little to do with them, only something inside Dodd set hard into an obstinate rock and wouldn't allow it.

Heneage was watching him very shrewdly. 'Yes,' he said, mainly to himself. 'You do know something. Well, that's good.' He smiled. 'Come along, now, we haven't got all day.'

Dodd was not at all surprised to find his arms being manacled behind him by one of Heneage's men who then prodded him in the back. Heneage swept out of the Fleet prison with Dodd in the middle of his entourage and out into Fleet Lane where a carriage stood, drawn by four horses. Somebody opened the door, somebody else shoved Dodd up the steps and into the dimness, forced him to sit on a leather-covered bench. The carriage creaked sideways on its leather straps as Heneage and another man got in and sat down on the bench facing him.

'Lie down,' said Heneage.

'What?'

The other man's gauntleted hand cracked across Dodd's face. 'Do as you're told.'

Slowly, staring at Heneage all the time, Dodd laid himself awkwardly down, sideways on the padded leather, sniffling at the annoying blood trickling out of his nose. Heneage's subordinate put a blanket over his head, something that must have been used for horses in the past because the smell of them was pungent. Dodd found it comforting, it reminded him of home. What would Janet do when she heard she was a widow? Marry again, certainly, being the heiress she was, probably she would forget him since she hadn't even a bairn to remember him by. The men of his troop might drink to his memory a couple of times, Red Sandy would remember him, but in a few years he would fade as others had. Even Long George had left more of a mark than he would.

Would he go to heaven? Privately he doubted it, especially after his sin of venery with the whore, so that was no comfort either.

When he was dead, he would face an angry God who would know exactly how many of his bills were foul.

The carriage jerked and bounced along the streets, its iron-shod wheels clattering and scraping where the way was paved and then rumbling and squeaking and bouncing even worse where the road was dusty and rock hard from the sun. Dodd didn't know which way it was going since he didn't know where Chelsea was and the movement and the stifling darkness of the blanket were making him feel sick.

Should he tell Heneage about Edmund Carey? Would it help? No, he decided it wouldn't, because if Heneage was like Richie Graham of Brackenhill, admitting that much would only convince him Dodd must know more and that would make everything worse, not better.

There wasn't anything he could do except hope that the Courtier, who had run like a rabbit from the bailiffs that morning, would find a way of helping him. Would he? The Carey that Dodd knew in Carlisle would, he thought, certainly. The Carey Dodd had seen in London – he wasn't sure. He didn't know the man so well. Liked him even less.

The coldness Dodd felt inside wasn't helping him against the heat of the day and the blanket, and the wool suit didn't help either. Drops of sweat were trickling down his back and chest under his shirt and his left arm was going to sleep because he was lying on it. He tried to move into a more comfortable position and was kicked in the shins. He sighed. There wasn't any point in frightening himself even more by imagining all the things that might happen to him and at the moment there wasn't anything else he could think of. All he could do was wait. Luckily, he was good at that.

Dodd relaxed and did what he always did when he was lying in ambush. He thought back to when he was a boy in Upper Tynedale, an unimportant middle son in a string of them that made his father proud, a cheeky bright lad that his mother insisted on sending to school to the Reverend Gilpin when he was in the area. When he wasn't learning his letters and listening to the Reverend tell him of the hellfire that waited for reivers, he was running about the hills, herding cattle or sheep, potting the occasional rabbit with his sling, fishing in the Tyne, fighting his brothers, playing football. His mother as he remembered her then was plump and almost always either suckling a babe or round-bellied with another one, plodding in stately fashion after the particular hen she had decided to kill for the pot. She would corner it against the wooden wall of their pele and then squat down and wait patiently for the stupid creature to stop fluttering, calm down and start scratching, at which point she would grab, pull and twist and the hen would be dead. Dodd smiled fondly under his blanket; she had told him once when he had asked her in childish awe if she had a special charm for chickens, that people always wasted a lot of effort chasing after something that would come to them if they waited.

The rocking and jolting stopped and Heneage pulled the blanket off his captive, only to find him fast asleep and smiling. It faded the smug expression on his face more effectively than any defiance and he punched and slapped Dodd awake like a schoolboy.

Dodd who always hated being woken, reared up and tried to headbutt him, only to be stopped by his henchman after a confused scuffle.

'Och, whit the hell d'ye want?' he demanded.

'Edmund Carey's whereabouts,' said Heneage, straightening his gown and dusting himself off fastidiously. 'Or his brother's.'

'Piss off. Ah dinna ken where they are.'

Heneage sighed and shook his head with theatrical regret and waved at the henchman. 'Keep clear of his face,' he said. 'And don't kill him.' He went down the carriage steps, making it lean and creak again, and at his nod, another heavyset man went up them, holding a short cosh in his hand, shut the carriage door behind him.

There was a short silence and then Heneage heard the northerner's voice, sullen and contemptuous. 'Och, get on wi' it then.'

That was followed by a crash and a series of thumps and grunts that made the carriage rock. Heneage looked about him. They were parked in a corner of Salisbury Court, where the noise of the carpenter's yard next door in Hanging Sword Court would disguise most of the noise. The people passing through the court were mainly

Frenchmen, servants of the French ambassador and the rest were men who worked for Heneage, watching the Papists' coming and going. He had decided against going to Chelsea immediately simply because it was a long way and took several hours in a coach and he wanted to be able to get back to Whitefriars before the London gates shut officially. He had driven around the lanes and streets for a while to see if the motion of the coach would upset the northerner's stomach, but that had been a failure. The blasted yokel had gone to sleep.

It was always a difficult balance to strike. Given enough time, Heneage could guarantee to crack any man, usually without even having to damage him too much, so he could be executed without the fickle London mob feeling too sorry for him. He had found that lack of sleep, hunger and thirst would do the job more effectively than Topcliffe and all his ingenuity. But Heneage had a strong feeling that he didn't have very much time. He was walking on a thin crust over a quicksand and there were too many things he didn't know: Marlowe was supposed to arrest Sir Robert Carey, Marlowe knew him well, and Marlowe had managed to arrest this useless northern bumpkin instead. How was it possible? Marlowe was usually far more reliable than that. Had he betrayed Heneage? Surely not, surely he wouldn't dare.

As a result, Carey was still loose in London and had been for several hours when Heneage had thought he was safely caught. What had he been doing? Had he managed to reach his father, despite the cordon of watchers around Somerset House? Surely he hadn't worked out what was going on? Had he found his brother? Had Edmund Carey come out of hiding and met him? There were so many perplexities, the whole thing depended now on Heneage finding Edmund Carey first, damn the man for an unreliable drunk and a thief.

The rocking carriage had settled down to a steady rhythm. Heneage watched, thinking of ways and means. After a while, he banged the flat of his hand on the carriage door.

'That's enough, open up,' he ordered. After his henchman had swung down from the carriage, he climbed the steps and looked at the northerner who was on his knees on the narrow floor, hunched

in a ball and making the soft pants and moans men make when
they think they're being stoically silent.

'Get him on the bench, I want to talk to him again.'

Heneage's man kicked the northerner. 'Get up.'

The northerner stayed where he was, probably hadn't heard.
'You'll have to help him.'

In the end it took both of them to heave the northerner back
onto the bench, where he sat still hunched and wheezing.

'You're being very foolish, you know,' Heneage said sadly.
'I'd always thought Borderers were sensible folk who know when
something is quite hopeless.'

The man lifted his head and made a coughing noise which
Heneage realised was actually a breathless chuckle. He said
something indistinct. Heneage reached across, took a handful
of hair and lifted his head a bit more.

'What did you say?'

'Ah said . . . ye dinna ken any of us then.'

'Edmund Carey,' said Heneage. 'Where is he? I know you know
where he is. Tell me and this will stop.'

The Borderer showed his teeth in a grin and spat as copiously
as he could in Heneage's face.

Mistress Julie Granville had been sewing ruffs for a long time and
quite enjoyed the work. Sitting in the shade of an awning with
the other respectable women in the gaol, her fingers flew as she
hemmed the narrow twelve yards of linen that would eventually
decorate somebody's neck. She didn't even need to look at what
she was doing any more, her fingers worked automatically making
a very soft rhythmic sound, of the prick as the needle went in and
out, the tap of her thimble pushing it, the drawing sound as the
thread passed through. She was sitting where she could watch the
gatehouse to see the return of the man who had promised to help
her unfortunate gentleman in Bolton's Ward. She was worried
about him. The gaol servants had grabbed him in the way they
used when they were about to give someone a beating. For all she
knew he might be in the Hole already though generally Newton
made a big production of it when he was ill-treating some poor

creature, he would make sure everyone knew so they would fear him more.

Some people were at the gate, haggling with the guard there over the garnish he wanted to let them in to visit their friends, as they said. It was only about an hour after the northerner had been taken away, but her ears caught the different sound and rhythm from one of the servingmen, the same sound Henry Dodd's voice had had.

She looked at him, hoping it was Dodd. It wasn't. This was somebody taller, dressed country-style in a completely fashionless suit that didn't fit him properly and a leather jerkin, somebody with wavy dark red hair. She blinked and squinted, catching her breath: he looked so like Edmund when he first came to the gaol, only younger and less stocky, so much the same swagger in his walk, the same humorous smile, the same . . . She knew she had gone pale and then flushed. Of course she had been lonely in the summer and she knew how wrong was the heady rush of feelings that had struck her like a summer storm when she talked to Edmund that first time, after her son had accidentally hit him with a flung stone meant for a rat . . . But he had been rueful and sympathetic, allowing her to bandage his ear where the stone had clipped it, even interceding to save the little boy from her anger. When he looked at her she felt he looked at her as if she were another man, not just a woman to be seduced or ignored. No, that was wrong: not another man, but as if she were his equal, as if he thought of her as a person and was prepared to like her. He had been gentlemanly, he had made none of the usual suggestions that the men in the gaol routinely tried on all the women not over the age of sixty nor deformed, he had been respectable and friendly. It had been the most seductive experience of her life. In her heart she had fallen into sin at once, without any coaxing from Edmund.

Now here it was again, unmistakeable: the same energy, the same flamboyance, though subtly different. After Edmund took sick with the gaol-fever and she had nursed him, he had raved in delirium about himself, his brothers, his father, his mother, as men do when they don't know what they're saying. That was when she had learned his true name and begged him to write to his father to bail him out and he had adamantly refused. He had spoken of his younger brother with a wistful, envious admiration and then as the fever disordered his brain more and more, with a touching concern, begging her not to let Robin or Philly see him in such a state . . .

Julie Granville put down her sewing carefully on the piece of canvas she used to wrap it in when she wasn't working. Then she stood up, dusted off her skirt, adjusted her cap and ruff and walked across the courtyard to where Edmund's brother was squatting, talking gently to some of the children playing knuckle bones in the dust.

'. . . a man in a blackberry-coloured suit, a bit shorter than me and stronger-built with a very glum face and funny way o' talking like this? Have you seen anyone like that? I might pay as much as a shilling to someone who could tell me about him . . .'

'Yes, I seen 'im, sir,' said one of the urchins. ' 'E was the one wot Mr Gaoler Newton's men was going to give a leatherin' to, they took 'im out of the courtyard an hour ago.'

'Where did they take him?'

'Mr Newton's lodgings, and there was strangers here, a fat man in brocade and velvet wiv lots of servants . . .'

Ceremoniously Edmund's brother handed over a sixpence. 'I'll give you the other half of the shilling if it turns out you're telling the truth. Now have any of you seen another man, a gentleman who looks like me . . .'

She shouldn't address him as Sir Robert. He was wearing a country farmer's clothing and his face and hands were dirty, he must be in disguise, though his boots fitted him far too well to belong to a farmer. She coughed and held her hands tightly together over her apron. He looked up at her cautiously, smiled, stood, took off his hat and just stopped himself at the beginning of what would surely have been a very magnificent court bow.

'Are you . . . are you called Robin?' she asked.

The intensity of his blue gaze shook her. 'What of it, mistress?' he asked with a strong northern sound in his voice.

She must be careful. What if he was one of Edmund's enemies, one of the men he was hiding from. Just because he looked so like

Edmund didn't necessarily mean they were brothers, and perhaps there was some other urgent reason why Edmund didn't want his family told. Family members could hate each other more bitterly than mere enemies, as she knew to her cost.

How could she check? Inspiration came from one of the many nights she had spent sitting next to Edmund as he fought and raved, trying to cool him down with Thames water, fanning him with her apron.

'Goodman, can you tell me who taught you to ride?' she asked.

Blue eyes narrowed, the man frowned. 'It was my brother, mistress, why?'

'What was his name?'

'Edmund.'

'Can you tell me what . . . how you treated him at the first lesson?'

The frown got heavier. Oh God, what if she was wrong? What if this was Heneage's man . . .

'Why?'

'Please, bear with me.'

'Well . . .' he grinned infectiously. 'I'm afraid I bit him. I'd fallen off and he was making me get back on again, so I bit his ear. Drew blood too.'

'What happened?'

'No, you tell *me* what happened.'

She smiled, pleased that he had good sense. 'He shouted, the pony bolted and you both got into trouble because it broke into a garden and ate the peas.'

He had caught her arms, was leaning down to stare into her eyes and she caught a faint spicy lavender smell from him, under the normal musk that no man produced naturally, which confirmed her opinion that he was not wearing his own clothes.

'Where is he, mistress? Yes, my name's Robin, I'm his brother. Can you take me to him? Did he send you?'

It was the shadow of desire to feel Edmund's brother's hands on her and she flushed, stepped back. He let go at once.

'Please, mistress, I've been combing London for him ... Is he all right? Is he still alive?'

For answer she turned, led him across the courtyard to the steps down, paid an ill-afforded penny to the gaol servant who was dozing there on a stool to let them in. Robin looked up and around at the darkness and stink of Bolton's Ward, his nostrils flaring. She went across towards where Edmund lay, and saw him move feebly, trying to turn away, hide his face. Robin spotted him too, lengthened his stride and was there first, kneeling on the slimy stones, bending, catching his brother's shoulders, lifting him, embracing him. She smiled to see it, then turned away so they could have some privacy.

When she approached Robin had sat back on his haunches.

'What the hell were you playing at?' he was demanding in a furious whisper. 'Father's been searching for you for weeks, why the devil didn't you send a message? Why in hell did you stay in this shit hole, you could have died ... You can't mess around with gaol-fever, it nearly killed me and I had the two best nurses in the world looking after me, for Christ's sake ...'

His rage convinced her more than his affection had, but it was distressing Edmund who was lying back on his grubby pillow, panting.

She touched Robin's shoulder and he whipped round, glaring at her. 'Mistress, why didn't you ...'

'He begged me not to, sir,' she said firmly. 'I tried my best to get him to write to your father, but he wouldn't, even when he was lucid. And most of this time he has been too ill to do anything.'

'You might have done it on your own, got him out of this filthy place.'

His anger shook her, though she knew it was really a diffuse fury that wasn't aimed at her.

'S ... sir, I didn't know what to do. I didn't dare reveal who he was or contact your father because he was so desperate that I shouldn't. How could I go against what he said? He pleaded with me not to betray him, said if I sent any message to my lord, the spy in his household would make sure Heneage found him first ... And he was so afraid of Heneage. And in any case, I think he was ashamed. He said many times he wanted to die.'

'Oh Christ.'

'He very nearly did, sir, and is still not recovered. This is the most dangerous time with gaol-fever; if he strains himself too much now, it will come back and probably kill him. Please be gentle with him.'

It was touching and made Julie want to smile at them. Although Robin was still fuming, Edmund's frail hand had crept out from under the blankets and into his brother's. They were holding hands like children and neither of them had noticed.

'Yes, you're right,' Robin said eventually. 'I'm sorry, Ned, I should have thought. I suppose it probably was right to lie low, but . . . for God's sake, why in this place? Why not the Eightpenny Ward?'

'Most of his money was counterfeit and somebody stole the rest,' Julie explained.

'Bastards.'

Edmund said something with a faint smile.

'No, you're damned right nobody would have thought to look for you in here. I didn't. How could you possibly bear it? It's worse than below decks in a ship. It's like . . . it's like a circle of hell.'

Again Edmund whispered something to his brother with a look at her that Julie knew meant she was the subject. She could feel herself flushing.

Robin listened for a moment. 'One question,' he said. 'When did you understand Heneage's game?'

'When I . . . paid my tailor with the gold we made . . . I thought we'd made . . . and he weighed it and threw it back in my face for a forgery . . . I suddenly saw it . . .' came Edmund's creaking breathless voice,' . . . saw how it used me against Father. All I could think of was to hide and the only place I thought they might not look at first was in gaol, especially . . . in a different name. I made a deal with the man to arrest me for the debt in mother's name, as Edward Morgan.'

Robin nodded. Edmund lay back and panted, white with

exhaustion. Very gently, Robin released his brother's hand, put it under the blankets, tucked him up like a child and then stood, dusting his fingers and his legs.

'Mistress Granville,' he said quietly to her. 'I don't think we have much time. I want you to go to the courtyard and find a man there, by the name of Kit Marlowe. He's almost as tall as I am, velvet peascod doublet slashed with peach taffeta, but he looks like a cocky smug bastard and that's exactly what he is. When you find him, tell him . . . tell him to go to my father and fetch reinforcements.'

Edmund was plucking at the blanket, the cords of his neck straining to lift his head. Robin saw and patted him. 'I know, I know, Marlowe's Heneage's man. He says he wants my help to get him in with Essex and just for the moment, I believe him. All right?'

Edmund let his head fall back and closed his eyes. They looked sunken and his colour was bad. Robin looked down at him with a worried frown and then at her.

'Please, mistress, hurry,' he said. 'I'm staying with Ned. If a plump-looking man in a fine marten-trimmed gown asks you where he is, even if he says he's Mr Thomas Heneage, the Queen's Vice Chancellor, lie.'

She nodded, frightened at the large stakes these men were playing for . . . Defying the Queen's official? Well, she could do it for Edmund.

In the end, it was lucky that Heneage had brought no thumbscrews with him, because he had expected to be able to capture Sir Robert Carey and put the next part of his plan into operation. It meant he had to send one of his men to fetch some to use on his prisoner. While he waited, he decided to see if painting word pictures of some of the effects and refinements of thumbscrews would have any effect on the yokel. He had been talking for ten minutes when he realised that the blasted man had somehow managed to doze off again, lying sideways on the carriage bench.

His first impulse was to use his dagger on the man's eyeballs, see if that would keep him awake, but he controlled himself.

He was absolutely certain the northerner knew where Edmund Carey was hiding. The spittle he had carefully scrubbed off his face before snatching his henchman's cosh and using it for five satisfying minutes on the bastard northerner's kidneys, that infuriating childish gesture confirmed his instinct that he was dealing with defiance and not ignorance.

He was planning how to use the thumbscrews to break Carey's man quickly, considering other places you could use them than merely fingers, when it occurred to him to wonder how it was a northerner could know where Edmund Carey was when nobody else did.

The answer came to him from God, as simply as the sun rising. He actually laughed, because it was so obvious.

He leaned out of the carriage and called his second in command over to him, told his driver to whip up the horses again. He called to where his henchmen were standing in a group, sharing a leather bottle of beer and practising knife throwing at the swollen corpse of a rat lying in a gutter. Then he kicked the northerner's shins to wake him up.

'Edmund Carey's in the Fleet, isn't he?' he said, and saw the telltale change in the man's eyes. 'You really should have told me before, it would have saved you some pain. And you would have told me in the end, you know; people always do. Probably after we'd crushed one or both of your balls.'

'Ay,' croaked the man. 'Ay, he's in the Fleet. Deid and buried, wi' gaol fever.'

Heneage laughed at this nonsense. 'Oh, really,' he remonstrated. 'If that was true, you'd have told me at once, you're not mad.'

'Mr Heneage,' said the man, breathing carefully. 'I wouldnae willingly tell ye where yer ain arsehole was, not if yer catamite begged me to.'

Heneage blinked at him. 'When I've finished with Edmund Carey and his interfering brother, I will take you apart, piece by piece.'

The carriage jolted into motion, causing the northerner to whine through his teeth very satisfactorily as he fell helplessly off the bench and in a huddle onto the narrow floor. Heneage left him there, so he could get the benefit of the bone-jolting movement of the coach. Generally anybody but an invalid or a woman would prefer to ride but for some purposes, such as privately transporting prisoners, a carriage was unimproveable.

Julie Granville heard the hammering on the prison gate and went to look, along with a crowd of children. When Newton opened the postern a plump man was standing there, four square in fur-trimmed velvet and at his back at least eight hard-faced men at arms.

He stood with his arms folded while Newton bowed and scraped and tried to argue in a wheedling tone of voice about his authority and his position and his properly paid-for office.

One of the men at arms stepped forward and cuffed Newton. 'Don't delay Mr Vice Chancellor,' he said. 'This is in the name of the Queen.'

Newton cringed and stepped back. The men at arms filed through with the Vice Chancellor in the middle.

Julie picked up her skirts and ran across the courtyard, down the steps to Bolton's Ward. The gaol servant now sitting there was an odious man she had had dealings with before who leered at her bodice and told her he didn't want a penny for garnish, but a nice loving kiss. For a moment she couldn't think what to do, whether she should let him or not, but her guts revolted at the thought. She could hear the sounds of the upper parts of the gaol being searched while the prisoners were harried into groups according to ward in the courtyard. Her children would be frightened without her, but one of her gossips would look after them, she knew. Meanwhile she didn't have time to argue with a lecherous gaoler.

She went up close to him, putting up her mouth as if yielding, and when he reached for her she kneed him as hard as she could in the balls. He made a pleasing *oof* noise and reeled against the wall, and she took the keys off his belt, opened the heavy door with it.

Her eyes took a few minutes to adjust to the dimness, but she could see Robin Carey over near his brother, sitting cross-legged, talking quietly to him. He looked up as the door opened, saw her and came instantly to his feet.

'What is it, mistress?'

'The Vice Chancellor ... Mr Heneage ... he's searching the gaol.'

For a moment Robin looked astonished.

'But he's only had Dodd for a couple of hours ...' he said to himself in a voice of bewilderment. Then he stood absolutely still and she had no idea what he was thinking because his face had gone stiff like a mask.

He looked at her considering. 'Mistress,' he said, quite conversationally. 'Will you help me?'

She hesitated. What would happen to her, to her children? Could she, dare she trust him? His family were important and rich, perhaps they might help her? Or perhaps they would simply use her and forget her. She didn't know.

She saw Edmund was raising his head again, looking at her. His eyes were less vividly blue than his brother's, more of a sea-grey colour, but the memory of the kindness and laughter in them steadied her.

Her heart was thumping hard. She came in, shut the door behind her and locked it with the key, then came across to him.

'That won't hold them very long, I'm afraid. Newton has the master keys,' she said.

'Do you have the key for his ankle chain?'

'Probably.'

They tried a couple, found the right one and unlocked it, revealing a wide bracelet of ulcers on the bony ankle. Robin bit his lip when he saw it, then raised his head and looked around. Some of the other beggars and sick men in the ward were looking up, a couple of them were moving anxiously as far away from the brothers as they could, being tethered.

'Over there,' Robin said, pointing at an alcove under one of the high semi-circular barred windows that were at ground level of the courtyard. 'I'll carry Edmund, you bring his bedding.'

Edmund was trying to struggle upright, but his brother simply picked him up in his arms and straightened his knees.

'Oh, shut up, Ned,' Robin told him. 'You don't weigh anything like as much as several of the women I've carried into my bed.'

259

Julie scooped up the straw pallet that had cost her sixpence, trying not to think about its likely population of lice and fleas, took the pillow and the blanket and followed as Robin carried his brother briskly over to the alcove, apologising politely as he stepped over prone bodies and cursing once when he nearly slipped on a turd. Julie put down the pallet and Robin laid Edmund gently down on it, arranged the blanket and pillow and then stood and leaned his arm on the pillar of the arch. There was a querulous tone in Edmund's voice, though Julie couldn't quite make out the words.

'Ned, you're a prize idiot. Heneage isn't going to get you and nor are you going to hang for coining. I'm going to hang you myself for causing me so much trouble. Mistress Granville,' Robin added gently to her. 'I really think you ought to leave.'

'I don't want to,' she blurted out, cut to the quick that he would dismiss her like that.

'Mistress, life might get a little tense in here for a while. Those other poor sods can't escape but you can.'

She sniffed at him, turned her shoulder and went resolutely, holding her breath when necessary, to unlock all the other ankle chains in the room. Some of the beggars were too far gone to move, but those that could instantly crawled or staggered out of the way to the stone benches at the side of room. Robin watched her without further comment. She came back and sat down on the stone floor next to Edmund, spread out her skirts and put her knife in her lap. Then she took Edmund's hand in her own and stroked it.

'You know he's married, mistress,' she heard Robin's voice above her. He was looking down, not unkindly.

'So am I, sir,' she said.

Whether Edmund's brother would have been tactless enough to ask the question he must have been wondering about, she never found out. Somebody tried the door, found it locked, hammered a couple of times and then there was a sequence of shouts as others were sent scuttling off to find the gaoler and Mr Vice Chancellor.

'Oh, bollocks,' Robin said, mainly to himself, drawing his sword and stepping out a little to block the alcove's opening with his body. She heard him muttering to himself and thought he might be praying, hoped fervently that the Lord God of Hosts would hear and perhaps send a few angels to help, then smiled at herself for being childish. It was odd she could do it. Her heart was thumping so hard and her hands had gone cold.

The gaoler's keys scraped and clattered in the lock, it was flung open and two men at arms came in, clubs in their hands. They stopped when they saw Robin standing there, waiting for them, sword bare.

'Good afternoon, gentlemen,' he said, and Julie could hear that he was smiling.

The Vice Chancellor pushed past and stood between his two henchmen, his little mouth pursed and pouched with anger.

'What do you think you're doing, Carey?' he demanded. 'Your brother is guilty of forgery, which is a hanging offence, witchcraft which is a burning offence, and treason which is a . . .'

'Hanging, drawing and quartering offence,' drawled Robin. 'Yes, I know.'

'Are you going to hand him over to me in a sensible fashion or are you going to be stupid?' demanded Heneage.

'Oh, normally I'd instantly decide to be stupid,' said Robin. 'But first I want to know who you're after.'

'Your brother, Edmund Carey. He stole property which is mine and he . . .'

'Edmund Carey? That's not him. That's Edward Morgan. Didn't you check the book?'

'I know your mother's maiden name as well as you do, Carey, if that's what she was and . . .'

'You know, if you insult my mother I'll simply have to kill you, which I could do, right now, if I wanted to. And then it would all be very inconvenient, I'd hang for it if I lived, which might upset my father, but you would be dead and facing God Almighty and all the poor souls you've destroyed with torture and ill-treatment. And then you would go to hell for the rest of eternity. So don't you think you ought to try to be polite, hm?'

'The sick man that you are standing in front of is Edmund

Carey and I want him,' said Heneage impatiently. 'I'm going to take him, so get out of my way. I won't tell you twice.'

'You're going to take him, are you? Who? You personally? I don't think so. You haven't the stomach and you haven't the strength for it. So who's going to do it?' Again Julie could hear the smile in his voice as he moved his head to look lazily round at the men-at-arms crowding the stinking cellar and making it even more airless. 'Are you?' he asked the nearest one. 'Or you? Or you, over there? Or the two of you? I think that's all you could get in on me at once, given the way this cellar's built. Such inconvenient pillars, aren't they? Whyever did they build it like that? So you see, it isn't really very easy for your men, Heneage. They've got clubs and knives and I've got a sword and I'm sure they'll knock me down eventually, but in the process I should be able to kill at least one, maybe even two of them. Maybe I'll maim a few more of them, you never know. This is a broadsword: it's not perfect for close-quarters work but it's quite sharp and it has two edges as well as a point and I'm in excellent practice with it.'

He looked round again, balancing on his toes and looking quite relaxed. 'So who's it to be? Which of your men love you, Heneage, which ones would follow you into battle?'

You could feel the tension in the air and also the way uncertainty spread among the men around Heneage. They were looking at each other, assessing Robin's stance, deciding whether he was telling the truth, wondering why he was talking so much. Julie knew. He was acting, playing for time. Edmund's bony fingers were gripping hers tight enough to hurt.

'Maybe we could just fight it out, Heneage, eh?' Robin was moving now, waving his sword in elaborate arcs and making it flash hypnotically in the sunlight filtering down through the window, shifting his feet like a tennis player. 'You and me, sword to sword, or knife to knife. That would be fun, very chivalric, very old-fashioned. Or use guns. I can see you're not a fighting man, more of a desk man really, aren't you? Standing back while other men do your dirty work, get themselves killed in your service? But you could probably fire a gun, couldn't you, something light like a dag, only weighs a couple of pounds, you could do that. Maybe you could even aim it straight? I'm not as good a shot as I should be, you'd have a chance.'

Heneage's mouth tightened. 'Don't be ridiculous. In the name of the Queen I order . . .'

'Don't drag my cousin into this,' said Carey pointedly and Julie had to hide a smile because of the expression on some of the men at arms' faces.

'Webster, Oat, arrest that man.'

Two of the men at arms moved forward uncertainly. Heneage seemed to expand with rage like a pigeon's neck. 'And you, Potter, get him out of there.'

The men-at-arms were advancing in a circle on Carey who had stopped his little dance and taken up a fighting crouch, the open *en garde* with sword and poignard recommended for more than one opponent. He was grinning at them, showing his teeth like a fox at bay.

'I'll give twenty-five shillings to the man who subdues him,' said Heneage. Carey laughed.

'Christ, Heneage, you're cheap. The Borderers are offering ten pounds sterling for my head.'

That was when everything got confused. Julie noticed that the men-at-arms at the back of Bolton's Ward were distracted, they were looking over their shoulders. Heneage was listening to one who was whispering in his ear, there was the sound of boots on the stairs, shouts. Meanwhile the men at the front hadn't realised anything was happening, they were focused on Carey and nerving themselves. Suddenly they made their rush, two of them from either side with their clubs high. One swung down, one swung sideways, Carey blocked the higher one with his blade, leaped sideways to avoid the worst of the sideswipe, used his poignard to stab for the man's face when his sword got stuck in the cudgel's wood and the man fell backwards away from Carey's stab while the other two tried to hit him as he tried to shake the cudgel off his sword. Julie flung herself forwards trying to catch the boots of one of them as Carey took a blow on the shoulder and faltered; she caught them and got a kick in the face though she brought the man down.

There was another man-at-arms in the fight; Carey had dropped his sword, dodged a club, kicked someone in the kneecap and then somebody had caught his arm, he was hit again, shrewdly with the thrusting end of a cudgel in the belly and he doubled over. One man at arms lifted his club high to bring it down on Carey's head and finish the fight. It bounced off the sturdy haft of a halberd thrust out by a broad elderly man in black velvet and brocade. There was a sweep of tawny satin and flame-red velvet gown as the elderly man whirled, punched the man-at-arms and knocked him down.

Carey was upright again but obviously couldn't see properly, hadn't realised he could stop fighting now, he was lungeing towards the newcomer with his poignard. Julie put her hand to her mouth, but the old gentleman stood his ground with the halberd held in defence across his body and roared, 'ROBIN.'

It was almost comical to see Carey stop almost in mid-air, skidding on the slimy floor, fighting for balance. One of the new men at arms in a blazing livery of black and yellow put out a hand and stopped him from falling over.

'F . . . Father,' he wheezed as his sight cleared, looking round him at his father's men, some of whom were grinning. 'Where the . . . hell have you been?' He sheathed his poignard carefully at the back of his belt, and leaned against the wall, tenderly cradled his midriff, easing his shoulder and wincing, shaking his head to clear it.

Lord Hunsdon looked at his son for a moment, obviously assessing him for serious damage, and then he turned to Heneage who had suddenly seemed to shrink in size and had drawn back. The place was so full of men now, it was hard to move, every one of Heneage's men countered with one of Hunsdon's.

Hunsdon stared coldly at Heneage for several seconds. 'Mr Vice Chamberlain, I'll deal with you later,' he said. 'Where's Ned?'

Carey gestured wordlessly, still working on catching his breath. Julie picked herself up from where she had been nursing her painfully bruised cheek, curtseyed as low as she safely could to Lord Hunsdon.

'He's here, my lord,' she said. 'Be careful, don't go near him if you've never had gaol-fever. He's been terribly ill with . . .'

Quite gently Hunsdon put her aside, went over to his son and embraced him. Only Julie heard what he said which was, 'There now, poor boy, you bloody idiot, there now.'

The next moment Hunsdon had turned round and was giving a dizzying series of orders which cleared Bolton's Ward as if by magic, Heneage standing blank-faced in a corner under guard, his men at arms told they'd get in no trouble if they went and stood quietly in a corner of the gaol courtyard, some of Hunsdon's men sent running to find and hire a litter, no bloody new-fangled carriages mind, they could ignore the useless contraption standing in Fleet Lane.

Hunsdon went over and clasped his youngest son to him as well. Carey was recovering quickly now, bright eyed and rather pleased with himself until something occurred to him and his face clouded.

'Where's Sergeant Dodd, Father?' he asked anxiously. 'Have you found him?'

Heneage's second-in-command scooped up Carey's sword, pulled the cudgel off the blade and gave it to him, hilt first. 'If you mean the northerner, sir, he's in the carriage.'

Carey turned and ran out of Bolton's Ward, up the stairs. Hunsdon nodded at two of his men to go with him. Heneage looked down at his boots.

Another of Hunsdon's men came trotting in to report that the litter was ready in the courtyard. Hunsdon took his magnificent gown off and wrapped it around his son before two of the men picked him up carefully under the knees and armpits and carried him up the stairs.

Hunsdon nodded to Julie and offered her his arm. They were all at the door of Bolton's Ward, ready to leave, when Carey came back down the stairs two at a time, went over to Heneage and, without preamble, lashed out with his fist. Heneage fell back grabbing at his nose and Carey followed up, quite silent, white to the lips, crowding him against the wall, punching him with a blinding flurry of short cruel blows. Heneage cringed, wailing, 'I didn't touch him, he didn't tell me, I worked it out, I never hurt . . .' The words ended in a gargle as Carey put his hands round the man's neck and started to squeeze.

'Stop him,' ordered Hunsdon wearily and it took three of his men to do it because Carey was deaf and blind to anything except killing Heneage. Julie had never seen a gentleman go berserk before and she found it very ugly and frightening. Edmund would not have lost all control like that, used such barbarous violence.

Hunsdon went close to his son who was still struggling white-faced.

'Is your man dead?' he asked. He asked the question several times before his son could be sane enough to answer him.

'No, I . . . no, he's not.'

'Is he crippled?'

Carey's eyelids fluttered as he thought. 'I don't . . . think so.'

'Well, thank God for that. You've a good man there. Now you know you can't throttle the Queen's Vice Chancellor, she wouldn't like it.'

Robin was breathing hard and shakily. 'One of . . . one of Heneage's servants was there, with thumbscrews.'

'But they hadn't been used.'

Robin shook his head.

'Well, thank God for that too,' rumbled Hunsdon, putting his hand on his son's shoulder and shaking him gently back and forth. 'Thank God.'

Heneage was pinching at the bridge of his nose, bent over to keep the blood away from his fine clothes, his handkerchief darkening.

'I'll see you in Star Chamber for this,' he said huskily. 'How dare you . . .'

'How dare you touch my man?!' roared Carey, swinging round to him and making his father's men grab at him again to stop his lunge. 'If he dies I'll make sure you follow him, you'll swing for it or I'll kill you myself, you fucking piece of . . .'

'ROBIN!' bellowed Hunsdon, nose to nose with Carey. 'Do I have to hit you to calm you down?'

Carey was breathing heavily through his nose again but he was trying to regain his self-control. Julie saw him trembling all over like a nervous horse with the effort.

Heneage was still muttering sulkily and stupidly about law-suits for battery and assault. Hunsdon looked over at him contemptuously.

'Be quiet,' he ordered. 'This is unseemly. We shall discuss these matters somewhere more private.'

That reminded Julie of the secret Edmund had given her to hold. She turned aside to lift up her kirtle and take it out of the pocket of her petticoat where it had been weighing her down for weeks. She held the heavy little package out to Lord Hunsdon.

'My lord,' she said. 'Ned . . . Mr Carey gave me this to hold for him.'

Hunsdon took it, looking puzzled. Carey reached out his hand. 'My lord, may I?' Hunsdon gave it to him, he opened it, glanced at it and nodded. Heneage watched and for the second time Julie saw real fear in his face. Carey held one of the little round lumps of metal up to the light and squinted.

'The Tower mark,' he said. 'I thought so.' He smiled so cruelly at Heneage that Julie decided she didn't like him at all. 'We can destroy you now, Mr Vice, you know that don't you?'

Heneage didn't answer.

In a manner that brooked no argument, Lord Hunsdon took over the gaoler's lodgings. Julie felt that perhaps she should withdraw now, go and see to her children who were staring at her from behind the skirts of the woman who ran the ruff-making circle. But Hunsdon insisted that she stay with him even after Edmund had been loaded barely conscious into the horse litter and sent off at a sedate walk down Fleet Lane towards Somerset House, past the row of tethered horses that had brought Lord Hunsdon and his men to the Fleet. Another litter was being fetched for Robin's henchman, who was sitting in the sunlight on the steps of the carriage, bent like an old man and looking putty-coloured and ill. Obstinately he insisted in his guttural, almost incomprehensible, voice that if they would just get him a decent horse he could ride, for God's sake, what did he want wi' a litter like a woman, he was nae sae bad, he'd been worse, dinna fuss, and forebye he didnae want to go back to Somerset House until he knew what the hell

267

had been going on ... In the end, to stop his complaints, two of Hunsdon's men helped him into Newton's living room and sat him on the best padded chair, with a cushion to ease his back.

There Carey paced up and down in front of his father who had taken the only other chair and was sitting behind Newton's table like a judge.

'As you know, my lord, Mr Heneage wants to be Lord Chamberlain and have control over the Queen's courtiers, her security arrangements and her mind, if possible.'

Hunsdon grunted at this in a way which indicated he was neither surprised nor shocked nor very impressed. Carey answered the comment with a smile.

'I know, my lord, it's pathetic, isn't it? But still. He wants to remove you, and since you won't oblige him by committing treason, raping a maid of honour or going to Mass, he's been looking for some way to blackmail you into resigning your office.'

'I protest at these outrageous accusations. I have never been so insulted ...'

'Oh, be quiet,' growled Hunsdon. 'Let the boy ... let my son tell his tale.'

'Under protest, be it noted.'

'Noted, noted. Yes, Robin?'

'Dodd pointed out to me the similarity with some of the gangsters we have in the north. If a man is too strong to attack directly, they kidnap one of his near relatives and apply pressure that way. King James does something similar when he takes noble hostages off his Border lords.'

'Dirty business.'

'Effective, though, my lord. If Mr Heneage had succeeded and taken Edmund into the Tower on some trumped up but believable charge, you might have been willing to exchange the office of Lord Chamberlain for him.'

'Certainly not,' said Hunsdon, and glared at Heneage.

Carey didn't comment but continued. 'This summer Edmund was inveigled into a project by two men who called themselves alchemists. The plan as presented to him was to use the Philosopher's Stone they claimed to have discovered to create a large quantity of gold blanks. They wanted him to lay his hands on a set of Tower coin dies: that way, they said, what they did would not be forgery. The blanks would be gold, the coin dies would be genuine, so the coins they struck would be no different from the Queen's money in any way.'

Hunsdon sighed heavily at this. 'He fell for it?'

'I'm afraid he did, my lord. Of course they needed some seed-gold to work the transformation, which Edmund got for them somehow. And the coin dies – well, by a remarkable coincidence, Edmund knew a man who had just retired from being one of the Deputy Mint-masters at the Tower and who had kept a pair of dies that should have been cancelled because they were an old design.'

'Heneage's man?'

Carey smiled. 'Of course. Edmund bribed the man to get the dies. He witnessed the transformation, which he found very impressive since he knew nothing at all about the goldsmith's art. What he saw was a method called parcel-gilding. According to the goldsmith I talked to, it's a very simple thing to do if you know how to control a furnace and the main problem is to keep the mercury fumes from escaping so you can resublimate it and reuse it. An alchemist's pelican does the job perfectly.'

'At the end of it he actually had a pile of parcel-gilt pewter blanks, but he thought they were genuinely gold?'

'Yes, my lord.'

'Why in the name of God didn't he weigh them himself to make sure?'

Carey waved an arm. 'I don't know, my lord.'

Hunsdon rolled his eyes and sighed heavily. 'Go on.'

'Well, then they struck coins from the blanks using the Tower dies and of course the coins looked perfect. Edmund believed that the whole operation was nearly official; one of the alchemists had a warrant from Heneage and the idea was that the coins would be used to help pay for the expenses of his intelligencing which the Queen will never give him enough money to run properly. Edmund took a fee for his part in getting the seed gold and finding the coin dies.'

'And then he tried to spend it and found . . .'

'Quite so. They were straightforward forgeries. His tailor weighed them and told him what they were.'

Hunsdon was staring coldly at Heneage. 'Of course uttering false coin is a hanging offence.'

'Which the Queen takes very seriously.'

'Very seriously indeed. She would be enraged,' said Hunsdon. 'The most I could have done would have been to beseech the mercy of the axe for Edmund. She might also have been suspicious of me.'

'Precisely, my lord.'

Hunsdon nodded. 'Well, it's clever, you have to give him that,' he rumbled. 'It might have worked.'

'I think Heneage planned that Edmund would be arrested for coining. He would then offer to you the services of his pursuivants to find the alchemists responsible, in exchange for your resignation from the Lord Chamberlainship. Possibly he might even have found somebody to take the blame.'

Hunsdon nodded again. 'Under such circumstances . . . Hm.'

'Only at last, Edmund started to use his brain. When the tailor accused him, he worked out what had been going on, what the whole elaborate coney-catching operation was about. He isn't stupid, he's . . .'

'He has no common sense. Whatsoever.'

Carey coughed. 'At that point he panicked. He knew Heneage must be behind the business because of the warrant. All he could think of was to lie low somehow. It seemed to him that he might be safer in gaol than out of it, so he struck a deal with the tailor to be arrested in a false name.'

'But why the devil didn't he come to me?'

'He was afraid of your anger, my lord, and also . . . He was ashamed. He knew how stupid he'd been.'

'Urrrh.'

'Also, in the summer you were on Progress with the Queen and very hard to contact. Gaol might not have been such a bad idea, as a temporary measure, until you came back. Unfortunately, within a week of coming here to the Fleet, he had caught a gaol-fever, his true money had been stolen or, more likely, he had gambled it away, and Newton, who didn't know who he was, had slung him in Bolton's Ward. There he might have died had not Mrs Granville here nursed him and supported him.'

In his pacing, Carey had come close to where Julie stood, drawing her forward. He smiled encouragingly at her, but she looked down, not liking him any more.

She curtseyed to Lord Hunsdon.

'Is this true, mistress?'

'Yes, my lord.'

'You kept my son alive through a gaol-fever in that pesthole he was lying in?'

'Er . . . that was God's Will, my lord, I only nursed him.'

'Why?'

'Well . . . er . . .' she knew she was flushing and she hoped Edmund's father would just think she was shy. 'He was kind to my children, sir, and very patient when Johnnie accidentally hit him with a stone on the ear, and . . . er . . .' Edmund's father had a look of amused understanding on his face. 'We are both married, my lord,' she added hurriedly. 'There was nothing improper . . .'

'You weren't working for Mr Heneage?'

That angered her. 'No, sir, certainly not.'

'I hardly think so, my lord,' drawled Carey. 'Since she saved my skin as well just before you arrived, by bringing down one of Heneage's men when they attacked. She also kept safe the packet of coin-dies and the warrant which Edmund gave her, which she would undoubtedly have given back to Mr Heneage if she had been working for him, since that was one reason why he was searching for Edmund.'

'Mistress Granville,' said Lord Hunsdon, with a little bow from his chair, 'I apologise for suspecting you. I am deeply in your debt and unlike most of my sons, I pay my debts.'

She didn't know what to do except curtsey again.

After a pause to glare at his father for the covert jibe, Carey continued. 'So Edmund had disappeared and with him the Tower coin-dies and the warrant which incriminated Mr Heneage, since he had access to them and Edmund didn't. Heneage was looking for him, you were looking for him . . .

Incidentally, my lord, why did you employ Robert Greene about the business?'

Hunsdon harumphed. 'I thought Edmund might have gone on a binge and you set a drunken gambler to find a drunken gambler. Greene has investigated for me in the past; he's good at it, when he's sober, or nearly.'

'I see,' said Carey in a tone that skirted very close to being an insult. 'Well, after he had also drawn a blank, you sent for me, very inconveniently, from Carlisle.'

'How was I to know how many warrants for debt you had waiting for you? None of you idiot boys will ever tell me how bad your position is.'

You could see Carey didn't like being called a boy by his father, Julie thought, and also this clearly was a sore point. Carey scowled. 'We fear your wrath, sir.'

'Oh, do you, by God?' growled Hunsdon, scowling back. 'Well, spend less then. Or engage in some halfway sane investments.'

Just for a moment there looked to be the fascinating prospect of father and son leaping into battle against each other. Somebody cleared his throat.

'Ay,' droned a doleful northern voice. 'But how was it yer man Michael got hisself strung up on the Hampstead Hanging Elm?'

Carey looked thoughtfully at Sergeant Dodd. 'It was a mistake. One of Heneage's men paid the footpads that infest the Heath to stop him and wasn't specific enough about how, so they shot him. They didn't have time to bury him so they strung him up so that if our horses spooked at the smell, we wouldn't wonder at it.'

He looked back at his father who was shaking his head regretfully. 'Poor Michael,' Hunsdon said. 'His wife's taken it very hard. Presumably Mr Heneage wanted you, so he could use you to winkle out Edmund.'

'Precisely, sir. I think you know most of the rest of the story.'

That obviously wasn't true if Hunsdon's expression was any guide, but Julie saw him take the hint. He swung round on Heneage.

'Mr Heneage. Have you anything to say?'

Heneage put away the blood-soaked handkerchief he had been

using on his nose. 'This is not a court of law, my lord,' he said thinly. 'But I will say this. Every word of Sir Robert's ridiculous tale is a lie. I have nothing but respect for you, my lord, and for your family, nor would I ever engage in such preposterous plots against you.'

Carey's hand had gone to the hilt of his sword. 'How dare . . .?' he began through his teeth. Hunsdon waved him down.

'Mr Heneage, do you want my son to call you out?'

'I would not accept the challenge, my lord, since duelling is against the law and the clearly expressed will of Her Majesty the Queen. I will however consult my lawyers in case there is a suit for slander that can be pursued, in addition to the charges of assault, battery and false imprisonment for which I have a cast iron case.'

'How do you explain the Tower Mint coin-dies?'

Heneage shrugged. 'I can't, my lord. Nor do I intend to try. Doubtless you or Sir Robert best know what happened. Neither they nor the warrant amount to evidence because a warrant can be forged and the coin-dies might have been come by in a number of ways.'

There was a frustrated silence before Sergeant Dodd spoke up again.

'Ay, well, sir,' he said, his voice compressed. 'I dinna ken what all yon fine courtiers and cousins to the Queen can do agin ye, Mr Heneage, but I think I have as good a case agin ye for assault, battery and false imprisonment and better. And I'm sure my lord Hunsdon will see me right wi' a good lawyer to take the case.'

'With pleasure,' said Hunsdon.

'Possibly I made an unfortunate mistake with you, Dodd . . .'

'Och, did ye now?' said Dodd, sitting forward with a wince. 'Did ye, by Christ? I was slung in gaol in mistake for Sir Robert and ye came along and took me oot on nae warrant whatever, pit me in yer foul contraption of a carriage, and had yer men beat the hell out of me on the suspicion I knew where Sir Robert's brother was. Ye threatened me wi' torture. Ye beat the hell out of me yersen, sir, d'ye recall, personally, wi' a cosh? It's no' gentlemanlike to get yer hands dirty, but ye did and since ma kith and kin are hundreds o' miles away and I canna raid ye and burn yer house down about yer ears, I'll go the southern way to ma satisfaction, and I'll see you in court, sir.'

'I might be . . . er . . . willing to pay compensation to you, Dodd, for a very unfortunate . . .'

Outrage burned in Dodd's face, propelled him out of his chair.

'By God Almighty!' he bellowed, fists on the table. 'I am the Land Sergeant of Gilsland and I have had enough of yer disrespect, Mr Heneage. Ye can call me Sergeant if ye wish tae address me.'

Heneage looked taken aback. 'Er . . . Sergeant.'

'Incidentally, I think the offer of compensation is rather close to an admission here,' said Carey drily. 'Which was witnessed. Do you still want to take me to court, Mr Heneage?'

Heneage's mouth was pinched. 'Possibly we could come to some arrangement.'

Dodd sat down again in the chair quite suddenly. 'Jesus,' he muttered and rubbed at his lower back.

Hunsdon leaned forward and put his forearms on the table. 'We are going to come to this arrangement. You will drop any and all lawsuits against my sons, rescind any warrants you have sworn out regarding them, and in all ways hold them harmless for the events of these past few weeks. In return we will drop any and all lawsuits against you and I will use my best endeavours to persuade Sergeant Dodd of Gilsland to be merciful to you in the matter of his own lawsuit, which is of course a separate issue.'

Heneage sneered. 'I wish to consult my lawyers . . .'

'Why?' snapped Hunsdon. 'Be your own lawyer in this case.'

'And if I refuse?'

'Mr Heneage, you know me. I prefer a quiet life now I'm old. But if I'm stirred to it, I like a fight as well as any man. I think I have the resources and the friends to tie you up with parchment and paper from one end of Westminster Hall to the other.'

'And the Queen?'

'I will not lie to my sovereign. But she'll hear none of this affair unless she asks me about it, so you had better hope she doesn't ask.'

'So had you,' said Heneage venomously. 'She hates coiners.'

Hunsdon tilted his head noncommittally.

Heneage gestured at the warrant and the Tower Mint dies, holding his hand out for them. Hunsdon's eyes half-hooded themselves and he passed them to Sir Robert.

'I want the coin-dies,' said Heneage. 'And the warrant.'

'You admit they were originally yours?' asked Carey.

'No, Sir Robert. I want to suppress false evidence.'

'If they're false, then they can do you no harm,' growled Hunsdon. 'If they're true, then you should certainly not have them since the coin-dies may tempt you to trespass again. I'll keep them safe for you.'

Heneage departed in his carriage, his men jogging along beside it, heading west for his house in Chelsea. Hunsdon's men mounted up in a flurry of circling horses while Hunsdon conferred with the lawyers he had summoned as back-up to the brute force of his henchmen. They conferred at length with Gaoler Newton who proved obstinate now he had the real Sir Robert Carey physically in his power. Eventually, he agreed to release both Carey and Mrs Julie Granville and her children on bonds of a thousand pounds each. Lord Hunsdon uncomplainingly wrote out bankers' drafts for both sums which Gaoler Newton sent straight round to the Exchange to be checked, before putting them in his strongbox.

Mulishly, Sergeant Dodd rejected the expensively hired litter and climbed slowly aboard a quiet-paced mare, where he sat grimly staring ahead of him. Julie refused Sir Robert's courteous offer that she should ride pillion behind him, but accepted the same offer from Lord Hunsdon. Her children came tumbling and squeaking with excitement out of the gate and John her eldest instantly agreed to go up in front of Sir Robert.

The cavalcade trotted sedately down Fleet Lane, over the little bridge and down Fleet Street, threading out to single file at Temple Bar and then going straight in at the main gate of Somerset House. Until that moment, when Lord Hunsdon handed her down with immense ceremony to his waiting steward, Julie had not been able to let herself believe this was anything other than a dream. She looked around at the courtyard with its fine diamond windows shining with sunset, at the strapwork in the brick and the wonderfully elaborate chimneys and she found herself clasping her children as they jumped down or were lifted from the horses and laughing at the madness of it all.

Sunday, 3rd September 1592, late evening

9

Hunsdon's stately Portuguese physician had prescribed bed rest and cold cloths to be applied to Dodd's belly and lower back. The surgeon had been ordered to let eight ounces of blood from Dodd's left arm to prevent infection. The doctor had also prescribed the drinking of tobacco smoke to ease his kidneys, which were very painful. Dodd had pissed some blood when the doctor asked to see his water, which had terrified the life out of him, until Dr Nunez explained that as it was dark and not bright, that meant it was corrupt blood being expelled rather than healthy blood, which was a good sign, generally speaking. He had left, leaving a long list of dietary orders, such as forbidding beer and recommending watered wine, and settled an astonishing bill with the steward which included a very large fee for going on to visit Barnabus's relatives in the City.

Carey was lounging on a chair sharing the long clay pipe with Dodd. He had changed out of Dodd's homespun clothes into an old doublet and hose he used for fowling, and which he had been pleased to find was now a bit loose in the waist and tight on the shoulders.

He blew smoke expertly out of his nose and frowned. 'Smells a bit funny, not like the usual tobacco.'

'Ay,' said Dodd, taking the pipe and sucking smoke cautiously into his lungs. If he did it too fast it made him cough which hurt. 'The doctor mixed some Moroccan herbs and incense with it, said it added the element of earth to the smoke, or some such.'

'Is it helping?'

'Ay,' Dodd admitted reluctantly. 'It is. Ay.'

'Hm. I think my shoulder's feeling better too.' They both watched blue smoke curl up in ribbons through the last rays of the sun, an elegant and calming sight. Dodd leaned back on a pile of pillows and sighed. Being bled had left him feeling as weak as a kitten, never mind the aftermath of Heneage's persuasions, and the pipesmoke was making his head feel quite light, as if he was mildly drunk.

'All right,' he said. 'Did yer dad hear any more about yer man Michael?'

Carey gave an eloquent lift of his shoulder. 'Apparently somebody turned up yesterday to claim his money and blame it all on the footpads we killed. It might well have been them, after all.'

'Ay.'

'Interestingly, the man insisted on being paid in silver, not gold.'

'Hm.' Dodd chuckled a little at that, and wondered at himself. Really, this tobacco-smoke drinking wasn't so bad; if only it weren't so expensive he might take more of the medicine. 'How did ye ken it was the little bald poet that playacted Dr Jenkins?'

'Well, he is a player, after all. But there was another thing. Do you remember Cheke explaining how dewdrops of Mercury transfer themselves into your clothes during the reaction?'

'Ay.'

'That's how there were beads of the stuff in Edmund's clothes chest, of course. But there was also Mercury in the inside pocket of your leather jerkin.'

'Eh?'

'Of course, I knew you couldn't have been there for the coining. But you carried Mr Shakespeare's *billet doux* to Mistress Bassano and there might have been Mercury on that from Shakespeare's best suit. It was the only connection I could think of.'

Dodd tilted his head in acknowledgement that this made sense.

'And was it him that killed Robert Greene, then?' he asked.

Carey smiled lazily. 'How do you make that out?'

'It's nobbut a guess. The apothecary said he died o' poison and d'ye mind ye left Shakespeare guarding him the day we found him drunk. Maybe he put poison in his meat or beer then.'

'What makes you think he'd want to?'

'Och God, he was telling and telling me all about how Robert Greene was stopping him at his poetry-writing and how he hated his guts. I think I may even have advised him to . . . er . . . kill the man.'

Carey reached into the breast pocket of his doublet and pulled out a chased silver flask. 'Remember this?' he said. 'Robert Greene's flask. He had it on him when we found him and he was drinking from it most of the night. He got it refilled by the tapster with aqua vitae and no doubt drank some more on his way home and for a nightcap before he went to bed. The next morning he sickened and died.'

'Ay but it could ha' been the eels,' Dodd pointed out from sheer perversity while Carey smoked.

'Could have been,' said Carey and sighed. 'Only it wasn't. Barnabus and Simon didn't have plague. Heneage sent men to capture me and found only Simon, with Barnabus already dead the same way as Greene.'

'How d'ye ken that?'

'I broke into my lodgings.'

Dodd winced at this plain admission of madness. 'But are ye sure it wisnae plague?' he asked on a rising note of panic.

'Certain. We found Simon trussed up like a chicken with Tamburlain roosting on the bed and Barnabus . . . Well, it was easily recognisable, what he'd died of. And under Barnabus's pillow, I found this flask.'

Dodd narrowed his eyes. It took him a while, thanks to his wooziness, but he worked it out. 'Och, Barnabus and his light fingers.'

'Precisely,' said Carey giving him back the pipe. 'I've told him thousands of times that his habit of thieving whatever didn't belong to me and wasn't nailed down would kill him in the end, and it did. But it's certain there was poison in the flask, for there was nothing wrong with Barnabus before and he didn't have plague.'

'So yon Shakespeare killed both Robert Greene and Barnabus?'

'I think so.'

'Can ye prove it?'

Carey shook his head. 'I've nothing but suspicion. Shakespeare had the chance to put poison in Greene's flask – that doesn't prove he did it. And he can't have known in advance what Barnabus would do, so he's hardly to blame there.'

'Will ye ask him?'

'I got hold of him while the doctor and the surgeon were seeing to you and Edmund. I think hearing he'd killed Barnabus by accident shook him a bit, but then he denied everything, the whole boiling lot and challenged me to arrest him for it.'

'Ay, well, he would.'

'Of course he would.'

'Och.' Dodd was shaking his head, more in amusement than disapproval, 'I've allus said ye cannae trust poets.'